D0423323

The Sociology
of Public
Administration

The Sociology of Public Administration

Michael J. Hill

Crane, Russak & Company, Inc.
New York

© Michael J. Hill 1972
Published in the United States by:
Crane, Russak & Company, Inc.
52 Vanderbilt Avenue
New York, N.Y. 10017

Library of Congress Catalog No. 72-80114
ISBN 0-8448-0024-4
Printed in Great Britain

Contents

Preface

The sociological study of complex organisations has been rapidly advanced in recent years. Many sociologists who are working in this field have sought to develop theories or hypotheses which are applicable to organisations of all kinds. Yet most of the research work in this area of investigation has been done in industrial organisations, and primarily on the shop floor in manufacturing companies. Very little research has been done in public organisations engaged on the making and implementation of government policies, a fact that has not, in the United States, deterred sociologists from formulating generalisations which are claimed to apply to such organisations.

In Britain, sociological studies in the field of administration are almost nonexistent. The study of public administration continues in this country to involve merely the provision of historical and descriptive accounts of the machinery of government, together with informed but unsystematic speculation about ways in which the civil service works in practice.

The object of this book is to suggest ways in which modern developments in sociology are applicable to the study of public administration. Organisational sociology does not provide an entirely satisfactory framework for this exercise, but nevertheless it is felt that students of public administration have a great deal to gain from looking at some of the theories and some of the empirical work that is being done in this field. Accordingly, this book engages in the difficult exercise of introducing some of the topics which have been given attention by sociologists, while at the same time pointing out the drawbacks associated with too wholesale an acceptance of some of the more all-embracing propositions of organisational sociology.

One possibility at this point in the evolution of public administration in Britain is that civil servants will turn for assistance with some of their managerial problems to some of the theories which have been developed in the United States by social scientists who have studied industrial management. One of the best features of the traditional British approach to the study of public administration has been that the subject has been regarded as closely linked with the study of politics. It would be most undesirable if the kind of sociology which came to the attention of civil servants was wholly preoccupied with issues of organisational behaviour in a nonpolitical context. There is therefore a need to build up a field of study which links the insights that organisational sociology can provide with the traditional concerns of students of public administration. This book is an attempt to do this. It takes some areas of concern in the field of public administration and attempts to throw a new light upon them by examining them from a sociological perspective.

The basis for this book was provided by a course I gave, entitled 'The Sociology of Public Administration', to undergraduate students in the Sociology Department at the University of Reading. I am grateful to Professor Andreski for enabling me to develop my special interest in this subject. The original suggestion for the course came from Martin Albrow to whom I am deeply indebted for encouraging me to develop this subject, and for all the help he has given me since I started on the book. I think the text makes clear how much I owe to his writings in this and allied fields. I am grateful to HMSO for permission to quote from the Fulton Report on the Civil Service.

Since I have been at Oxford, Olive Stevenson has given me valuable encouragement and support which have helped me to complete the book. I should like to thank her too for her comments on the manuscript, and also the following people who have commented on all or part of various versions of it: Alan Fox, Dennis Marsden, Tony Sargeant and my brother, Christopher. I am also grateful for the efforts of Mary McMahon and Connie Sansom who have battled with my handwriting to produce the typescript.

The book is dedicated to my wife, Betty, who has helped a great deal with the preparation of the manuscript, but whose most important contribution has been the support and encouragement she has provided throughout my academic career.

1

Bureaucracy and Democracy: The Theoretical and Philosophical Debate

The first two chapters of this book are concerned with some of the broad theoretical issues that have concerned sociologists and allied social scientists who have been aware of the importance of the complex administrative machinery of the state for the distribution of power and influence in developed industrial societies. The first of these two chapters will deal with what may be described as the European tradition of macro-sociological concern about the relations between bureaucracy and democracy; while the second will be concerned with theories about the internal structure of organisations which have largely been developed by Americans interested in problems of management (although they draw to some extent upon the German Max Weber and treat him as one of their founding fathers).

In the discussions of specific issues in the remainder of the book both these intellectual traditions will be drawn upon, and it will be stressed that a study of public administration founded upon only one of these traditions will be inadequate.

The relationship between bureaucracy and political democracy has been debated at great length during the last century and a half. In the course of this debate three extreme positions have been taken, all of which involve treating the study of the detailed working of public administration as irrelevant. The 'liberal' tradition in political science has tended to assume that there are no real problems in securing a civil service that carries out the will of its political masters without question. On the other hand, there has at the same time developed a pessimistic line of thought, which treats bureaucratic power as a fact of modern life about which little can be done. The third point of view on this issue is the

Marxist one, regarding it as self-evident that in capitalist societies both representative institutions and administrations will be
effectively controlled by the bourgeoisie, and seeing administration
as unproblematical in socialist societies.

In the following discussion the conflict between the protagonists
of these three positions will be described in some detail, though
in practice it will often appear as a two-cornered rather than a
three-cornered fight, largely as a result of the tendency of the
liberals to duck into either corner and leave the more tough-
minded combatants in the other two camps to fight it out. It is in
fact the strong liberal tradition in British political science, with its
blind faith in representative government, that has led to the neglect
of public administration as anything other than a historical and
descriptive subject, in which it is taken for granted that organisations operate in ways prescribed in their formal constitutions and
that political/administrative relations are unproblematic. Of course,
some attention has been given in Britain to the other way in
which representative institutions may be undemocratic, when the
relationship between electors and elected is a tenuous one. It is
recognised that this is also an important issue, but it is largely
ignored here as beyond the scope of this book.

Albrow[1] has shown how, in the nineteenth century, the development of a representative democratic system of government was
seen as ensuring that the European 'disease' of bureaucracy did not
occur in England. He quotes Carlyle as saying[2] 'I can see no
risk or possibility in England. Democracy is hot enough here.' It
may be taken as a common view at that time that England had
democratic government, while Germany had bureaucratic administration because she had not yet acquired a fully representative
system of government. The dangers of bureaucratic government
were recognised by the English students of government like Mill
and Bagehot, but they saw the political system as supplying sufficient protection against them.

For Marx and Engels this 'representative government' provided
no more than a vehicle for the reinforcement of the powers of
the bourgeoisie. Their position is summarised in the following form
in the *Communist Manifesto*: 'The executive of the modern state
is but a committee for managing the common affairs of the whole
bourgeoisie.' Therefore to them the debate about the relations
between democracy and bureaucracy was irrelevant, and the presence in central Europe of autocratic administrative systems was

no more than a survival from the pre-capitalistic era. They argued that[3] 'all struggles within the state, the struggle between democracy, aristocracy and monarchy, the struggle for the franchise, etc, etc, are merely the illusory forms in which the real struggles of the different classes are fought out among one another.'

Notwithstanding their aloof position in regard to the liberal concern with the relations between state power and democracy, Marx and Engels recognised the coercive nature of the state, and regarded it as one of the evils of capitalist society, an instrument to ensure bourgeois domination. Accordingly, for them, the eventual revolution, the eventual overthrow of the bourgeoisie by the proletariat would take care of the state too. In the words of Engels:[4]

The state, then, has not existed from all eternity. There have been societies that did without it, that had no conception of the state and state power. At a certain stage of economic development, which was necessarily bound up with the cleavage of society into classes, the state becomes a necessity owing to this cleavage. We are now rapidly approaching a stage in the development of production at which the existence of these classes not only will have ceased to be a necessity, but will become a positive hindrance to production. They will fall as inevitably as they arose at an earlier stage. Along with them the state will inevitably fall. The society that will organize production on the basis of a free and equal association of the producers will put the whole machinery of state where it will then belong: into the Museum of Antiquities, by the side of the spinning wheel and the bronze axe.

The main assault upon the positions taken by both Marxists and liberals developed between the last years of the nineteenth century and the First World War, as a number of writers produced evidence of the growing importance of the administrative, or bureaucratic, machinery in industrialised societies and argued from that evidence that the bureaucracy represented a social and political force of increasing importance.

Probably the most important of these writers was Max Weber. Weber's discussion of bureaucracy is associated with his analysis of types of authority. He postulates three basic authority types: 'charismatic', 'traditional' and 'rational-legal'. 'Charismatic authority' is based upon[5] 'devotion to the specific and exceptional sanctity, heroism or exemplary character of an individual person'. It is a transitory phenomenon associated with periods of social turmoil; the essentially personal nature of the relationship between leader and follower makes the development of permanent institutions impossible and accordingly it succumbs to processes of 'routinisation' which transform it into one of the other types of authority. 'Traditional authority' on the other hand rests upon[6] 'an established belief in the sanctity of immemorial traditions and the legitimacy of the status of those exercising authority under them'. While charismatic authority's weakness lies in its instability, the weakness of the traditional authority is its static nature. It is thus the case that the 'rational-legal' type of authority is superior to either of the other two types.

Weber states that rational-legal authority rests upon[7] 'a belief in the legality of patterns of normative rules, and the right of those elevated to authority under such rules to issue commands'. The maintenance of such a system of authority rests upon the development of a bureaucratic system of administration in which permanent officials administer, and are bound by, rules.

Weber regards the development of bureaucratic administration as intimately associated with the evolution of modern industrialised society. Bureaucratisation is seen as a consequence of the development of a complex economic and political system, and also as a phenomenon that has helped to make these developments possible. Therefore in his view it is a phenomenon with which exponents of theories of representative government must learn to come to terms.

Students of Weber have differed in the extent to which they regard him as a theorist who believed that bureaucracy can be subjected to democratic control. The view that he was doubtful of the capacity of the liberal ideal to survive, as well as being a critic of the Marxist position, is expressed by Bendix, who draws attention to Weber's observation that:[8]

bureaucracy had turned from an ally into an enemy of capitalism. At the time of the absolute monarchies the bureaucratisation of government made possible a 'wider range of capitalistic activity'. But today one can expect 'as an *effect* of bureaucratisation a policy that meets the petty bourgeois interest in a secure traditional "subsistence", or even a state socialist party that strangles opportunities for private profit.' Along these lines Weber anticipated some kind of reversion to patrimonialism. The dictatorship potential implicit in mass appeals added to the desire for a secure subsistence which would result in a centralised bureaucracy under a dictator, a vast army of state pensioners, and an array of monopolistic privileges.

Clearly, then, Weber stressed the importance of the authority system, where Marx was concerned solely with the system of production, to explain political relations in an industrialised state. Moreover, Weber implied that the bureaucracy gave the state power to shake itself free of bourgeois control. But he also went further to express scepticism about the Marxist claim that the state would 'wither away' under socialism. According to Weber, say Gerth and Mills,[9] 'Socialisation of the means of production would merely subject an as yet relatively autonomous economic life to the bureaucratic management of the state.'

Part of Weber's thesis about the growing power of bureaucratic officials is illustrated with reference to one specific political area by Roberto Michels. In his book,[10] *Political Parties,* Michels set out to show that power in democratic mass parties becomes concentrated in a few hands. A key part of his argument is that full-time officials in socialist parties and trade unions are in a very strong position as 'professionals' relative to the 'amateurs' who may challenge them from the ranks of their supporters. A logical extension of this argument is to point out that permanent civil servants are in a similar strong position relative to politicians. Moreover Michels argues that radical and socialist politicians tend to become conservative, compromised by the bourgeois comfort of their own positions. They enjoy a situation in which they are at least partially accepted by the established order which they were elected to challenge, and inevitably many of them identify with one-time 'class enemies' rather than with their own mass supporters. In such cases they are ill-equipped to offer an effective challenge to civil servants who do not share their political commitments.

The primary target for Michels' attack was the democratic socialists, aspiring to achieve peaceful social change through control of the state by a mass political party, but his argument does hint indirectly at the problems that face the proletariat in controlling their own political apparatus in the Marxian post-revolutionary situation. Mosca,[11] on the other hand, was concerned to show much more directly that a socialist state would inevitably centralise power, and that mass democratic institutions are unable to control those at the centre of the political system. His argument implies either that permanent bureaucrats will enjoy a powerful position relative to politicians or that politicians will become, in effect, bureaucrats rather than 'servants of the people'. While the actual institutional structure may vary, the ultimate tendency will be for politicians and bureaucrats to become indistinguishable, and as far as democracy is concerned it will matter little whether what has happened has been the 'bureaucratisation of the politicians', or the 'politicisation of the bureaucrats'. To prevent this happening it is necessary to prevent the monopolisation of political power. The development of a powerful central bureaucracy must be checked by other independent institutions providing a source of 'countervailing power'. What this seems to involve, in particular, is the continued existence of economic power outside the control of the state. In this sense, Mosca's position, at least in the later editions of his work, involves taking issue with socialists, both revolutionary and democratic, in favour of representative institutions reinforced by capitalist power. In this way he was one of the first theorists to emphasise the inevitably different position on state power that had been taken by the social democrats, as opposed to the traditional exponents of the theory of representative government. Mosca is in effect arguing that liberals must not become subject to the temptation to develop too elaborate a welfare state.

The main twentieth-century defender of the Marxist faith, Lenin, was, not surprisingly, more concerned about the attacks on Marx and Engels' theory of the state from social democrats, than from theorists like Weber and Mosca who were well to his right. In his book,[12] *The State and Revolution,* it is Kautsky who is subjected to a particularly vituperative attack.

Kautsky was not a gradualist, in the sense that he did not share the views of British social democrats nurtured on the theory of representative government that capitalism could be transformed by an accumulation of minute political acts, but he did see violent revolution as unnecessary. He argued[13] that bureaucratisation was gradually delivering the capitalists into the power of the state, and that therefore all the proletariat had to do was to seize power by democratic political means, or failing that by a mass strike. The proletariat must seize the state machine, but could not expect to destroy it.

Lenin attacked Kautsky for what he saw as his failure to acknowledge the Marxist doctrine that 'the state is an organ of class rule' and that the only way to deal with the bourgeois state is to 'smash' it. Yet in an attempt to remove some of the ambiguities in Marxist theory which the social democrats had exposed, Lenin introduced a significant amplification of the doctrine that the state would wither away after the overthrow of capitalism. He argued that in the aftermath of revolution: [14] 'The proletariat needs state power, the centralised organisation of force, the organisation of violence, both to crush the resistance of the exploiters and to *lead* the enormous mass of the population—the peasantry, the petty bourgeoisie, the semi-proletarians—in the work of organising the socialist economy.'

Thus, in this restatement of Marxist theory, the 'withering away of the state' accompanies the completion of the work of social transformation. In this way Lenin opened a gate that Stalin drove a cart and horses through when he espoused the doctrine of 'revolution in one country' to explain the fact that the state did not wither away on account of its encirclement by bourgeois powers, and the consequent fact that the final attainment of socialism had to await world revolution. As realistic revolutionaries, Lenin and Stalin both found it necessary to acknowledge to some degree bureaucratic realities and to repudiate the anarchist tinge to the theories of Marx and Engels.

Of course the Leninist and Stalinist position on the state still involves no suggestion that there might be a split between the proletariat as executive—and hence nominal controllers of the state—and their officials as administrators—and thus perhaps the real controllers of the state. The role given in both pre- and post-revolutionary society to the 'party' by Lenin and Stalin, and their adoption of the notion of 'democratic centralism' as an organising principle, led the communist movement in such a direction, in a way which they obviously were not prepared to acknowledge. It was left to a Yugoslav Communist 'renegade', Djilas, to spell out what was really happening to the power structure of communist societies in his book, *The New Class*.[15]

Djilas argued that the party runs communist society by means of a bureaucratic structure which elevates party officials into the position of a new ruling class. While it is possible to quarrel with Djilas' use of the concept of class, it has proved more difficult to find fault with his general analysis of the way in which power is distributed in communist societies. Confusion does arise, however, over the fact that, formally speaking, party bureaucracies and state bureaucracies operate side by side in the communist states, with the former interpenetrating the latter. The degree of inter-penetration varies and there is some evidence, at least for Yugo-slavia,[16] of a dual system providing some checks and balances, which may evolve into a new kind of 'plural' power structure.

Djilas' claim to have identified a new 'class' in communist societies resembles a more general argument about both commu-nist and capitalist societies developed a few years before by an-other former Marxist, James Burnham.[17] While primarily con-cerned with arguing that managers are replacing owners as the dominant group in capitalist industry, Burnham widened his argument to suggest that members of the 'managerial class' he claimed to identify were beginning to dominate the state bureau-cracy in all advanced industrial societies. He argued that the extension of state activities had helped to accelerate this trend, by widely extending the power of administrative bureaux. Thus he wrote:[18] 'Laws today in the United States, in fact most laws, are not being made any longer by Congress, but by the NLRB, SEC, ICC, AAA, TVA, FTC, FCC, the Office of Production Manage-ment ... and the other leading "executive agencies".'

Burnham's position represents probably the most extreme of all the 'pessimistic' arguments about bureaucratic inevitability. He paid little attention to the possibility that bureaucracies may differ in kind and may be dominated by different kinds of people. As Gerth and Mills argue:[19]

... much of the cogency that Burnham's thesis has is due to the simple fact that the form of organisation all over the world is, perhaps increasingly, bureaucratic. But the ends to which these structures will be used, who will be at their tops, how they might be overthrown, and what movements will grow up into such structures – these are not considered; they are swallowed in the consideration of the *form* of organisation, the demiurge of history, the 'managerial world current'.

Outside the communist bloc, modern sociologists have not been disposed to dispute the evidence that bureaucratic organisation is increasingly important and that it tends to concentrate power into the hands of officials. But there have been a number of positions taken up on the precise consequences of this trend for national power structures. Marxists have continued to support sophisticated versions of the basic doctrine that the state is the 'executive committee' for the bourgeoisie. A school of sociologists and political scientists who are often known as the 'pluralists' have argued that power centralisation is prevented by competing interests. The 'pessimistic' line of thought has been defended, too, by theorists, some of whom have sought to stress the chinks of light, in an otherwise dark picture, provided by the ways in which individual or cultural values may influence bureaucratic behaviour. Let us examine these three positions in a little more detail.

In Bottomore's book, *Elites and Society*,[20] there is an attack on the view that bureaucrats and managers constitute a 'new class'. Bottomore's argument with regard to civil servants is primarily based upon evidence from studies which show that recruits to the higher branches of civil services are largely drawn from the upper middle classes, and have educational backgrounds that suggest that they will identify themselves closely with bourgeois interests. The evidence is not as unambiguous as Bottomore seems to imply, and in any case the main drawback of this kind of argument is that social origin does not necessarily determine current identification, interest or commitment. In Chapter 9 the arguments about social origins are examined more fully, with particular reference to the backgrounds of British civil servants.

However, to supplement the necessarily rather weak argument from social origins, Miliband[21] argues that civil servants tend to be selected from people who are considered to have values lying within an ideologically 'safe' spectrum, that civil-service neutrality must involve an implicit commitment to the status quo and that, as the operators of the bureaucratic machine, civil servants become intrinsically suspicious of innovation. Miliband's Marxist position is naturally sustained primarily by a more general analysis of the social structures of western societies; his argument about civil servants is that, even if they are in a position of potential power, their neutral role sustains the status quo.

The Marxists have been able to knock down the 'managerial revolution' argument fairly easily, mainly because it is clear that capitalists do not continue in business once they cease to make profits. It is naive to believe that a class of people who often allow other people to manage their affairs do not do so primarily in order to further their own interests. On the other hand the Marxists make another mistake in failing to allow that any of the concessions that capitalists make to other powerful interests are of any importance. Most Marxists are stuck in a position in which they are unprepared to acknowledge that any change short of revolution is a real change. There are crucial questions to be asked about the degree of compromise, and the extent of the concessions made by the bourgeoisie in modern societies, and, for our purposes, about the extent to which civil services play a 'brokerage' role in relation to these concessions. The study of these questions is inhibited if one takes a rigid position either on the immutability of capitalism or on the irrelevance of the Marxist critique of the power structure of industrial society.

The Marxists have been one of the main targets for attack by sociologists of the 'pluralist' school of thought. Reference has already been made to Mosca's view that capitalist economic institutions prevent the centralisation of power he regarded as inherent in a socialist system, but Mosca's interpretation of the facts was remarkably close to that of a socialist theorist like Miliband. They might both agree, were they contemporaries, in interpreting American or British society as capitalist, and only differ in that Mosca would have seen the power of the capitalists as preventing the state becoming too powerful, while Miliband sees state power and capitalist power as both parts of a uniform system of class domination. But the modern 'pluralists' dispute the Marxist interpretation of the facts. Theorists such as Aron,[22] Lipset,[23] Dahl,[24] Dahrendorf[25] and Galbraith[26] identify other sources of power which they regard as important, such as the trade unions, the political parties, and other voluntary organisations, which they see as counterbalancing both the power of the state and the power of the capitalists. In this way they have developed a 'theory of democratic elitism',[27] an optimistic blend of political sociology and political philosophy, which may be contrasted with the conservative and pessimistic elitism of Mosca.

The 'pluralist' interpretation of the way in which western societies operate attempts to provide an answer to the doubts expressed by Weber, Michels and Mosca on the capacity of elected politicians to control the bureaucratic machine. The pluralist argument is that, in a democratic political system, elected politicians gain support from powerful forces outside the direct political arena. While this does not match up to any ideal of 'direct democracy', it does provide a situation in which a plurality of interest groups may check and counter-check each other, and limit the development of the power of the executive.

However, in this kind of political system, opposition to those in power will be strong, and majorities cannot readily override minorities. Such a situation has a conservative influence on government action in general, since any innovation may provoke many opponents. Moreover, it may be objected that democratic principles are violated by the fact that some interest groups, particularly those with money and those well placed to paralyse essential services, have more influence than others. Indeed Bachrach[28] argues that to regard such a political system as democratic is a one-sided view which derives directly from a tendency of political scientists to confine themselves to the study of power *within* the governmental system. They expect democratic government to be achieved in a situation in which some of the most significant actors have excessive power, deriving from their control over organisations which are governed in a manifestly undemocratic way. Such actors are primarily interested in ensuring that the power of the state is used in ways that do not threaten their own areas of private power.

Probably the most significant exponent of what was earlier described as the 'pessimistic' line of thought about bureaucracy was C. Wright Mills. He pointed out in vehement terms the irrelevance of the competing political philosophies which we have identified as underlying many theories of bureaucracy:[29]

Liberalism has been concerned with freedom and reason as supreme facts about the individual; Marxism with supreme facts about man's role in the political making of history. But what has been happening in the world makes evident, I believe, why the ideas of freedom and reason now so often seem so ambiguous in both the capitalist and the communist societies of our time ; why Marxism has so often become a dreary rhetoric of bureaucratic defense and political abuse ; and liberalism, a trivial and irrelevant way of masking social reality. The major developments of our time can be adequately understood in terms of neither the liberal nor the Marxian interpretation of politics and culture.

Mills then goes on to argue that this irrelevance is particularly a result of the development of bureaucracies, which neither kind of political theory adequately deals with, and so he claims:[30]

Great and rational organisations — in brief, bureaucracies — have indeed increased, but the substantive reason of the individual at large has not. Caught in the limited milieux of their everyday lives, ordinary men often cannot reason about the great structures — rational and irrational — of which their *milieux* are subordinate parts.

Accordingly they often carry out series of apparently rational actions without any ideas of the ends they serve, and there is increasing suspicion that those at the top as well – like Tolstoy's generals – only pretend they know.

Mills saw the only hope of preventing the massive bureaucracies of the USA and USSR from racing on to the point where they destroy us all in the fact that centralised decision-making is possible within them. Accordingly he argued that, paradoxically, these juggernauts, which are currently being run 'without reflection' by 'cheerful robots', can be brought under control. He wrote:[31]

In the polarised world of our time, international as well as national means of history-making are being centralised. Is it not thus clear that the scope and the chance for conscious human agency in history-making are just now uniquely available? Elites of power in charge of these means do now make history – to be sure 'under circumstances not of their choosing' – but compared to other men and other epochs these circumstances do not appear to be overwhelming.

So Mills called upon the[32] 'intellectuals, the scholars, the ministers, the scientists of the rich societies' to assume political responsibility and control their bureaucracies.

It is easy to deride Mills' faith in the reason of intellectuals; as Bachrach argues,[33] it is hard to see how the intellectuals can avoid being bought off, as Mills himself argues they are now, or how they can reach a value consensus that will enable them to act concertedly to influence events. What, however, is interesting about Mills' argument is that it focuses upon the fact that centralised decisions are taken in bureaucratised systems of government, and that therefore there are key decision points which are open to influence. The conclusion this suggests is that before rushing to any of the available macro-sociological conclusions about the role and control of bureaucracy in modern society it is necessary to study precisely how decisions are taken and who is able to influence them.

Some of the sociologists who readily acknowledge the importance of state bureaucracy in modern society have drawn attention also to the extent to which the actual power and behaviour of administrative bodies vary from country to country. Their arguments tend to involve using that most difficult of sociological concepts, culture; a concept that tends to be used when it is difficult to explain a phenomenon in more concrete terms. The important point to be made in this context about administrative systems is that they vary in the kinds of value systems which they have developed, and in the extent to which they can be said to have played a part in imposing their kinds of value systems upon the culture of the societies in which they are found.

In the essay that has already been quoted extensively, Mills comments that[34] 'in neither the USA nor the USSR is there a senior civil service firmly linked to the world of knowledge and sensibility and composed of skilled men who in their careers and in their aspirations are truly independent.'

Does he believe that such a civil service may be found elsewhere? A number of writers will be mentioned in this book who clearly consider that the British civil service provides such a case, and Nettl has gone so far as to suggest that it has been able to achieve a position of cultural dominance which makes it the leader of the 'national consensus':[35]

In Britain it is, I maintain, presently a Whitehall consensus. It was not always so. But the political emasculation of the aristocracy as a condition of its survival, together with the remarkable decline of importance of formal politics (House of Commons, Party Conferences, grass roots) in favour of the executive and its chief, the Prime Minister, have led to the quiet emergence of the Snowmen, the upper civil servants and their mores. Their influence on the professions was socially logical and predestined, their influence over business a more drawn-out and difficult process. Efforts are being made to draw in the Trade Unions and the arts, though with only limited success as yet.

In America it is just the other way about. There is consensus too (though weaker) and it comes *from* the business community. Top businessmen join the administration – not to be businessmen (like Beeching) but to be administrators (Macnamara). When Americans think of 'organisation' or 'administration', they visualise big business as often as government....

Bendix developed a rather similar argument about the cultural dominance of the German civil service, again comparing it with the American civil service. At the end of this discussion he argued,[36] 'Without attention to the divergent bureaucratic culture patterns, we cannot understand the significance for each society of bureaucracy as an ideal type of administration under the rule of law.'

Bendix recognised that these different culture patterns have their roots in different historical experiences. This is where our subject becomes so very obscure, for, clearly, an observed bureaucratic culture pattern is not just a 'given' for the analysis of events in the present, it is also both partly the creator and partly the creation of the present social and political structure. However, the main point of raising this topic in this chapter has been to emphasise that bureaucratic government is not just a uniform phenomenon with a uniform impact upon any country in which it develops, and that therefore it is wise to be alert to cultural factors which may either modify or enhance its impact upon any individual country.

This chapter has presented a variety of theories and points of view on the power of public bureaucracy in the modern state. Many of the views that have been quoted can be tested by empirical studies of public administration and in particular by the examination of the relationships that exist between bureaucrats and politicians, and between these two groups and society. Hence they have provoked research into these topics. There have been three main types of approach to this research. The simplest approach has involved the study of the social characteristics, and social and political affiliations of public servants. A more complex approach has been concerned with relating the characteristics of bureaucratic systems to the cultures of their own societies. The third approach is exemplified by research that seeks to study the actions of bureaucrats and to relate those actions to the pressures upon them from inside and outside their organisations. These three approaches represent successively more direct, but at the same time more complex levels of investigation of the relationship between public administration and society. The more complex approaches are often not adopted because of the level of difficulty involved, because it is far from easy to provide objective and unambiguous evidence on such topics, but above all because social scientists are rarely given access to the information they need to tackle such questions.

Because the third approach is in many respects the most satisfactory, considerable attention is given in this book to the discussion of what goes on inside public bureaucracies. It is for this reason that the second of these two introductory chapters is devoted to a discussion of some of the main theoretical issues in the sociological study of organisations.

2

Organisation Theories

In the previous chapter, the work of Max Weber was mentioned as one of the most significant attempts to show the importance of an elaborate system of organisation, or bureaucracy, in the political structure of the modern state. Weber specified in some detail an 'ideal type' bureaucracy, and in so doing provided subsequent students of organisations with a model which has had a considerable influence on organisational sociology.

The strength of the bureaucratic form of administration, according to Weber, rests upon its formal rationality, a notion which a number of modern students of organisations have equated with efficiency. This translation of Weber's concept has led to some useful discussions of the relationship between formalism and efficiency but has also given currency to a rather unsubtle characterisation of Weber's theory. Albrow shows how this confusion arose and provides the following clarification of Weber's position:[1]

The real relation between formal rationality and efficiency can best be understood by considering the means by which efficiency is commonly measured, through the calculation of cost in money terms, or in time, or in energy expended. Such calculations are formal procedures which do not in themselves guarantee efficiency, but are among the conditions for determining what level of efficiency has been reached. At the heart of Weber's idea of formal rationality was the idea of correct calculation, in either numerical terms, as with the accountant, or in logical terms, as with the lawyer. This was normally a necessary though not sufficient condition for the attainment of goals; it could even conflict with material rationality.

The next few pages will be as much concerned with what leading students of organisations thought Weber meant as with what he really meant; nevertheless it is important to draw attention to the way in which formal rationality and efficiency have been confused because there seems to be a continuing tendency in our culture to assume that the adoption of certain kinds of formal procedures necessarily produces efficiency. In so doing, three mistakes are made: first, it is assumed that organisational ends are normally clearly specified and understood so that the adoption of efficient means guarantees the efficient attainment of ends; second, efficiency itself is treated as an unambiguous concept which, given the competing character of ends and their complex relation to means, it is not; and third, the simplifications which are involved in giving formal procedures an internal logic are overlooked.

Weber's theory is seen as providing a number of simple propositions about the formal structure of organisations, a misconception that has contributed to his usefulness to students of organisations but which does not do justice to the depth of his understanding of the critical issues in organisational sociology. As he was concerned to outline the characteristics of an organisational type that is important in complex societies because of its formal rationality, he naturally stressed the strength of that type rather than its weakness. In contrast, many of his nineteenth-century predecessors emphasised its weakness and used the term 'bureaucracy' in a purely derogatory sense.[2] His aim was to define a widespread kind of organisation and explain why it was growing in importance, offering thereby sociological analysis rather than political polemic.

Weber lists a number of characteristics which, taken together, define bureaucracy. Those characteristics are as follows:[3]

1 A continuous organisation with a specified function, or functions, its operation bound by rules. Continuity and consistency within the organisation are ensured by the use of writing to record acts, decisions and rules.

2 The organisation of personnel is on the basis of hierarchy. The scope of authority within the hierarchy is clearly defined, and the rights and duties of the officials at each level are specified.

3 The staff are separated from ownership of the means of administration or production. They are personally free, 'subject to authority only with respect to their impersonal official obligations.'

4 Staff are appointed, not elected, on the basis of impersonal qualifications, and are promoted on the basis of merit.

5 Staff are paid fixed salaries and have fixed terms of employment. The salary scale is normally graded according to rank in the hierarchy. Employment is permanent with a certain security of tenure, and pensions are usually paid on retirement.

The 'debate with Max Weber' which has been so important for

the development of the sociology of organisations has focused upon two issues. One of these has been the issue of efficiency where, as shown above, criticisms of Weber have been based upon a misunderstanding of his work. However, in this context, it is fruitful to look at these 'criticisms' because they involve important observations about the nature of large-scale formal organisations.

Those people who see bureaucracy as an inefficient instrument base their arguments upon two points, that bureaucratic procedures are slow and that bureaucratic organisations develop rigidities that undermine effective action. The critics of bureaucracy do not, in general, suggest a form of organisation that would be superior to the bureaucratic organisation as Weber defines it. Either they make points about the need for flexibility in the general model—many of these are quite valid and will be discussed below—or they fulminate against large-scale organisations in general, just as they rage against the large-scale and complex society that makes them necessary.

The identification of bureaucracy as slow raises a more fundamental problem.[4] The careful attention to rules and precedents which Weber regards as so fundamental to rational bureaucratic action makes it inevitable that procedures will tend to be slow.

The argument that bureaucratic organisations tend to develop rigidities,[5] however, represents a more fundamental case against the notion of bureaucracy as an efficient instrument. It is argued that individuals within a bureaucratic organisation tend to evade decision-taking to avoid having responsibility for incorrect or unpopular decisions. The hierarchical nature of the organisation makes it easy for them to do this by passing matters up to their superiors for decisions. The evidence on this point is highly ambiguous since it is difficult in practice to separate evasion of responsibility from justifiable reference to superiors. Moreover, the truth is confused by the fact that bureaucrats frequently seek to protect themselves from hostility in a face-to-face relationship by implying that the responsibility for their decision lies with a superior. Furthermore it is necessary to recognise that the complexity of the task performed by an organisation, the demands of the social and political framework within which the organisation operates, and the characteristics of its personnel, may each be sources of rigidity independent of, or interacting with, organisation structure.

The second issue on which critics of Weber have focused is connected with the argument about efficiency, and thus is partly based upon the misunderstanding of Weber, but involves at the same time a rather more significant point about the logic of Weber's model. It is suggested that the hierarchical nature of the structure of the bureaucratic organisation makes it inevitable that it will under-use experts. It is argued that Weber's model contains a basic contradiction between hierarchy and expertise as organisational principles. Attention has been focused upon this contradiction by Parsons and by Gouldner, in particular. Gouldner made this point in the following way:[6] 'Weber, then, thought of bureaucracy as a Janus-faced organisation, looking two ways at once. On the one side it was administration based on expertise: while on the other, it was administration based on discipline.'

It may be objected to this criticism that Weber is in fact suggesting that these two organisational principles do not conflict, that in bureaucratic organisations the most expert tend to occupy the most senior positions. But even if this is Weber's view, it can still be argued that he fails to resolve the fundamental incompatibility of these two principles. Bureaucratic organisation is founded upon the need to make the maximum use of the division of labour. Such division is based upon the need to subdivide a task either because of its size or because it is impossible for a single individual to master all its aspects. In fact, in most cases both these reasons apply. The principle of hierarchy rests upon the notion of the delegation of responsibility to subordinates. If the superior could himself perform the whole of the task he delegates, he would not need to have subordinates. He will be delegating part of the task either because he has not the time to do it himself, or because he has neither the time nor the knowledge to perform certain parts of the task. Inasmuch as the latter is the case, it is obvious that in respect of at least part of the task the superior is less expert than his subordinate. But even in the former case this may also be true, since, particularly as far as tasks that require decision-making are concerned, the subordinate will be in possession of detailed information which, in delegating responsibility, the superior has chosen not to receive.

It is for these reasons that, as far as detailed parts of an organisation's functions are concerned, it must be recognised that expertise resides primarily in the lower ranks of a hierarchy. And it is for these reasons that it is inevitable that there tends to be conflict between authority based upon expertise and authority based upon hierarchy in bureaucratic organisations.

This particular unresolved inconsistency in Weber's theory has helped to provoke several valuable studies of conflict between experts and administrators within organisations. Of particular note here are two recent books by Presthus[7] and by Victor Thompson.[8] An allied topic that has also been explored is the conflict that exists for experts between professional orientation and organisational orientation in their attitudes to their work.[9] These topics will be explored again later in the book.

Perhaps the key issue in contemporary research into organisations has been the exploration of the extent to which informal social systems exist within formal organisations. For this sort of work Weber's formal model has provided an ideal starting point.[10] In attempting to explain why the organisations they study do not correspond to Weber's ideal type, researchers have discovered ways in which formal rules are modified or evaded.

Weber's ideal type of bureaucracy involves a number of propositions that are rather similar to the principles of organisation recommended by what Simon calls 'classical administrative science.'[11] The classical approach to administrative theory involves the setting out of formal principles of organisation which take no account of human variability or irrationality. Certainly there is no place in the organisational model provided by the classical theorists for the notion of the informal structure of organisations. The work of industrial psychologists and sociologists, in revealing this as the main weakness of the model provided by early management textbooks, has clearly influenced those sociologists who have sought to apply Weber's model in the study of organisations. Two intellectual traditions—one, largely sociological, concerned with demonstrating the fact that Weber's formal model does not neatly fit the realities of organisational forms, the other, rooted primarily in social psychology, concerned with showing how human behaviour will not readily fit into a formal organisational pattern— have been brought together in contemporary discussions of organisations.

Management thinking has been transformed by research which reveals that informal group structure has an enormous impact upon individual work behaviour. The work carried out under Elton Mayo at the Hawthorne works in Chicago during the late twenties and early thirties is often credited with effecting this revolution in industrial sociology.[12] This is an over-simplified view. The Hawthorne researchers were influenced by research on morale carried out during the First World War.[13] They were also well aware of the progress being made in social psychology between the wars, and in particular they were influenced by the more sophisticated approach to human motivation that Freudian psychology helped to produce. The development of a more complex approach to social structure at this time, by sociologists and anthropologists under the influence of Pareto, Simmel, Durkheim and the 'Functionalists', also had some impact upon their work, and particularly upon the Bank Wiring Room research. In some ways, too, their thinking had been foreshadowed by the writings of Mary Parker Follett on management.[14] For these reasons it makes more sense to say that the Hawthorne researches represent the most significant *single* advance in the understanding of human behaviour in a work context. The Hawthorne researches have had a colossal impact upon subsequent workers in this field, and it is only natural that the process of the simplification of the history of ideas has led to their being accorded a significance out of proportion to their true contribution.

The starting point for Mayo and his associates was the failure of an earlier piece of research, carried out by the firm, to explain a pattern of responses of a group of employees to variations in lighting. Both increasing and decreasing the light had led to increased production. So the responses of a team of female workers, in the Relay Assembly Test Room, to a whole variety of changes in working hours and conditions were studied in great detail. As a result of this study Mayo's team came to the conclusion that the most significant influence upon the behaviour of the workers was the fact that they were being studied. The interest shown in them by the research team, who took over responsibility for them from their supervisors, had a positive effect upon both the morale and the output of the workers in the Relay Assembly Test Room.

This research was followed by an interviewing project carried out throughout the factory. Employees were encouraged to express their grievances in nondirective interviews. It was found that general personal problems figured far more prominently than specific grievances in the interviews. Nevertheless employees expressed pleasure that the company was sufficiently interested in them to listen to their points of view.

Finally, Mayo and his fellow-workers decided to try to observe work behaviour in as natural a context as possible. They sought to study behaviour within a group of workers in the Bank Wiring Room, over a long period of time, making it clear that they were not identified with the supervisors in any way. This research revealed the importance of a group structure, bearing no relationship to formal roles within the work team, in determining the behaviour of the individual workers. In particular it was found that the group recognised a production norm, comfortably below their physical capacities, and that the only individual who refused to acknowledge this norm was socially isolated. The social relationships that existed within this group, and in particular the various games they played together at intervals during the working day, made a considerable contribution to their satisfaction with their jobs.

The general significance of the Hawthorne researches lies in their emphasis upon the importance of interpersonal relationships in the work situation, both between workers and their superiors and amongst the workers themselves. It is this that is relevant for this book. There is no need, therefore, to get involved in the controversy that has surrounded Mayo's emphasis upon 'human relations' as the key to all management's problems,[15] an emphasis which involves ruling out the suggestion that at least some of the conflicts between management and workers may arise from irreconcilable interests.

The Hawthorne researches demonstrate the need to analyse organisations as living social structures. They indicate that, just as to discover that there are such and such a number of farmers, shopkeepers and labourers living in a village and that x works for y and so on is not to find out a great deal of significance about the social structure of that village, so to regard an organisation as merely a pattern of formal roles is likely to make it impossible to fully understand the determinants of behaviour, even formally prescribed behaviour, within that organisation.[16]

Although these findings relate to the shop floor, to the lowest level in an organisation's hierarchy, subsequent research has demonstrated the validity of these findings for all levels. Interpersonal relationships within groups of office workers[17] or within management[18] have equally been found to determine work behaviour in a way that formal organisational rules in no way anticipate. However, to suggest that such behaviour necessarily involves rule violation and opposition to hierarchical demands is to adopt far too simple an approach to the formal/informal dichotomy. An important aspect of the work of the next theorist to be discussed, Chester Barnard, is that the role of the informal structure in the functioning of an organisation is recognised and explored.

The Functions of the Executive was first published in 1938.[19] Barnard was a senior executive whose work, overtly at least, owes little to the academic developments in the social sciences that were occurring at the time he wrote his book. Yet his analysis of organisational behaviour represents a systematic approach to many of the issues raised by Mayo and his co-workers.

The Hawthorne researches involve the discovery that the co-operation of employees is not something management can take for granted, or even easily buy. The importance of Barnard's work is that he treats the cooperative relationship as something that is essentially problematical, and seeks to examine the bases upon which human cooperation within an organisation can be achieved and maintained.

Barnard's book starts with a painstaking analysis of this relationship, building his analysis up from the most elementary forms of cooperation. The reader should not be deterred by the tedious and rather obvious detail of this part of the book, as the argument does gradually develop to more complex organisational forms. Barnard wishes to make it quite clear that the same principles apply to relationships within complex organisations as to simple two-person cooperative relationships.

Thus Barnard points out that continued cooperation of personnel within an organisation depends upon each individual achieving a satisfactory balance of advantages over disadvantages in respect of his participation. He goes on to suggest that such advantages, or 'incentives', will not only consist of the obvious ones, acquisition of pecuniary rewards, prestige and power. They will also include 'ideal benefactions', the satisfaction of personal ideals such as pride in craftsmanship or pride in the achievement of organisational goals. Furthermore, they will include satisfactions derived from social relationships in the work situation, satisfactions that may be provided by 'informal' social relationships.

Barnard develops this analysis in terms of 'incentives' by suggesting that for the organisation as a whole there exists an 'economy of incentives'. One of the important problems for organisational leaders is the allocation of *scarce* incentives in such a way as to maintain effective contributions from personnel. As far as monetary incentives are concerned this will be an obvious point. But Barnard maintains that it has equal validity if other sources of satisfaction are treated as incentives, for example the satisfactions derived from informal personal relationships. The development of what another writer has called an 'indulgency pattern'[20] within an organisation may occur when management turns a blind eye to minor forms of rule infringement. The lengthening of breaks, fooling around while at work, swapping of jobs and so on may contribute to making work more congenial, and intelligent management may recognise that such behaviour makes a contribution to keeping down labour turnover, absenteeism, labour disputes and other personnel 'problems'. However, there must be a point at which behaviour of this kind proves a serious threat to efficiency. Barnard's notion of the 'economy of incentives' thus involves recognition that management is limited in the extent to which it can provide any kind of incentive without damaging the organisation. The above example has been drawn from a field in which the point about the 'economy of incentives' can be most easily made, the shop floor in industry. But equally the analysis may be applied to the relationship between efficiency and employee morale in the field of public administration. Organisational success depends upon keeping up the balance of advantages for all personnel, yet if the level of incentives is pushed too high, organisational functions will suffer. In public administration this sort of situation occurs when personnel, at any level, are able to adopt an exploitative approach to the organisation; when they are able to use it as a vehicle for their own satisfactions, which are not only monetary ones, to the point where it can no longer function effectively.

An important aspect of Barnard's analysis of organisational behaviour in terms of cooperation is his treatment of the concept of authority. To Barnard, authority must be analysed as something recognised by the recipient of a communication, and depends upon both the source of the communication and its contents. This stands in particular contrast to the common notion of authority as something exercised by x over y. For Barnard, authority must be seen as something y acknowledges x as having, under certain circumstances. Within an organisation, Barnard suggests that an individual will accept the authority of his superior so long as the demands of his superior fall within certain limits.

The limits within which the individual will accept this authority Barnard calls his 'zone of indifference'. The size of this 'zone' will depend upon the individual's commitment to the organisation and upon his susceptibility to social pressures within it.

Useful as Barnard's contribution to the understanding of authority is, the concept of the 'zone of indifference' has a certain arbitrariness. Commands cannot simply be divided into acceptable ones, to which the individual is indifferent even if he disagrees with them, and unacceptable ones which the individual is unwilling to obey, preferring the alternative of severing his connection with the organisation if he does not get his own way. Unacceptable commands must be analysed along a continuum. At one end of that continuum is the situation in which the individual gives in after briefly querying the command with his superior. The only effect of this command is to marginally weaken the individual's commitment to the organisation. Its effect will be to slightly tilt the advantage/disadvantage balance and thus narrow the 'zone of indifference' for future commands. At the other extreme of the continuum are, of course, the commands that will be treated by the individual as totally unacceptable and will lead to him severing his connection with the organisation unless the command is withdrawn. Between these two extremes there can be many different situations. Commands that are evaded, commands that are partially obeyed or that are made the subject of compromise, commands which are obeyed after appeals to third parties and so on.

It has been made clear in various parts of this discussion of Barnard's book that he recognises the importance of the 'informal' structure of organisations. Two important aspects of Barnard's discussion of this concept are; first, that he acknowledges that informal relationships may be just as important at the top as at the bottom of organisations, and second that he recognises that there is a dynamic relationship between the formal and the informal structure of an organisation. On this second point he points out that formal organisations often emerge from informal ones, and that in the process new informal organisations will be created. He suggests, moreover, that informal organisations 'are necessary to the operation of formal organisations as a means of communication, of cohesion, and of protecting the integrity of the individual'.[21]

The importance of Barnard's contribution to organisation theory lies in his attention to the importance of securing cooperation from subordinates in order to run an organisation effectively. He makes it clear that the manager or administrator should pay attention to the motivation of his staff as well as to the formal principles upon which their deployment is based.

Barnard's weaknesses are that, like Mayo, he ignores the possibility that there may be irreconcilable conflicts of interest within an organisation, and that he pays no real attention to the impact of the world outside on the organisation. His theories have a neatness which derives largely from the fact that they are based upon classical economic theory, which means that, even though he is not treating the organisational participant as a rational economic man, he is assuming that a similar, if more complex, kind of calculating process occurs. Furthermore, the calculating process involved in the 'economy of incentives' is one that cannot be translated into numerical terms and therefore cannot be empirically tested. The neatness of the theory is attractive but perhaps misleading.

H. A. Simon has devoted much of his life to trying to advance, from a similar position to that taken by Barnard, to the development of a sophisticated 'general theory' of organisation. In his book *Administrative Behavior*, published in 1945,[22] he calls for the development of a systematic study of administrative behaviour based upon the analysis of decision-making, and derides 'classical' administrative theory as vague and unscientific, founded upon 'proverbs', statements that are superficially true but ambiguous and indefinite when applied to reality.

After the rather grandiose claims Simon makes for his own theories, one must feel that his book is rather disappointing. It does, however, contain incisive discussions of some of the key issues in the study of administration. *Administrative Behavior* is important because it raises some of the main issues which any theory of administrative behaviour must tackle, but it raises problems rather than providing answers. In his later work Simon tries to move towards the formulation of a coherent body of organisation theory, but what in practice this amounts to, in a book entitled *Organizations* produced in 1958 in conjunction with J. G. March, is the setting out of a large number of separate hypotheses and not in any sense a linked 'theory'.[23]

In *Administrative Behavior* Simon stresses the need to make the study of decision-making a central part of the study of administration:[24]

B

... it has not been commonly recognized that a theory of administration should be concerned with the processes of decision as well as with the processes of action. This neglect perhaps stems from the notion that decision making is confined to the formulation of overall policy. On the contrary, the process of decision does not come to an end when the general purpose of an organization has been determined. The task of 'deciding' pervades the entire administrative organization quite as much as the task of 'doing' – indeed, it is integrally tied up with the latter.

Simon attacks the notion of decision-taking as external to administration, the notion that decisions are taken by politicians leaving administrators to put those decisions into 'action'. He points out that administration involves continual decision-taking. Such decisions can be seen as organised in a hierarchy, minor decisions being consequent upon major ones. Thus any particular major decision, say a decision by a local authority to build a new school, creates a need for a succession of lesser decisions, on siting, design, staffing and so on.

Simon presents decision-making not as a process of 'maximising', as in economic theory, but as a process in which individual rationality is limited: 'The central concern of administrative theory is with the boundary between the rational and the non-rational aspects of human social behaviour. Administrative theory is peculiarly the theory of intended and bounded rationality – of the behaviour of human beings who *satisfice* because they have not the wit to *maximise*'.[25]

Simon pays particular attention to the fact that decisions are based upon premises and that these premises will involve both factual and value elements. He recognises that it is often difficult to separate these elements but suggests that in ordering the hierarchy of decisions, deciding which decisions are the key ones which should form the premises for lower-order decisions, administrators should try to give priority to value premises. He suggests that the best approach to the problem of how to separate administration from politics, a problem that political scientists have puzzled over ever since Woodrow Wilson tried to come to grips with it in a pioneering essay on administration,[26] lies in seeking to reserve for politicians the taking of value decisions wherever possible. Simon's prescriptions on this point are examined in more detail in Chapter 10 of this book.

The importance of Simon's analysis lies in the fact that he draws attention to the difficulties involved in separating facts and values, and not in his own rather unconvincing attempt to indicate how, with regard to decision-making, facts and values may be disentangled. It is a pity that his own analysis does not lead him to deal with the more concrete problem of conflict between administrators' values and the values of politicians and/or the values of sections of the public. In fact Simon, like Barnard, limits his attention to what goes on inside administrative organisations and pays little attention to their relations with the outside world. Value issues are presented as abstract issues unrelated to the conflicts of interest with which they are associated in the real world.

His emphasis upon decision-making means that Simon sees organisational leadership as having as a primary function the setting of the context within which subordinates will make minor decisions. Such action involves determining some of the 'premises' upon which future decisions will be based. And most decisions, particularly those taken at lower levels within a hierarchy, are largely predetermined by 'premises'. Efficient decision-taking occurs whenever all the relevant decision-making premises are taken into account. Simon provides an interesting discussion of training and rule making—both processes of establishing decision-making premises—as alternative approaches to the control of decision-making by subordinates.[27]

Simon deals with the issue of authority in a very similar way to Barnard, using the concept of 'area of acceptance' where Barnard talks of 'zone of indifference'. He regards the magnitude of the 'area of acceptance' as determined by 'sanctions', but makes it quite clear that within the scope of sanctions he includes the social phenomena discussed by Barnard. Thus Simon says: 'At least as important as the negative sanctions—physical and economic force—are community of purpose, social acceptance and personality.'[28]

The main attempt to elaborate organisation theory in a similar way to Barnard and Simon whilst building in some assumptions, lacking in their theories, about the impact of the environment has been provided by a school of sociologists who have become known as the 'structure-functionalists'. The best known theorist of this school, Talcott Parsons, has paid relatively little attention to organisation theory and seems quite unprepared to acknowledge that public organisations can be regarded as in any sense different from other kinds of organisations.[29] Indeed, since the great weakness of Parsonian theory lies in its failure to deal adequately with social conflict, it is not surprising that he has little relevant to say about a kind of organisation which is often in the centre of conflict. A writer who is often regarded as belonging to the structure-functionalist school but who has paid particular attention to public administration is Philip Selznick. Moreover Selznick has not been concerned to derive his organisation theory from a general sociological theory, so that in dealing with the relations between organisations and their environment he is not constrained by a general assumption about social equilibrium.

Selznick's main contributions to this subject will be found in *TVA and the Grass Roots*[30] and in *Leadership in Administration*.[31]

Selznick emphasises the need to study an organisation in relation to its social environment, in his words 'as an institution':[32]

The term 'organisation' thus suggests a certain bareness, a lean no-nonsense system of consciously coordinated activities. It refers to an *expendable tool*, a rational instrument engineered to do a job. An 'institution' on the other hand, is more nearly a natural product of social needs and pressures – a responsive adaptive organism.

In this way Selznick relates organisations both to their external environment and to the informal social systems that develop within them. But he goes an important step further, to relate external environment directly to the internal social system. Individuals within an administrative organisation bring with them certain social commitments and attachments. Then, in the course of their administrative duties they have to take actions that affect the public. Their particular 'public' may be single individuals or powerful organisations. The reactions of the 'public' to any administrative actions must be taken into account, particularly if they have any bargaining power. In the course of time a pattern of complex relationships may grow up between an individual and those people and organisations who constitute his 'public'. At the same time the individual will be involved in a similar network of relationships with his colleagues, who will also be likely to be involved in a series of 'external' relationships of the same kind. A similar kind of analysis to that provided above is possible if one substitutes for 'individual' a single department within an organisation. The web of relationships will constitute, to use

Simon's terminology, important 'premises' for any decisions that are required to be taken.

Selznick's functionalism lies in this emphasis upon the constraints upon organisational action. His position is well summarised in the following quotation from *TVA and the Grass Roots:*[33]

All formal organizations are moulded by forces tangential to their rationally ordered structures and stated goals. Every formal organization — trade union, political party, army, corporation etc. — attempts to mobilize human and technical resources as means for the achievement of its ends. However, the individuals within the system tend to resist being treated as means. They interact as wholes, bringing to bear their own special problems and purposes; moreover the organization is embedded in an institutional matrix and is therefore subject to pressure upon it from its environment, to which some general adjustment must be made. As a result, the organization may be significantly viewed as an adaptive social structure, facing problems which arise simply because it exists as an organization in an institutional environment, independently of the special (economic, military, political) goals which called it into being.

Thus Selznick is important as a theorist whose concept of an organisation as a system does not lead him into ignoring the fact that the direction in which it moves as a system is a result of conflicting forces both inside and outside it.

Selznick has been attacked for emphasising the way in which organisations can be diverted from their stated objectives. Gouldner links him with Michels as a theorist who 'seems to imply that survival is possible only in an icy stasis, in which "security", "continuity" and "stability" are the key terms.'[34] But it is probably more seriously misleading to imply that organisations work undisturbedly towards the goals which their founder set for them. Selznick has in fact replied to Gouldner that his intention was to emphasise dangers not to resign to pessimism, and *Leadership in Administration* was concerned to explore how men can give purpose to organisations if they learn to come to terms with the forces that may divert them.[35]

Before leaving a discussion of Selznick's work, attention must be paid to two concepts he developed in the course of his analysis of the experiences of the Tennessee Valley Authority, the concepts of 'administrative constituency' and 'co-optation'.

An 'administrative constituency' is defined as:[36]

a group, formally outside a given organization, to which the latter (or an element within it) has a special commitment. A relation of mutual dependence develops, so that the agent organization must defend its constituency and conversely. The relation gains strength and definition as precedents are established in behaviour and in doctrine, and equally as the constituency itself attains organized forms.

For the Tennessee Valley Authority, the large farmers of the area formed such a 'constituency'.

Co-optation is a 'process of absorbing new elements into the leadership or policy-determining structure of an organisation as a means of averting threats to its stability or existence'.[37] There are two forms of co-optation, 'formal' and 'informal'. 'Formal co-optation' involves adding people to an organisation for the purpose of lending it legitimacy, sharing 'responsibility for power rather than power itself'. 'Informal co-optation', on the other hand, involves yielding to a source of power; generally in practice this means accepting representatives of special interest groups. Such co-optation will alter the character of an organisation.

These concepts form a crucial part of a valuable approach to the analysis of the adjustment of an organisation to its environment. It is this that constitutes Selznick's special contribution to the sociology of public administration.

In the last part of this chapter, the work of three theorists, Barnard, Simon and Selznick, has been selected for special attention from the large body of work which is often described as 'organisation theory'. If this were an account of the development of sociological thinking on organisations over the past thirty years this focus upon the work of only three writers would clearly have been inadequate. In other places in this book the reader will find reference to specific propositions formulated by writers who claim to be providing 'organisation theory'. It is important to point out that there is no single systematised body of organisation theory, but rather a large number of theoretical propositions many of which have been formulated quite independently of each other. This means that the student in search of organisation theory will find a large number of books in which writers expound theories of their own, and that furthermore he will also find books which —while they may claim to perform a systematising function—will in fact bring together a number of comparatively unrelated hypotheses or theories. An account of the wide range of work found under the organisation theory umbrella would be inappropriate here.[38]

The practical administrator who decides to study organisation theory can easily be overwhelmed by the tower of Babel he discovers. Many of the theories are too abstract to be susceptible to practical applications. Others build too much around a small number of simple propositions. Some books that claim to order the subject merely confuse it because of the multiplicity of the propositions contained within them. The large number of 'readers' available in this field is particularly confusing because each contains a diversity of points of view inadequately integrated. Finally there is a number of books, which purport to provide insight into organisation theory, but in fact knock down such theories as do exist and provide in their place 'models' or 'frames of reference' masquerading as theory.

Having subjected himself to this 'learning experience' it will not be surprising if the administrator adopts one of the more straightforward theories emanating from the period before the American intellectuals really moved in on the organisation theory field. The 'proverbs of administration', the formal theory so derided by Simon, still retain a considerable attraction for practical men. They provide straightforward organisational propositions uncomplicated by considerations of 'human nature'. They belong to an age of innocence before the psychologists and sociologists came along to argue that human factors, of importance but difficult to measure or predict, must complicate organisational functioning. Administrators will be tempted to argue for using the 'formal' rules approach, leaving modifications to allow for human factors to be made intuitively as and when they are necessary.

Alternatively many 'practical' men have been prepared to be a little more sophisticated, to go along one step further into the management theory jungle and acknowledge the importance of human relations in the sense emphasized by Mayo. Thus, they acknowledge that they need to develop some manipulative skills in interpersonal relations if they are to succeed in keeping close to the traditional 'formal' principles of organisation.

It will not be the objective of this book to advance the practical administrator any further down *that* road to organisational understanding, which the *main stream* of organisation theory claims to provide; on the contrary the author has a great deal of sympathy for the administrator who concludes that that particular road leads nowhere very useful. There is a great deal to be said for the view that administration is only to a very limited extent a science, inasmuch as there are few general organisational principles, however derived; and that therefore a combination of experience and intelligent guesswork will continue to be of importance in administration.

Naturally, this book is an attempt to persuade its readers, some of whom it is hoped will be practical administrators, that so total a rejection of organisational sociology is not appropriate. Organisational sociology has something to offer the study of public administration when, for example, it draws attention to the complexity of social structures, points out ways in which compliance may be problematical, or throws light upon the manifold ways in which formal structures are modified in practice. At the same time there is a number of special features of public administration that are not adequately dealt with in organisation theory, notably the very special relationship the public bureaucracy has with its environment, the extreme salience of value issues in its everyday working, and the fact that civil services employ very many individuals whose commitment to their organisation is neither as total as that of members of voluntary organisations nor as slight as that of many industrial workers. Accordingly there are grounds for scepticism about the applicability of such 'general theory' as is available to public administration, and selectivity must be adopted in sorting through the wide range of more partial theories, particularly where their origins lie in researches conducted in industrial workshops.

In addition to these general reservations about a tradition of organisational study which has its roots in industrial sociology, it is important to draw attention to a specific weakness of much work in this field. This is a failure to deal properly with the power dimension in organisations. Inevitably linked with this is a lack of emphasis upon conflict, a tendency to exaggerate consensus, particularly with regard to goals.

This weakness has been a source of criticism of industrial sociology, as a subject which often seems committed to a management point of view in which industrial harmony is regarded as a readily attainable goal and conflict springs only from individual irrationality. When an attempt is made to apply theories and findings from organisational sociology to the study of public administration, this failure to deal adequately with power and

conflict seems a particularly serious weakness. This is not because
there is necessarily a great deal of conflict within administrative
organisations—on the contrary there may be a fairly high level
of commitment to the organisations from the majority of the
employees—but because the goals and activities of these organisations are surrounded by a great deal of social conflict. It was for
this reason that this book started with a discussion of one of the
most fundamental political issues of our time, the relationship between bureaucracy and democracy. The sociology of public administration must deal with this issue if it is not to be merely
another kind of managerial sociology. Equally while civil servants
undoubtedly have a great deal to learn from management about
the use of certain practical techniques, it would be disastrous if
British public administrators became obsessed by managerialism
to the extent that their sensitivity to their political role was reduced. Without such sensitivity Mills' gibe about 'cheerful robots'
must be applicable.

Formal and Informal Organisation

The notion of making a distinction between formal and informal organisation derives very largely from the attack by Mayo and his associates on the classical organisation theories (see pages 19–22). This attack, which involved above all an exposure of the inadequacy of the formal principles of management proposed by the classical theorists, was discussed in Chapter 2. It was shown that Mayo's work is particularly important for revealing the extent to which an industrial work group forms a social structure of its own, over and above the structure which is laid down by management in providing for the organisation of the work task. Subsequent writers, notably Barnard, Simon and Selznick, have sought to generalise this observation and to apply this distinction between the formal and the informal to all aspects of organisational behaviour, pointing out that it is not merely factory workers and not just subordinate groups of employees who establish significant patterns of informal behaviour in the course of interaction with fellow members of their organisation.

However, even when generalised in this way, this distinction is misleading in some respects because it involves the assumption that organisations are always highly structured, with a clear-cut body of rules and procedures and fully recognised organisation plans, so that particular actions can be readily identified as in conformity with such structures or involving deviations from the patterns prescribed. In practice the lines that are drawn between formal and informal aspects of organisational behaviour are often arbitrary, and often involve either a prescriptive assumption that there is a formal structure which everyone *ought* to accept and that informal behaviour is deviant behaviour, or an assumption that there are two distinct structures when in practice the formal and the informal are interlocked.

Despite the unsatisfactory nature of the formal/informal distinction it is widely used in connection with the study of organisations. This provides one reason for discussing it here. More importantly, however, it is of value to study the viability of this distinction because by so doing it is possible to learn a great deal of value about how the complex organisations, which we find in public administration, actually operate. Exploration of the use made of these concepts will throw light upon organisational changes in response to the social environment, and in response to pressures from particular groups of participants; therefore it will provide an approach to the study of organisations in dynamic terms.

In many respects, this whole chapter is concerned with trying to define the terms formal and informal as used in this context. Their meaning can only be properly explained by reference to the use made of the concepts in describing particular aspects of organisational life. Nevertheless it is helpful to offer some short definitions at this stage, however inadequate they may subsequently be shown to be.

Weber's definition of bureaucracy provides perhaps the best definition of what is commonly known as formal organisation. It was summarised as follows on page 16:

A continuous organisation with a specified function, or functions, its operation bound by rules. Continuity and consistency within the organisation are ensured by the use of writing to record acts, decisions and rules. The organisation of personnel is on the basis of hierarchy, the scope of authority within the hierarchy is clearly defined, and the rights and duties of the officials at each level are specified.

Inasmuch as an organisation to some degree measures up to that definition it can be said to have a formal structure. Evidence of such structure will be available in the form of rule books, codes and manuals; records of decisions; organisation charts and so on.

The informal organisation can be defined by reference to the formal. As Simon, Smithburg and Thompson say: 'By *informal organization* is meant the whole pattern of actual behaviour—the way members of the organization really do behave—in so far as these actual behaviours do not coincide with the formal plan.'[1]

Unfortunately this neat distinction between the formal and the informal is much more easily made in theory than in practice. Hence it has come under considerable fire in recent years.[2] There are several reasons why it is difficult to make the distinction.

First, paradoxically enough, the use of these concepts is often associated with an excessively formalistic way of thinking about organisations. This presumably derives from the fact that the term informal was brought into use as a result of the discovery of the incompleteness of the formal. It derives from the expectation that the formal would be complete, whereas it is much more reasonable to expect the formal to be incomplete or to expect formalisation in any particular area to be very partially achieved. Hence it may be suggested that behaviour can be placed on a continuum between the formal and the informal as suggested in the following table:

Formal end	1. procedures that are recognised, codified etc.
	2. generally recognised practices that are not codified
	3. practices recognised by all or some persons in positions of authority but not given official recognition
	4. practices not permitted but not strenuously prevented
Informal end	5. practices not permitted against which preventative action is taken

Much behaviour within organisations, which many writers would describe as informal, falls within categories 2 and 3, and achieves a kind of permanency that would more appropriately justify the name formal than informal. Many writers seem to overlook the point that formalisation is often strenuously avoided in organisations. They have been led by their obsession with classical theory to expect formalisation where it is unlikely to occur.

A second reason why it is difficult in practice to distinguish between formal and informal is that the neat equation of the formal with the notion of a plan laid down by those at the top of the organisation, in conformity with the goals of the organisation, does not exist. Goals are seldom specific and clear, there is often conflict between the organisation's participants—even between top decision-makers—about goals, and even if goals are comparatively clear there may be disagreement about the means of implementing them (see Chapter 5).

Ambiguities will thus exist in the formal instructions to subordinates that open the door to informal practices, and significant aspects of the organisation's procedures will be left uncodified. Often formalisation will occur only when internal conflict or attack from outside forces it upon the organisation. Often too, contrary to the notion of formalisation originating from the top, pressure to develop routinised procedures will come from subordinates. This is particularly true of rules that safeguard employee interests, such as safety regulations and rules about conditions of service.[3] But as Merton has suggested it may be true of other matters too where rules protect the subordinate from insecurity.[4] Indeed, Merton goes further to suggest that bureaucrats use formal rules to secure the informal group against outsiders.

Furthermore, it would be wrong to imply that structures are left comparatively unformalised simply because of ambiguities or conflicts in the goal-setting or planning processes. Structures may well be quite deliberately left fluid in order to provide flexibility in the face of changing conditions. Burns and Stalker identified forms of organisation structure of this kind, which they called 'organic management systems':[5]

adapted to unstable conditions, when problems and requirements for action arise which cannot be broken down and distributed among specialist roles within a clearly defined hierarchy. Individuals have to perform their special tasks in the light of their knowledge of the tasks of the firm as a whole. Jobs lose much of their formal definition in terms of methods, duties, and powers, which have to be re-defined continually by interaction with others participating in a task. Interaction runs laterally as much as vertically. Communication between people of different ranks tends to resemble lateral consultation rather than vertical command. Omniscience can no longer be imputed to the head of the concern.

It has been made fairly clear in defining formal organisation that there are limits to the extent to which rules will be formulated to control every aspect of organisational activity, and that in most organisations there are likely to be large areas of employee behaviour unregulated by rules. To explore the factors which determine just where the limits to formalisation will be placed, two questions must be examined: first, why are formal structures developed at all? and second, given that formalisation is often avoided, what social factors provide resistance to the formalisation process?

The answer to the first of these questions is provided by Weber. As Albrow puts it:[6] 'Weber was sure that rational bureaucracy was bound to increase in importance. It had a series of characteristics—precision, continuity, discipline, strictness, reliability—which made it technically the most satisfactory form of organisation, both for authority holders and all other interested parties.' It is this notion of rationality which many interpreters of Weber have equated with efficiency, thus equating his approach to this issue with that adopted by the classical administrative theorists. The underlying philosophy behind the point of view of the classical theorists involves, say Miller and Form,[7] the assumption:

that formal organisation is necessary to achieve organisational goals. It is necessary because it is by nature impersonal, logical, and efficient. An organization can function best when individual idiosyncracies, sentiments, and prejudices do not interfere with official activities. Thus, if offices and roles are defined as a series of rights and duties, the individual element in social interaction is reduced.

These observations about the advantages of formal organisation must be related to the issues of size and complexity. Formal principles of organisation provide ways to cope with the problems raised by the expansion and elaboration of organisational tasks. In some respects it is impossible to answer the question 'why formal organisation?' without answering the more fundamental question 'why organisation?' As Barnard's analysis of the development of organisations suggests, the most basic principles of formal organisation—cooperation in a common task and the differentiation of parts of that task by division of labour—are inherent in the formation of organisations.[8]

There have been a number of accounts of the way in which voluntary organisations develop a formal structure as their functions increase in range and size. One particular aspect of this process is the formalisation that occurs as voluntary officials hand over responsibilities to full-time officials.

Much the same process can be detected in the evolution of public administration, as politicians have delegated responsibilities to officials. Such a process has been accelerated in public administration by the very extensive responsibilities taken on by governments; the political, social and moral pressures against corruption, patronage and graft; and the particular need for consistency in public administration in the light of the legal framework in which it operates. There are many historical studies of this process. A good general discussion of the processes involved is provided in F. M. Marx's *The Administrative State*.[9] More detailed accounts of the evolution of European civil services are provided by Barker[10] and by Chapman.[11] To provide some more concrete illustrations of the processes involved there follows a brief account of some aspects of the evolution of the British civil service. This discussion is largely based upon accounts by Cohen,[12] Kingsley,[13] Kelsall,[14] and Parris.[15]

Historians have traced the evolution of the British civil service back into the Middle Ages. For example, a classic work by Tout deals with the 'Civil Service' in the fourteenth century, showing how state offices emerged from the administration of the royal household.[16] However, the really significant developments in the formalisation of the civil service have occurred between the middle of the eighteenth century and the present day. Parris says of the term 'civil servant' that it[17]

can be found in contexts going back to the early middle ages. So long as this is understood to be a convenient shorthand way of saying 'those servants of the Crown who performed functions roughly analogous, so far as any comparison is possible, to those performed by the civil servant in twentieth-century Britain', no harm is done. Without some such reservation, the use of the term in relation to periods earlier than the half-century 1780–1830 is an obstacle to understanding. The 'permanent civil service' prior to that time differed from its modern counterpart in three significant ways. It was not permanent, it was not civil, and it was not a service.

In his essay, Parris then goes on to deal primarily with the first of the developments towards a more formalised civil service, the separation of offices within the administration from the political offices at the head of each ministry. Parris argues that there were important political reasons for these changes, in particular the desire to curb Crown patronage and the need of ministers, in an era of increasing political activity, to reduce their burdens by delegating administrative tasks. These changes created the conditions for the development of a bureaucratised civil service.

The late eighteenth century was also a period of rising government expenditure, particularly associated with the wars of that period. There was accordingly a rising demand for economy in the spending of public money. Such a demand was accompanied by considerable pressure for the improvement of standards of public morality. Hence movements for administrative reform particularly focused upon the need to develop techniques to prevent fraud and to eliminate sinecures and other public offices which were merely opportunities for individual profit-making.

Growing government activity in the early nineteenth century continued to arouse the anxieties of politicians, desirous, as ever, of curbing public expenditure. Hence, once the worst abuses of patronage had been abolished, attention increasingly turned to inefficiency. Various incidents testified to widespread maladministration, of which the Crimean War provided some of the most glaring examples. Moreover, the growing bourgeoisie became increasingly concerned about the unbusinesslike way public administration was conducted. In the words of Kingsley,[18]

Of significance, also, was the constant dissatisfaction of the commercial classes with the functioning of those branches of the government most immediately touching their interests: the customs and excise offices and the post office. It is of more than passing interest that middle class protests against administrative inefficiency were directed overwhelmingly at these agencies and that from 1833 onwards the Commons was deluged with petitions and protests concerning their management.

Hence the middle part of the nineteenth century saw some significant measures designed primarily at achieving greater efficiency by securing better recruits. Their objective was to eliminate the remaining vestiges of patronage and to provide formal processes of selection to regularised career positions. The most notable amongst these measures were those prompted by the Northcote-Trevelyan Report of 1853, the Orders in Council of 1855 and 1870, and by the Playfair Report of 1875, the Order in Council of 1876. Also important in providing a career service on the lines of Weber's model were the Superannuation Acts of 1834 and 1859.

The continuing growth of the civil service in the latter part of the nineteenth century and on into the twentieth century obviously led to continuing elaboration of the formal structure. Concern for uniformity and central control of the system led to the development of Treasury control of all aspects of the service. Recently some concern has been expressed about the extent to which the civil service has become dominated by bureaucratic forms of central control and, after the Fulton Committee[19] recommended it, the Treasury passed much of its control over the civil service to the Civil Service Department, to detach management of the service from financial control. The Fulton report also proposed that the very complex 'class' structure of the civil service should be radically modified. However it would be inaccurate to represent these proposals as involving any real dismantling of the formal structure of the civil service. On the contrary they are accompanied by other proposals for more efficient management, by the use of organisation and methods techniques, job evaluation, planning units and a more scrupulous attention to costing, that will inevitably lead to increasing formalisation.

Finally, no account of formalisation in the British civil service would be complete without some mention of the significance of pressure by staff for the establishment of clear-cut conditions of service, pay scales, pensions and so on. Since the middle of the nineteenth century a number of staff associations and trade unions have sprung up in the civil service to represent the viewpoints of the various grades of staff. Perhaps the great landmark for these organisations came when the government agreed in 1919 to set up a system of 'Whitley Councils' both for the service as a whole and for individual departments[20]

to secure a greater measure of cooperation between the State, in its capacity as employer, and the general body of Civil Servants in matters affecting the Civil Service, with a view to increased efficiency in public service combined with the well-being of those employed; to provide machinery for the ventilation of grievances; and generally to bring together, with a view to free discussion of many diverse and complex problems, the experience and different points of view of representatives of many grades and classes constituting the administrative, clerical and manipulative Civil Service of the Country.

Interestingly, the relationship between the civil service and civil servants' trade unions provides an example of the impact of one formal organisation upon another. The unions' commitment to securing fair treatment for their members tended to force the civil service to ensure that its handling of its staff was consistent and fair enough to stand scrutiny. Significantly too it is from the trade unions and staff associations that much of the pressure comes to ensure that due regard is paid to seniority in promotions and other dealings with staff, thus helping to reinforce a bureaucratic characteristic of the civil service that is particularly widely criticised.

Any historical account of the development of the civil service is bound to present the landmarks of the formalisation process in terms of various Acts of Parliament, Royal Commissions and other public events. It is difficult to provide an account which does not exaggerate the significance of landmarks without getting deeply

involved in expounding the political history of our age. An underlying theme in the processes discussed above has been the ever-
increasing demand for positive government. The resulting pressure
has increased the size of the nonindustrial civil service from
around 16,000 in 1797, to 108,000 in 1902, 376,000 in 1938, and
over 700,000 in 1968.

Only a few examples of the complexity of the formal organisation today can be given. On the subdivision of staff into specific
classes Fulton reports[21]

The Service is divided into classes both horizontally (between higher
and lower in the same broad area of work) and vertically (between
different skills, professions or disciplines). There are 47 general
classes whose members work in most government departments and
over 1,400 departmental classes. Each civil servant is recruited to a
particular class ; his membership of that class determines his prospects
(most classes have their own career structures) and the range of jobs
on which he may be employed.

As an example of the body of formal rules which are typically
elaborated in a civil service department, the following account of
the bulk of instructions which junior civil servants in the National
Assistance Board (now the Supplementary Benefits Commission)
had to take into account in their day-to-day work provides some
insight:[22]

The job of the National Assistance Board was defined in the
National Assistance Act 1948, and in the regulations passed by
Parliament under the terms of that Act. However, for the Executive
Officer in a local office of the Board this basic statutory framework
had been enormously developed into a large number of instructions
found in the 'Codes'. The basic manual for day-to-day work on
applications for Assistance was the 'A' Code, a loose-leaf book of
several hundred pages that was subject to continuous amendment.
But this was supplemented by other 'Codes', in particular one in
which procedures for dealing with fraud and overpayments were laid
down and one giving instructions on procedures for attempting to
receive payments from missing husbands and fathers. Office procedures and personnel regulations were found in yet another code,
the 'G' Code, a manual largely derived from the Treasury's Estacode.
These codes were supplemented by circulars both from Headquarters
and from the Regional Office. Finally, on matters of local significance
the Manager also issued additional instructions from time to time.

It is impossible to give an account of any brevity of the complexity of the hierarchical structure involved in the modern British civil service. For an account of this the reader should consult Mackenzie and Grove's *Central Administration in Britain*.[23]

It has been shown that in order to build up the British civil service into a basically effective and reliable instrument of government it has been necessary to formalise it in various ways. This formalisation process has naturally been closely connected with its growth in size. Not only has increasing size made formalisation necessary but, equally, formalisation has made growth feasible.

Predictably, the work of those theorists who drew attention to the advantages to be derived from formalisation was seized upon and the following questions were asked: If formal organisation is so rational and efficient, why don't people do more to formalise organisational relationships? Why is formalisation often resisted? The answer most readily suggested to these questions, and implicit in Weber's equation of bureaucratisation with rationality, was that people are irrational; that in practice there is a kind of tension between rationality and irrationality in man, which produces both efforts toward the creation of the most rational and efficient forms of organisation and the sabotage of some of these attempts.

It is this point of view which dominated the work of Elton Mayo and the human relations school of thought. Their argument is that the formal approach to management is undermined by a failure to take into account the needs of employees, and to channel those needs from 'irrational' directions into a commitment to the 'rational' goals of the organisations.[24]

As explained earlier, Mayo's researches are of much greater importance for the advance of the study of human behaviour in organisations than his theory. Many writers[25] have pointed out that one of the flaws in Mayo's reasoning is the assumption that what is rational for the organisation is necessarily rational for the individual, or, to go even further, that it is really possible to identify what is rational for the organisation. In fact, it can be suggested that what Mayo and his associates revealed is that individuals within organisations cannot necessarily be expected to have any commitments to goals set by the needs of other individuals.

Thus, in explaining informal behaviour, it is not sufficient to have recourse to so simple a solution as that involved in explaining it in terms of irrationality; the 'human relations' approach, though not always wrong, does not provide complete answers for managers whose objectives are thwarted by the informal behaviour of their subordinates. A more realistic presentation of the relationship between the formal and the informal in organisations, which also involves recognition of the inevitable conflicts between organisational requirements and individual needs, can be found in the writings of Selznick. The following quotation, from his *Leadership in Administration*, presents a very neat picture of the relationship:[26]

An organization is a group of living human beings. The formal or official design for living never completely accounts for what the participants do. It is always supplemented by what is called the 'informal structure', which arises as the individual brings into play his own personality, his special problems and interests. Formal relations coordinate roles or specialized activities, not persons. Rules apply to foremen and machinists, to clerks, sergeants, and vice-presidents, yet no durable organization is able to hold human experience to these formally defined roles. In actual practice, men tend to interact as many-faceted persons, adjusting to the daily round in ways that spill over the neat boundaries set by their assigned roles.

The formal, technical system is therefore never more than a part of the living enterprise we deal with in action. The persons and groups who make it up are not content to be treated as manipulable or expendable. As human beings and not mere tools they have their own needs for self-protection and self-fulfilment — needs that may either sustain the formal system or undermine it.

There is another aspect to Selznick's approach which deserves mention here. The Hawthorne researches approach to the informal structures is very largely a psychological one. The focus of attention is the individual personality and its needs, or at most the small group. Little mention is made of the wider society within which the organisation operates. One specific criticism that has been made of these researches is that no attention has been paid to the level of unemployment outside the organisation in explaining commitment within it.[27] When considering the relationship between roles and the individual personality within the organisation, it must not be forgotten that the individual has other roles outside the work context. Thus, Dalton has studied clique structure within the management of a large firm in relation to the social roles, the membership of social organisations and so on, played by these persons outside the firm.[28] For a really full understanding of the pressures against the development of (or towards the breakdown of) the formal structure of an organisation, these factors also have to be taken into account.

Selznick's modification of Mayo's approach, then, suggests that the language of rationality and irrationality is largely inappropriate; that people may seek to create efficient organisational forms but must expect to find that social and psychological realities will modify those forms. But even this more complex proposition puts the issues too simply.

Any approach to this subject that suggests that a relatively rational process of designing organisational forms takes place, which is then subject to modification on account of the needs and personalities of subordinates, disregards the fact that the actions and goal conceptualisations of those who design these forms are themselves influenced by the fact that they too are enmeshed in a web of social relationships, and that they too may be responding to specific personal needs that shape their notions of organisational ends and means. As Josephson has pointed out,[29] 'both the classical description of the "ideal" bureaucracy and field studies of institutional behaviour neglect irrational leadership, in the first instance, due to exaggeration of logical behaviour, and in the second, by stressing irrational activity on the part of subordinates.' Further he argues, 'Ideally, bureaucracy assumes that in the process of "self-rationalisation" a participant will identify himself sufficiently with logical goals of an organisation to permit maximum rationalisation of behaviour. In practice, however, the process of identification may be reversed: the *executive* may identify the organisation with *his* goals and needs.'

However, even this very valid point made by Josephson is based upon the unsatisfactory rational/irrational dichotomy. Even if it is assumed that the people who design an organisation are entirely 'rational', seeking to relate structure to goals in the best possible way, it must be acknowledged that they will have very little idea what the best possible way is. Many sociologists have sought to show the flaws in Weber's formulation of it.[30] Simon criticised the 'proverbs' suggested by the formal theorists such as Gulick and Urwick,[31] yet he himself does little to advance us towards anything more concrete. Contemporary organisation theory represents further attempts to tackle this problem, yet anyone engaged in the practical task of designing a formal organisation would find their suggestions far too abstract. If the problem still defeats the theorists, surely people will not achieve the right approach to formalisation intuitively.

Consciously or unconsciously, the principles upon which organisations are built are generally the formal principles which were set out in classical theory. Hence 'rationality' consists of following a series of intuitive rules which have been given traditional endorsement and can be regarded as part of the western cultural heritage. Principles like the principle of hierarchy, or the separation of staff and line, or the separation of the public and private spheres of the lives of officials work in practice, more often than not, primarily because people are committed to making them work. This is not to say that certain social advantages have not been found to flow from the adoption of such principles but simply that there are no absolute tests of rationality or efficiency. Such concepts cannot be subjected to absolute tests because they can only be defined by reference to specific goals and specific side effects. Nepotism may to our eyes have a disastrous impact upon the working of a system of government but it may have some distinctly beneficial effects upon the working of particular family systems, whose disruption could have a more disastrous consequence for the stability of some systems of government.

Hence another weakness of Selznick's contrast between efficient organisational forms and social and psychological realities lies in the assumption that efficiency and adjustment to reality may be incompatible. Surely, to fail to adjust to realities is, from many standpoints, to be inefficient. To seek to provide rules for every eventuality if men dislike being utterly rule-bound is inefficient. Similarly, as Merton argues,[32] to bind men by rules in such a way that they cannot deal with novel situations seems a strange way to try to create an efficient organisation.

There is a distinct case for formalisation to enable organisations to become large and complex, and to handle their responsibilities in a coherent manner. But formalisation is in many ways an arbitrary and inadequate process, which is bound to be resisted by the very many people whose needs are unconsidered when rules are elaborated. There is here, then, a paradox. There is a case for formalisation, yet there are also evils resulting from over-formalisation. Politicians regularly fulminate against bureaucracy, but continue to build bureaucratic organisations. Newspapers attack bureaucratic rules but are quick to call for new rules whenever some disaster occurs. Most of us are enormously ambivalent towards the formal organisations of the state. It is possible to talk glibly about achieving the perfect adjustment, the right balance between these two extremes, but what does this really mean? If public satisfaction and employee morale is not being undermined by the over-formalised and arbitrary organisation, then it is being undermined by an inefficient and inconsistent but less bureaucratic organisation. The search for ideal bureaucratic forms must involve decisions about the desirability of different degrees of formalism which are based upon assessments of the consequences of the available alternatives. Rules cannot be formulated for any textbook of administration; on the contrary, value decisions have to be taken on the basis of likely consequences.

So far it has been made clear that the concepts of formal and informal describe aspects of organisations which are in dynamic relation to each other, and which shade into each other; that they cannot be equated with rationality and irrationality; and that organisations do not come anywhere near to formalising every aspect of the lives of their members. In addition, although it seems reasonable to expect that those in controlling positions in an organisation will be most closely committed to the formal structure, while those in the most subordinate positions will be most likely to be involved in informal structures and relationships, this correspondence will be far from total and there will be situations where the opposite applies. As Gouldner has shown, there are both 'superior' and 'subordinate' oriented rules.[33]

The next step in this analysis is to take a more specific look at the interaction between the formal and the informal within organisations. The first task is to look at informal groupings; this is followed by some comments on informal power and status. Dalton, describing informal groups as 'cliques', has suggested the following clique typology:[34]

    random

    horizontal—either aggressive or defensive

    vertical—either symbiotic or parasitic

Random cliques have no specific significance for the organisation as a whole. They grow up simply because members of an organisation do not interact with each other only in their formal roles. Friendship patterns grow up which cut across divisions according to department or rank. The extent to which these patterns develop will depend upon several factors. Their growth will very much depend upon the opportunities for contact between persons who are not in touch with each other in the course of undertaking their formal roles; they will thus depend upon the extent to which persons make casual contacts in the course of their working day, on the extent to which social mixing occurs in a canteen or social club attached to the organisation, and upon the extent to which such contacts are acceptable or taboo. On this last point it may be suggested that inter-rank social relationships tend to be frowned upon in some organisations, for example the armed forces. There are also probably certain social pressures which tend to make them less likely in Britain than in, for example, the United States. Such random contacts are also much more likely when an organisation is based in a small community than in a large one (for the obvious reason that out-of-work contacts will be more common) or when there are special aspects of the occupation which tend to bind members of the organisation to each other and separate them from other people.[35]

Although random cliques have no specific significance for the formal organisation, they make a contribution to solidarity and commitment to the organisation. Here they can be contrasted with the other types of cliques which are in many respects divisive. Random cliques are not united for conflict with other groups. They provide useful, yet relatively innocuous, channels of communication.

Horizontal cliques are groupings of equals within the organisation. Since Dalton was studying the managerial ranks of an organisation, these obviously consisted of more than groups of people working together. His distinction between aggressive and defensive horizontal cliques is less useful for the discussion in this book than the distinction between groupings of equals for some specific purpose—either aggressively to seek some concession or defensively to protect something—and groupings of a nonspecific kind. Significant examples of the latter kind include groups of subordinate workers who derive satisfaction from fooling around together at work, as in the Bank Wiring Room (see page 21); groups of employees who cooperate closely to help each other solve work problems, such as the federal agents studied by Blau;[36] groups of employees who develop close social solidarity extending outside the work situation, as described by Francis and Stone;[37] and groupings which are particularly important in providing a means of releasing some of the tensions associated with the work situation. On the last point, Blau has shown that the opportunity to complain or joke about clients provided this for the staff in a public welfare agency.[38]

The observations made above about random cliques being more likely when the social environment, or the nature of the job or work environment, bring people together will also apply to horizontal cliques. But, if there are pressures against inter-rank social mixing then this may act as a strong force towards horizontal grouping rather than random cliques.

Trade union groups provide the most obvious examples of horizontal groups held together by specific interests. A comment has already been made on the way in which trade union groupings tend to cut across the distinction between the 'formal' and the 'informal'. Trade unionism provides an approach to the legitimisation of horizontal groups, and it is through this mechanism that individuals find support to enable them to challenge a hierarchical authority structure. Naturally any subordinate who is able to say, when opposing his superior, that he has the support of colleagues is in a stronger position than when he is acting alone. But if he can also say he enjoys the support of a union, an autonomous organisation with members also from outside the limits of a single department or agency, his position is that much stronger. Above all, he is likely to be in a particularly strong position if his superiors have previously granted that union a right to bargain on his behalf. These are all fairly elementary points, yet it is important to make it clear that the general principles upon which the informal horizontal cliques described by Dalton are based are in practice the same ones upon which these most significant sources of countervailing power within hierarchical organisations are founded.[39]

It is also important to make this point because when horizontal groups within organisations are able to organise in this way, and to link up with comparable groups in other organisations, the end result may be so great an aggregation of power that they are able to make the maintenance of hierarchical principles of organisation impossible. The most widespread examples of this phenomenon come not so much from the trade unions organised by lower-level workers as from the associations which do so much to preserve the autonomy of professional employees. The power of professionals, and the way in which professional principles conflict with hierarchical ones, will be the subject of Chapter 8.

However, growing trade union power is gradually bringing about similar situations within the ranks of nonprofessional workers. Crozier,[40] in his study of a French nationalised industry, shows how the authority of supervisors has been undermined by trade unions which have been able to secure a situation in which rights and obligations are predetermined. The demand for participation in decision-making involves a demand for the recognition of the claims of horizontal groupings, the ultimate objective being the building of these groupings into a reformed formal structure. Crozier's study suggests that an alternative situation may occur in which the demands of subordinate groups of workers are recognised yet decision-making procedures are not altered, perhaps because management is forced to yield power but refuses to concede legitimacy. In this kind of situation, rigidity ensues with neither side being prepared to make the concessions that are necessary to move beyond stereotyped procedures. A kind of 'guild system' develops with stagnation based upon the maintenance of traditional prerogatives. Crozier describes the kind of grouping which develops in terms of a concept taken from Pitts[41] as a 'delinquent community' which protects itself from interference from those in authority, and in this sense possesses a negative kind of solidarity. Such a grouping may be described as a 'defensive' horizontal clique. Its peculiar features are ascribed by Crozier to the particular nature of French culture, but it may be that it is in general more feasible for a grouping of subordinate employees who acquire power as a consequence of their solidarity to operate in a negative rather than a positive way. Solidarity is more easily achieved on defensive issues; positive innovation tends to be much more difficult, and the occupancy of a subordinate role is in itself detrimental to initiative taking (in the sense that it may be said to involve 'alienation'). In short, it may be argued that successful subordinate challenges to a hierarchical structure may have a conservative rather than a revolutionary impact upon the organisation as a whole in that it will break it up into a series of informal groups intent on protecting themselves rather than on creating a dynamic new formal structure. A study of the impact of growing civil service trade unionism upon the flexibility of the public bureaucracy would be a valuable means of throwing light on this issue, to see whether the British system is evolving in the direction of the French system or whether there are other cultural, institutional or political factors which come into play to prevent such a process occurring.

A further point to be made about the tendency of horizontal groupings to occur for the purposes of joint action is that, apart from their relation to the authority structure of the organisation, and apart from the presence or absence of a 'normative commitment', groups vary in their readiness to act collectively. This variation is largely conditioned by cultural phenomena. In England, groups of manual workers and groups of routine clerical workers do not necessarily differ in the strength of their normative orientation to the organisation they work for, but they tend to differ in their readiness to consider collective action as a means of redressing grievances.[42]

Vertical cliques are cliques containing persons at different levels in a hierarchy. These cliques have a very real significance for the power structure of the organisation. The distinction Dalton makes between symbiotic and parasitic cliques refers to the fact that the latter often involve an exploitative relationship between persons, for example either a superior who uses friendship with a subordinate as an informal source of information and hence as a means of controlling subordinates, or a subordinate who exploits friendship with a superior as a means of gaining personal advantages.

Symbiotic vertical cliques involve one or more exchange relationships, where superiors gain the loyal support of certain subordinates in return for their readiness to consult those people and perhaps to sponsor them when opportunities arise for their advancement. Dalton suggests that these cliques are very important for decision-making within an organisation. He points out that when decisions have to be made, the key consultations and exchanges of information often occur rather more through the informal channels provided by symbiotic cliques than through the formal channels.

Dalton's study is rather exceptional in providing information about vertical cliques. This aspect of the functioning of an organisation is normally kept well hidden from the outside observer. Dalton made his study by becoming an insider, a course of action which some sociologists would regard as unethical and many would find impractical. All that can be said about vertical cliques in public administration in Britain is that it is certainly known that they exist amongst politicians, and that it is known too from the inferences drawn by journalists, such as for example the Insight team of the *Sunday Times*, that they exist as far as the relations between politicians and top civil servants are concerned. The extent to which they exist will depend upon some of the more general social and cultural features that have been discussed while considering other types of cliques. Thus, for example, in the civil service both relations between ranks and promotions are governed by a body of rules, and conditioned by an ethic of impartiality, which may well curb vertical clique development to a considerable extent, by contrast with much of private industry. Moreover grade consciousness in the civil service, a phenomenon not unrelated to class consciousness, may also tend to curb such developments. But these factors certainly are unlikely to eliminate vertical cliques altogether.

There is a tendency to regard vertical cliques as necessarily rather undesirable and unpleasant phenomena. This is connected with the particularly threatening character of personal conflicts, between people in senior positions within organisations, for the legitimacy of the management structure as a whole; as Fox suggests,[43] 'To recognize, and thereby run the risk of seeming to legitimize, open struggles between individuals for status and power may be perceived as too destructive of co-operative effort, management ideology and the notion of the unified team'.

Yet vertical cliques make possible informal consultations that avoid the premature making of formal commitments. They also provide means of control for superiors that enable them to avoid stepping up levels of formal supervision. And they provide subordinates with links with their seniors that enable them to raise grievances and make suggestions, without using formal procedures that may force their superiors to take hard lines to avoid losing face.

Of course there can be informal contact between superiors and subordinates without having clique formation, and it is often suggested that good management consists, amongst other things, of doing just this. Yet it must be recognised that the proliferation of informal contacts between levels in an organisation very often leads, sometimes even unwittingly, to vertical clique formation. Interaction between persons which is not subject to explicit formal rules will, of necessity, be moulded by interpersonal factors so that, for example, preferences for certain people may well bias relations with a group as a whole.

It has been shown that cliques, particularly vertical cliques, are important for the power structure as a whole. Since this subject was a central concern of Dalton's study of management it is helpful to follow further his suggestions as to why, in the organisation he studied, the real power structure deviated from what might be expected from a picture of the formal power structure. In his book he presents an interesting chart of the real power structure, built up from interviews with participants, which he contrasts with the formal power structure. He goes on to suggest a number of reasons why this difference occurs:

1 *Personalities*. Dalton suggests that personalities alone cannot have a significant effect upon the power structure, except in the case of two persons next to each other in rank where the lower of the two is a very much more dominant personality than his superior. This kind of situation is, of course, very common, and does not necessitate a detailed discussion. It is often referred to in discussions of the relations between ministers and civil servants.[44]

2 *Cliques*. The significance of vertical cliques within organisations has already been discussed. It only remains to add that if the clique system in an organisation as a whole is considered, it may be found that there exists what may be called an embryonic 'party system', so that in the event of a contest for power between two clique leaders, the supporters of the successful leader may find that they derive substantial advantages over the supporters of the unsuccessful one. There seems little doubt that in the British civil service, clique formation has been associated with conflicts over specific policy issues, the pro- or anti-Germans in the 1930s,[45] the pro- or anti-Arabs in the 1940s and 1950s in the Foreign Office,[46] or the pro- or anti-devaluation groups of 1964–7.[47] Is it too much to suggest that internal power positions have been affected by identifications on these controversial issues, and that resignations of key figures in these controversies have adversely affected the careers of some of their more junior supporters?

3 *The ambiguity of staff/line relations*. A characteristic of much of British central government is the dominance of 'line' officials. Professional roles often involve either a low position in the formal structure or a relatively high position where status is ambiguous and rights are unclear. In such a situation the professional may well find it necessary to use informal means to offset his relatively disadvantaged position.

Some attention has been paid recently to the problems of power and status which face advisers in government departments in Britain. In their evidence to the Fulton Committee, the Institution of Professional Civil Servants expressed its concern about the formal position of specialists very strongly:[48]

> The role of the 'specialist', however, is still largely subordinated to that of the administrator .... Despite interesting developments in some departments, the general position of 'specialists' is still grossly unsatisfactory.... It would be wrong to perpetuate or deify the wholly unwarranted mystique that it is only a member of the Administrative Class who can understand the machine and advise on policy.... No man should be effectively debarred at any level because of his speciality, whether it be science, engineering, medicine, law, administration or any other branch.

Exceptionally, a professional who is a very skilful organisation politician may succeed in exploiting the ambiguity of his position to make himself very powerful indeed. The classic case of this is reported by C. P. Snow in his account of the dominance of Lindemann as a scientific adviser during the Second World War.[49] Lindemann's success depended very much upon his ability to secure the ear of Churchill. In this respect he started with the advantage of holding the kind of ambiguous position which offers the possibility of securing special attention from the key decision-maker, a position which Dalton calls the 'assistant-to'.

4 *The ambiguity of the position of the 'assistant-to'*. In Dalton's study he found that the position of 'assistant-to' a senior manager was used in two very different ways, associated with marked differences in power and status. Some of the holders of these posts were themselves fairly senior members of the management team who had been pushed aside on account of incompetence into positions of no real power but some seniority, as an alternative to redundancy. But other 'assistant-tos' were young protégés of senior management who had been advanced from quite junior posts. They had been given positions of this kind partly because they provided opportunities for gaining experience of top management prior to acceptance for a very senior post, and partly because they could not have been considered for more regular 'line' posts because of the discontent that would have arisen from those who recognised that their advance had been excessively rapid and in disregard of the claims of more senior and experienced people.

These particular types of posts may well be peculiar to the kind of organisation Dalton was studying. Both 'near sinecures' and the rapid advancement of management's protégés are phenomena that cannot so readily occur in public administration without arousing political and public disquiet. However examples of ambiguous positions can be found in most large-scale organisations. In the British civil service, positions with particular responsibilities for personnel—establishments and welfare posts—and also posts in regional offices are often, rightly or wrongly, given to relatively senior occupants of the middle or upper grades who are not considered adequate for further advancement. Such posts may involve relatively less power than an officer of a comparable rank might expect to wield elsewhere in the service.

At the other end of the scale, comparatively junior officers who seem particularly promising are selected as private secretaries to ministers and permanent secretaries,[50] posts from which they may wield informal power considerably in excess of that normal for officers of their grade. But, though successful performance in a 'private office' may stand a civil servant in good stead for the future, such positions do not lead on to dramatic advancement.

Finally, politicians do, from time to time, bring into their ministries special advisers who will obviously expect to wield considerable power. Their fate is obviously very closely tied up with the fate of the ministers who bring them in, and their real power will depend upon the success of the minister in securing the adoption of policies with which he and his special advisers are identified. This is another point at which the logic of the formal/informal distinction becomes nonsense in that it may be suggested that there may be developed within government departments two 'systems', with the minister building up a team of advisers to counterbalance the official formal system. It would be nonsense to call the minister's team an 'informal structure', yet in practice the major difficulty they face is that they have to try to operate successfully in a situation in which an established permanent team of officials is accustomed to controlling the decision-making process. Both their strengths and their weaknesses lie in the fact that they are stationed outside the 'formal' system.

5 *Special relationships with head office*. Dalton's study was concerned with a branch office of a large nation-wide organisation. In that office were certain individuals who had been seconded from head office. He suggested that these individuals had a certain amount of informal power by virtue of continuing links with head office, the implication being that they were virtually spies from

head office. Such a situation again seems less likely in public administration, but individuals in local offices who have been transferred from a central office or individuals in specific ministries, who have come from the Treasury or the Civil Service Department, may well derive certain power advantages from having informal links with a dominant organisation outside their own. However, any advantages gained from such positions may well be counterbalanced by the fact that as former 'outsiders' their links with the informal structure of their new organisation may be weaker.

6 *Influence of outside status and groups.* In the discussion of random cliques it was suggested that groupings within an organisation may well be determined by groupings outside that organisation. Moreover, it must be recognised that status and power systems within an organisation may also be influenced in this way. This influence may take three forms: first, members of an organisation may be involved in status and power relationships in other organisations or social groupings that do not correspond with the formal authority structure existing in the organisation. This kind of situation is obviously often embarrassing to the persons involved, particularly the senior organisation members, and is normally avoided, except perhaps in small communities. In general, too, the complex relationship between, on the one hand, social status, personality, education, occupation, and, on the other, readiness to accept leadership roles in voluntary organisations will operate to make this kind of situation comparatively rare.[51]

The second form which this influence may take is that persons who are of different status in the organisation may be equals in social and voluntary organisation relationships outside the work context. Such relationships will contribute to vertical clique formation, as suggested above. They will also make an important contribution to overall solidarity within the organisation, as Dale has suggested is the case with the British higher civil service, and in this sense they will contribute to the stability of the formal structure. More insidiously they will also operate to exclude outsiders so that individuals who do not participate in certain forms of social life outside the organisation may find themselves at a disadvantage in internal power struggles.

These observations are pertinent to the view of the British higher civil service as possessing a caste-like structure, as suggested in Dale's account of the service,[52] within which 'outsiders' are at a severe disadvantage. The diversity of recruits to this service during the Second World War and the partial democratisation of education since that time have tended to make this an unreal view today. Chapman provides some important evidence on this point and makes some interesting contrasts between the data he collected and the image conveyed by Dale.[53]

Yet it is the case that some of the more 'professionally oriented' young administrative class civil servants of today have formed unofficial groups concerned with current administrative and political problems. This form of grouping, or indeed the better-known professional organisations like the Royal Institute of Public Administration, may provide a source of significant unofficial groupings inside the administrative machine.

The third form of influence by outside status involves the impact on an organisation of the overall social structure of the society in which it exists. Some sort of correspondence between high social status and high rank in a bureaucratic organisation may be expected, both because individuals from high-status backgrounds tend to achieve high-status occupations and because the achievement of a high occupational status contributes considerably to high social status. Informal groupings may become very important in situations in which this neat correspondence does not occur. Such situations are particularly likely to arise in societies where factors other than occupational status are important for the determination of social status. Two types of situation may arise, one involving an imperfect equation between social status and organisational rank which creates lack of respect for certain senior officials, and also perhaps excessive deference to certain junior officials, the other involving unequal relationships between rank equals so that low-status individuals are shut out from significant informal groupings.

The concern in this chapter so far has been with informal groupings and with the social and psychological factors which tend to make the real power structure of an organisation different from its formal authority structure. It is now pertinent to move on to discuss some specific examples of behaviour which has been called 'informal', behaviour involving the modification or evasion of formal rules. Two American studies have been particularly concerned with this aspect of informal behaviour in public bureaucracies, Blau's *The Dynamics of Bureaucracy* and Francis and Stone's *Service and Procedure in Bureaucracy*.

C

In his study, Blau suggests that three types of modification of formal rules may be found: 'adjustment, redefinition and amplification'.[54]

In their studies of public employment agencies both Blau and Francis and Stone draw attention to the way in which employees simplified the procedures they used for taking down particulars of job applicants in the interests of speed. Francis and Stone particularly see this as involving the sacrifice of procedure to service, though in Blau's study the importance of statistics of work done for the evaluation of employee performance offers a less altruistic explanation. Perhaps the most important point to make about these adjustments is that they are a response to situations in which the individual has to decide between conflicting requirements: to serve the public or to carry out the correct procedure, to work quickly or to work correctly.

Procedural adjustment, then, is not merely a process of avoiding doing unpopular things, rather it is a matter of choosing the more congenial of two alternatives. Individuals normally seek to justify their adjustments of procedures as explicit contributions to organisation goals. Blau's federal law-enforcement agents avoided obeying a rule which required them to report offers of bribes, seeing it as an illegitimate means of seeking the favour of superiors and as an infringement of what they regarded as the right way to treat the 'white-collar' persons with whom they were dealing.[55] They particularly justified this behaviour by reference to the strong psychological position the unreported refusal of such an offer put them in to enable them to complete their investigations successfully. The author has described a similar example of procedural modification in a discussion of the way National Assistance Board officers[56] dealt with suspected fraud by seeking to deter suspects from continuing to apply for Assitance rather than by using the formal procedures available for the investigation and prosecution of fraudulent applicants. The formal procedure was lengthy and elaborate and officers justified evading it because the fraud continued while evidence was being accumulated, prosecutions often did not follow charges, for legal or political reasons, and convictions rarely brought about restitution.

By the redefinition of a procedure or rule, Blau means a modification which 'deliberately sacrifices the original objective of a procedure in order to achieve another organisational objective more effectively'.[57] Thus the employment agents Blau studied

virtually abandoned counselling procedures in order to concentrate on a speedy placement service.

In trying to prevent redefinition and adjustment of procedures,
supervisors elaborated the rules relating to those procedures. This
is what Blau means by 'amplification' of procedures. He goes on to
suggest that the response of subordinates to 'amplification' is often
further 'adjustment' or 'redefinition' of procedures. It is in this
way that the running of a bureaucratic organisation involves a continuing dynamic relationship between the formal and the informal.

Individuals normally seek to modify and adjust rules that are
unsatisfactory and unpopular, rather than to evade them. Such
more subtle manoeuvres are less susceptible to detection and pre-
vention. To treat a rule as totally unworkable tends to require
either substantial support from one's peers, or a strikingly good
personal market situation, or the tacit support of those superiors
who are aware of such behaviour. Often, of course, these three
factors operate together, since collective market situations are
better than individual ones and wise superiors recognise when the
cards are stacked against them.

Gouldner has given the name 'indulgency pattern' to the kind of
behaviour in which superiors tolerate certain types of rule infringement by subordinates. He sees such behaviour as making a
positive contribution to employee morale. This will apply primarily to situations in which superiors could enforce rules but do
not, rather than with unenforceable rules which superiors have to
'indulge' because of their powerlessness. In practice it is difficult
to distinguish between these two types of situations because of the
ambiguous nature of many power situations—a problem that will
be discussed at the beginning of Chapter 6.

On the type of situation described by Gouldner, Blau makes a
further significant point that 'the toleration of illicit practices
actually enhances the controlling power of superiors, paradoxical
as it may seem.'[58] There are two reasons for this, one being
that the withdrawal of such toleration may be used as a sanction
in the event of the subordinate incurring his superior's displeasure
in some other way, the other being that 'by voluntarily relinquish-
ing some of his prerogatives, the supervisor ... [creates] social
obligations.'

The discussion of Blau's work on the relations between the
formal and the informal within organisations has involved a
certain disregard of the warnings about the misleading nature of

the distinction which were given at the beginning of this chapter. Blau's approach involves disregarding two important points about the formal/informal distinction.

In the first place Blau goes to great lengths to show that rule modification is not necessarily an irrational process. Thus he shows how law-enforcement agents disregard rules forbidding them to consult each other but comes to the following conclusion:[59] 'The fact that consultations were tolerated suggests that their unofficial character was incidental to their relative newness. To treat them as deviations from formal requirements may well be less fruitful than to consider them as modifications of the structure, a stage in its development. A basic reorganisation had actually taken place in this agency, and it was tolerated by superiors, although it had not yet received official sanction'. In other words the original rule was a stupid one which no intelligent supervisor would try to enforce. The true 'formal' position was that this area of behaviour was not rule bound.

Studies of bureaucratic organisations have been so obsessed with studying the impact of rules that insufficient attention has been paid to the very large number of situations in which rules have deliberately not been made, where the only 'rule' is that officials must use their discretion. The study of discretionary behaviour is a field of study in which the words 'formal' and 'informal' make little sense, yet the extent to which rules and procedures can be elaborated to control and limit discretion is a topic intimately related to the subjects discussed in this chapter. The exercise of discretion will therefore be the subject of the next chapter.

The second flaw in Blau's frame of reference lies in his apparent assumption that behaviour can be described as 'functional' or 'disfunctional' because it can be related to the goals of the organisation. Yet goals are often not clear, or are the subject of conflict, or are modified so that where formal or informal behaviour is related to goals one may find that the so-called goals are themselves problematical. The chapter after next will therefore be concerned with the setting and modification of goals in public organisations, and with the conflict and ambiguity which may surround such goals.

The next two chapters, therefore, must be considered in conjunction with this one in order to secure a complete idea of the strengths and limitations of the formal/informal dichotomy for the study of public administration.

4

Administrative Discretion

In Chapter 3 it was made clear that it is unrealistic to expect
to find that decision-making procedures will be entirely rule bound.
In practice very many decisions are left to be made by subordinate
officers in the light of their judgement, and do not involve a
routinised process in which specific rules have to be applied in the
light of specific facts.

The exercise of discretion must be clearly distinguished from
some other kinds of decision-making which are easily confused
with it. First, confusion can arise because, in Britain, very little
administrative decision-making can be regarded as being directly
prescribed or regulated by Parliament. Intervening between the
bare bones of Acts of Parliament and the decision-making of
individual civil servants there is a framework of rules which are
described as 'delegated legislation'. In other words administrative
bodies have powers which enable them to 'legislate'.[1] This point
may be illustrated by an example drawn from a field from which
many of the examples of discretionary behaviour discussed in this
chapter will be taken, social security. When an official of the
Supplementary Benefits Commission assesses the 'needs' of a
person who has applied for benefit under the terms of the 1966
Ministry of Social Security Act, he will base his initial calculation
upon a series of 'scale rates' given in his instructions. These scales
are not contained in the Act, they are set out in a Statutory Instrument which has been laid before Parliament and thus in a legal
sense has been 'passed' by Parliament. Although 'legislation' of
this kind is not subject to the kind of scrutiny given to an Act
of Parliament, and does in some sense arise from 'discretionary'
decisions made within a Ministry, it is misleading to use the term
in such a way.

The exercise of discretion must also be distinguished from
'maladministration'. In a sense, 'maladministration' implies dis-

cretionary behaviour in that it arises when an official uses his 'discretion' to ignore a specific rule. This sort of situation must be distinguished from many in which officials are explicitly required to exercise their own judgement. Confusion arises because the inequitable or biased use of discretion, in situations in which officials are left a large amount of decision-making freedom, is often mistakenly taken for maladministration. Some of the enthusiasm for the introduction of the Ombudsman seemed to stem from this kind of confusion, so that many people were unaware how limited his field of action would be. In the same way, while there is at present in Britain justifiable concern about the unsatisfactory nature of the complaints procedure dealing with police malpractice, it is often forgotten that if policemen are zealous in the pursuit of some kinds of offenders (say, for example, ones with black skins) and disregard other kinds of offenders, this is not a satisfactory ground upon which an individual can base a complaint if no malpractice is involved in *his* case.[2]

The exercise of discretion occurs when officials are required or permitted to make decisions without being given instructions which would in effect predetermine those decisions. There is naturally scope for further confusion because such decision-making is seldom entirely unregulated. In practice the official who is to exercise discretion may be expected to be subject to instructions, which determine limits to the scope of his discretion, and rules about the different circumstances under which he may or may not exercise discretion. He may also, by various means, be supplied with advice to help him to make his discretionary decisions. In other words, unlimited discretion is nonexistent (indeed it is a meaningless concept in this context) and the extent of discretionary freedom varies widely between different officials and between the different areas of responsibility each official has.

Studies of administration have paid little attention to discretionary behaviour, tending either to equate it with the kinds of administrative behaviour which are in practice, as suggested above, legislative behaviour, or to regard it as behaviour which can potentially be subjected to legislative or judicial control. It will be argued here that it is not the case that discretionary behaviour can easily be eliminated by rules, and that moreover the consequences of subjecting some areas of administrative decision-making to rules are of a kind which may, from many points of view, be regarded as undesirable. The control of discretionary behaviour will therefore be presented as much as a sociological and psychological problem, as a legal problem. Administrative law is concerned with the determination and regulation of the limits of discretionary decision-making not with the control of discretion itself.

There is a large number of examples in British government of issues which are the subject of discretionary decisions by civil servants. Examples quoted by the Justice report *The Citizen and the Administration* include decisions by the Ministry of Agriculture on the amounts of subsidies to be paid to individual farmers, decisions by the Ministry of Health on 'what may be called marginal benefits under the Health Service',[3] Board of Trade decisions on applications for import licences and decisions by immigration officials of the Home Office. All these examples involve complex decisions which are by no means entirely unregulated. In fact if, as Justice is, one is talking about departmental discretion, rather than the discretion of individual officers, it may be forgotten that in practice a wide range of operating rules has been developed inside the departments to control discretion. The public is confused by the reluctance of some departments to make their internal rules specific, and the individual who complains about a particular decision does not know whether his grievance has arisen out of a comparatively arbitrary decision by a junior official, a decision which has been the subject of careful consideration at a higher level, or a departmental rule. Much decision-making in the Supplementary Benefits Commission is regulated by internal rule books, or codes, of which the 'A code' is the most important. The Child Poverty Action Group attacked 'the secret rules which control the awards of supplementary benefits' and demanded their publication.[4] The Commission resisted this demand for some time, and eventually they published in 1969 a handbook which is a digest of parts of the 'A code.' It may be suggested that their reluctance to publish the 'A code' stemmed largely from the fact that it is a very ambiguous document, which sometimes gives clear instructions but often gives merely guidance to officers and in some cases merely sets out the alternatives which officers should consider. In other words the 'secret rules' are often not really rules, and in the hands of the public the 'A code' might convey the impression that there were more rigid prescriptions for decision-making than in fact there are.

To throw further light on the complicated relationship between the instructions given to a department by an Act of Parliament and the decision-making behaviour of junior officials who are required to operationalise that Act, the position with regard to Supplementary Benefits will be examined. This is a particularly good example to discuss because it involves a situation in which a distinct sector of social security policy is regulated by a single fairly short Act of Parliament, yet the implementation of the policy involves a large number of separate decisions on applications for help from people with a wide range of needs.

The Ministry of Social Security Act appears superficially to be giving clear instructions to the Supplementary Benefits Commission to make payments to claimants who prove their entitlement, but on close inspection it can be seen to be full of qualifications which give discretion to the Commission.

Thus section 4 of the Act states, 'Every person in Great Britain of or over the age of sixteen whose resources are insufficient to meet his requirements shall be entitled, subject to the provisions of this Act, to benefit...'; but section 5 says, 'The question whether any person is entitled to benefit and the amount of any benefit shall, subject to the provisions of this Act as to appeals, be determined by the Commission and shall be so determined in accordance with the provisions of Schedule 2 to this Act and the other provisions of this part of the Act and any regulations made by the Minister with the consent of the Treasury.'

But if Schedule 2 is examined to try to get out of this tangle of vagueness the following will be found, alongside a number of specific rules about the determination of entitlements:

Where there are exceptional circumstances –
  (a) benefit may be awarded at any amount exceeding that (if any) calculated in accordance with the preceding paragraphs;
  (b) a supplementary allowance may be reduced below the amount so calculated or may be withheld;
as may be appropriate to take account of these circumstances.

In addition to Schedule 2, section 5 mentions regulations made by the Minister as another source of rules. In this category the main item will be the latest Statutory Instrument laying down specific scales to be used in assessing claims. However in addition to rules of this kind, which come under Parliamentary scrutiny, there are a number of other levels at which rules are made which limit the discretion of the officers responsible for specific decisions.

The body to which the Act specifically delegates decision-making powers is the Supplementary Benefits Commission, a committee of laymen set up in order to try to insulate the day-to-day implementation of the Act from political interference. Obviously this body and its senior advisers play a crucial role in making decisions which restrict the scope of discretion at lower levels. Nevertheless a statement to a member of the public that the Commission has made a decision will in most cases be no more than a statement that a subordinate member of staff has made a decision within the terms of a brief given to him by the Commission. The same is true of the great majority of statements that commence 'The Minister has decided . . .' which emanate from other departments. The important point to make here about the role of the Commission in relation to Schedule 2 to the Act is that they have pin-pointed in the Codes a number of examples of situations in which officers should regard circumstances as 'exceptional'.

Before going on to give examples of 'exceptional circumstances' calling for discretionary decisions it should be pointed out that there are, for the officers who are required to take most of the day-to-day decisions in the SBC, the executive officers in local offices, two other sources of rules in addition to the Codes and circulars emanating from the policy-making divisions close to the Commission. Regional Controllers exercise a measure of supervision over local office work and issue circulars from time to time to regulate decision-making in their region, and in the same way managers in local offices also provide interpretations of discretionary rules to fit local circumstances.

In the straightforward case, the allowance paid to a claimant is made up of (1) the 'scale rates', specific amounts laid down by Parliament—so much for a married couple and so much for each child, varying according to age; and (2) the rent allowance—normally the full rent paid less deductions for services provided with the tenancy, but special rules exist to provide 'rent allowances' for owner-occupiers and for persons who are not householders. Any income or capital possessed by claiments is partly offset against their 'needs', and again the basic rules on how this should be done are in regulations emanating from Parliament.

Determination of entitlement thus primarily depends upon ascertaining a series of normally unambiguous facts about a claimant, and then carrying out a simple calculation. But the SBC official has also to determine whether there are exceptional circumstances which justify a departure from such a simple deci-sion. Therefore even a 'normal' decision involves a discretionary element in deciding that there are no exceptional circumstances. There may be significant differences between officers in the extent to which they look either for exceptional needs or for reasons for reducing allowances.

One particularly difficult area in which discretion may be exer-cised in relation to a claim which does not on the face of it involve exceptional circumstances concerns the treatment of sus-pected fraud. The straightforward approach to suspected fraud involves granting an allowance on the basis of the facts provided and then investigating to establish the true facts. If it is concluded that there is evidence that the claimant did not tell the truth, he is then charged and perhaps prosecuted. But there are a number of situations in which this straightforward approach is not in fact adopted. The alternative approaches involve discretionary situa-tions of a highly ambiguous kind, approaches which are difficult to discuss because of their ambiguity but which must be mentioned because they illustrate very clearly a difficulty involved in disting-uishing between officially approved discretionary behaviour and what may be called 'informal behaviour'.

An SBC officer is taught that efficient interviewing and investiga-tion of claims helps to prevent fraud; what does he do therefore if in the course of an initial interview his suspicions are aroused? Of course he is likely to act on the proposition that it is better to prevent crime occurring than to let it occur and then prosecute, so he strives to get the claimant to reconsider his statement or to withdraw his application. The problem is how can a line be drawn between zealous interrogation, which may be described as designed to help a claimant get himself out of a false position, and something very much more officious which may involve bullying to get someone to forego his rights. SBC officers are therefore in a position in which deterring applications seems a simple and attractive way of preventing fraud, since the alternative is a ponderous and not very effective procedure. The main check upon such behaviour on the part of SBC officers is the fact that some claimants will complain to their superiors if they act too offi-ciously in this respect. One of the problems here is that many claimants are ill-informed of their rights and unprepared to press their claims at all hard, so they are unaware of ways to fight back against such treatment. The 'right' to benefit is much more clearly set out by the 1966 Act than it was in its predecessor, the 1948 National Assistance Act, but this does not mean that in general people are aware of a difference.

One particularly important issue here is that, in certain cases, people against whom the SBC has certain evidence are refused payment, without the SBC having to go to court to prove its case. On the contrary the onus is on the claimant to establish before an appeal tribunal that he has been given an incorrect decision.

The most difficult issue falling in this category concerns what the SBC calls 'cohabitation', and in particular the situation in which a woman claims that she has no male partner, or at least no male partner who is prepared to maintain her, whereas it is the SBC's view that she and a man are living 'as man and wife'. In such a situation the SBC will terminate the woman's allowance and her only redress will be through her right of appeal.

The undisclosed common-law marriage raises particular problems for the SBC because it cannot prosecute an 'unmarried husband' for failing to support an 'unmarried wife', and it cannot prosecute a woman in this situation without something that is well nigh impossible to achieve, evidence that her man is assuming responsibilities for her material needs. The SBC is left in a position in which, in order not to give the participants in a common-law marriage advantages which they would not have in a legal marriage, it is forced to try to develop a definition of 'cohabitation', taking account of more than just casual sexual relations, which justifies it in refusing payments to a woman on the grounds that she is really in the same position as a married woman.

Dealing with this issue in relation to the SBC's predecessor, whose policy was much the same if perhaps a little less liberal, Marsden argues:[5]

The National Assistance Regulations, or officers' application of them both in the N.A.B. office and in the treatment of cohabitation, have the appearance of seeking to defend marriage: officers ensure that drawing an allowance shall not be easy, and that common-law marriage or extra-marital sexual relations shall not be economically preferable to legal marriage.

It has been shown above that the moral issue here is not quite as simple as Marsden makes it out to be; however, it is not surprising that under many circumstances the exercise of discretion by individual officers in respect of an issue of this kind becomes in practice an attack on the privacy of the unmarried mother or deserted wife.

There are other situations in which claimants are refused benefits which do not involve suspicion of fraud of any kind. For example, fit single men under forty who are registered for unskilled work and live in areas where work is presumed to be available are refused further benefits after four weeks. Here the key discretionary decision has actually been taken by the Commission and is enshrined in instructions to local officers but a series of subordinate decisions have to be made at the local level in the course of applying this rule to individual cases. This involves a judgement that specific individuals *could* get work without difficulty if they wanted to. This example is a good illustration of the kind of special ruling which can be made to deprive people of their apparent statutory right under the Ministry of Social Security Act.

There is a number of situations in which benefits may be paid at levels below those prescribed in the Act. In the National Assistance Board wide discretion was given to officers dealing with applications made in the local offices from individuals claiming to be 'in immediate need'.[6] This involved quite chaotic decision-making processes with the amounts paid out to such applicants being arbitrary and often determined by the principle that payments should be as low as the authorising officer could make without having a row with the applicant. Such decision-making has been more fully described in the author's article on the NAB.[7] In the SBC the amount of low-level discretion involved in dealing with personal applications at local offices has been cut down considerably by the decision that circumstances of this kind should not normally be regarded as 'exceptional' and that therefore full 'need' payments should normally be made. Furthermore the Codes lay down special scale rates to be applied in situations in which there is doubt as to whether the full facts about an individual's circumstances are yet available. Hence discretion is confined to deciding whether an individual should get a full payment or should be paid on one of the two provisional scales. Snap judgements are still required about the authenticity of particular claims, but the whole system is more closely regulated.

There is one element in the ingredients of the basic assessment of need carried out by the SBC about which discretionary decisions have to be made, that is the allowance for rent. Some minor problems are posed by variations in the facilities provided in return for rent payments, but a much more critical discretionary problem is raised by a policy decision that rent allowances should be restricted in cases where rents are deemed to be unreasonably high. Discretion on this issue is carefully controlled by the Regional Offices and by Headquarters, but the way in which this control is exercised may have significant implications for the outcome of individual decisions as the following discussion of the operation of this rule in the NAB makes clear:[8]

The rent allowance could be limited in certain cases where it was felt that the rent was excessive in relation to the kind of accommodation occupied, or if it was felt that the applicant for Assistance was occupying accommodation at a rent level and of a standard out of proportion to his normal requirements. An interesting social consideration entered here. It was recognised that it was reasonable for an elderly lady who had known better times to live in a private hotel on the south coast, but that most Assistance applicants should expect to occupy accommodation of a comparatively poor quality. Clearly then, on this point Executive Officers were required to make an assessment of people that was to some extent subjective. Such an assessment might be influenced by the values of the officer involved, but it might also be influenced by his assessment of the amount of pressure that would be likely to be put on him if he made a decision unfavourable to the applicant....

For the benefit of officers responsible for implementing these instructions at the local office further guidance was provided in the form of circulars from the Regional Office. Throughout most of the period the author worked for the NAB there was in operation a policy within his region which required that, in all cases where rents exceeded a given level, the rent allowance should be restricted to that level temporarily and that the 'case' (the papers relating to the application for Assistance) should be sent to Regional Office for decision. In this kind of case the procedure was for the Executive Officer to make a recommendation which the Manager would then endorse or comment upon before sending the papers to the Regional Office. This temporary refusal to give rent allowances in full, together with a tendency for the rent ceiling to be too low in some areas (remember this was during Rachman's heyday) came under fire in a *New Statesman* article. Soon after the publication of that article the procedure was changed. Under the new policy, Executive Officers were instructed to give rent allowances in full unless they felt the rent was unreasonably high, in which case they were to restrict the allowance temporarily and submit the papers to Regional Office together with arguments for restricting the allowance. This was a significant change of policy, which the individual who was 'temporary Manager' of the office at that time presented as 'merely a change of procedure'.

There is a number of ways in which SBC officers have to exercise discretion in deciding whether to grant additions to the basic allowances. These additions take two forms, regular weekly additions to allowances to meet continuing special needs, and single payments—known as 'exceptional needs grants'—to enable people to make particular expenditures. A good example of a weekly addition is an amount added to the allowance paid to a diabetic to enable him to meet the extra cost of his diet, while the great majority of the exceptional needs grants are sums granted to families to buy children's clothes.

There are several points that need to be made about these apparently straightforward examples of discretionary additions. First, it must be remembered that decisions of this kind are made frequently by a large number of officers at the executive officer level in the SBC; accordingly there are inevitably wide variations in the circumstances in which special additions are deemed necessary so that the overall pattern may contain inconsistencies. Officers differ in the extent to which they regard the official doctrine that the basic allowance should meet all normal expenditures as a tenable one. Similarly the people in receipt of supplementary benefits differ, in a way not necessarily related to need, in the extent to which they ask for additional or exceptional payments. Furthermore the fact that some people 'manage' their incomes and expenditures better than others means that the 'bad managers' may be more demanding but seem to some SBC officers to be the least 'deserving'. In other words it is natural that the Victorian notions of the 'deserving' and 'undeserving' poor will still have some relevance for decision-making simply because officers often have no satisfactory way of assessing the strength of an exceptional need and will tend to be thrown back on value judgements related to how sensibly the last grant was used, how well expenditures are planned and so on. Exceptional needs grants for clothing are particularly problematical because of the difficulty in assessing the extent to which it is reasonable to expect such expenditures from the basic grant. If such grants are made frequently then they may come to be regarded as a normal right of benefit claimants, with the result that particular refusals of 'exceptional grants' will be regarded as denial of 'rights'. The SBC has been criticised for just this, criticism that seems unfair from the inside but is indicative of how widespread exercise of discretion in a particular way creates a presumption that a deliberate policy exists and that such decisions are to be *expected* in future. In this way, too, welfare rights campaigns tend to expose the inevitable inconsistencies in discretionary decision-making of this kind; such a policy works best in paternalistic situations in which the poor passively accept other people's assessments of their needs. When individuals press for their rights, officers have to try to relate the strength of demands to the strength of need, if people start pressing collectively, the whole discretionary system could collapse.

Administrative discretion is not, of course, only concerned with the giving or withholding of monetary grants to members of the public, and even the SBC officer is required to make some discretionary decisions which are not of this kind. The requirement of the Act that the SBC should exercise its functions 'in such manner as shall best promote the welfare of persons affected by the exercise thereof', is an instruction which is highly ambiguous and which raises the unresolved question of whether the SBC's priority is the protection of public funds or the protection of the interests of its clients. This requirement does, however, suggest one discretionary function for the SBC which is not so controversial— welfare referral. The Seebohm Committee suggested,[9] 'A natural and helpful division of responsibility emerges between the Commission and the new social service department. We consider that the Commission's officers should refer cases to that department and should not attempt to undertake social work themselves.' This proposition sounds straightforward, but in practice (1) SBC officers must face difficulties in identifying social work 'cases', (2) monetary problems and other 'welfare' issues are often inextricably entwined, and (3) it may sometimes be the case that the SBC's approach to individual 'cases' and the social worker's approach may be in conflict. Olive Stevenson has written of 'a kind of tension between guarding the public purse and encouraging self-reliance on the one hand, and, on the other, compassion for the individuals about whose predicaments the social worker must always, by definition, be deeply concerned.'[10] In the exercise of his discretionary role the SBC officer does not just work to safeguard the public purse, the tension is also therefore to some extent built into his role.

There is a large number of situations in social life in which individuals have to exercise judgement. People have to take decisions which involve discriminating between people yet often cannot base those decisions on rigid rules. One of the best examples of such an unavoidable decision is provided by the academic examination. Here the examiner may find himself in a situation in which he is forced to (1) rate the performances of individuals on a continuum, and (2) set one or more dividing lines between pass and fail or between degree classes in relation to that continuum. Furthermore he may not have either any clear means of rating performances, such as is provided where all answers can be marked either right or wrong, or any firm rules on the proportions of students to be passed or failed. In other words the system in which he is operating has set a series of rules which force him into a situation in which he has to exercise his judgement. This sort of judgement is not normally called 'discretionary' yet it is similar in kind to the sort of discretionary judgements with which this chapter is concerned; its inherent arbitrariness is disguised by reference to academic expertise so that academics are treated as the legitimate guardians of certain qualitative standards.

The Supplementary Benefits Commission's refusal to meet unreasonable rents whilst recognising that varied conditions and standards of life make it impossible to fix an amount which may be considered too much and its policy of refusing grants to unmarried women who are cohabiting, which involves an unclear criterion of what exactly constitutes cohabitation, both involve very similar decision-making processes to that involved in examining. The examiner feels that academic standards would be undermined by a refusal to judge and fail people, the SBC feels that it must be protected from people who expect it to pay the rent of 'palatial' accommodation or to subsidise common-law marriages when it would not subsidise legal ones. Cohabitation at the Savoy is the ultimate threat! There are ethical judgements, about not giving degrees to those who have not earned them or payments to those who try to exploit the system, which lie behind these policies; discretion comes in because it is not so easy in practice to define an inadequate student or an exploitative claimant. Similar judgements are required of immigration officers who cannot easily identify immigrants with forged papers, or doctors who cannot, at the margin, distinguish between the fit and the unfit. In all these cases there are only two ways of eliminating discretion, fixing an arbitrary test to do the discriminating or accepting that discrimination is impossible (i.e. passing everyone, meeting everyone's rent, letting all immigrants in).

Whereas in the cases discussed above the policy makers have found ethical issues which stand in the way of the elimination of discretion, perhaps a more common source of discretionary rules lies in situations in which resources are limited. Here the problem lies in the difficulty of finding criteria which can be used to predetermine the operation of rationing procedures. Here again the point can be most clearly illustrated by selecting an example of what is superficially a very different kind to the exercise of discretion in the SBC, the discretion exercised by the police. As far as the police are concerned the scarce resource is personnel, as Lambert says:[11]

> The theory is that laws apply to all men and the police must enforce the law always, everywhere equally.
>
> Yet *full* enforcement is not possible. Law breaking is so common that to investigate every infringement, to prosecute every known offender, would require police forces of a size, and involve expenditure on a scale, that would be impracticable and intolerable. So small police forces with small budgets have to enforce laws selectively. Both as an organisation and as individuals, the police have considerable choice about how to organise, which crimes and criminals to prosecute, how to allocate what number of men to different law enforcement tasks and so on.

A rigid rule-bound approach to police decision-making would involve such obsessive attention to minor offences that the machinery of justice would grind to a standstill, the police would encounter a much higher level of public obstruction in carrying out their tasks, and minor offences would take up an excessive proportion of police time.

There is a number of fields of decision-making in public administration which involve a similar kind of discretion to that exercised by the police; there is, for example, a number of law enforcement tasks performed by civil servants, e.g. customs officers and factory inspectors. Furthermore officials such as tax and national insurance inspectors have to decide where they will concentrate resources in order to check statements and claims.

But while these examples apply where the scarce resource is

manpower, a closely similar rationing process operates where scarce resources are involved; with the distribution of, for example, social security benefits or farm subsidies. There are two ways in which a rationing process of this kind may operate. It may be decided that there is a specific global sum to be allocated so that individual allocations are planned in relation to an overall ceiling, or estimates may be made of the extent of individual needs which it is considered appropriate to meet so that the global sum to be spent is merely estimated. The two alternatives are likely to structure discretionary behaviour in markedly different ways. The first alternative is a characteristic of local authority budgeting in Britain and of much social security budgeting in the United States, while the second alternative is typical of central government budgeting in Britain, and thus of the British social security system.

In a situation in which an upper limit is set for departmental expenditure for a year, the *context* within which discretionary decisions are to be taken is much more likely to be set by political processes. A local authority social service department has powers to give cash payments under the Children and Young Persons Act of 1963. The Act does not make clear the extent to which these powers should be exercised, and there is no doubt that social service departments could do very much more under the Act than they are doing at present.[12] The present constraints come not from the Act but from the limited financial allocations of individual local authorities. Amounts of individual grants have to be decided in relation to an overall allocation, and arbitrary decisions may be made at the end of the year, for example, which are based not so much upon need as upon the amount left in the kitty. Similarly, individual members of staff may be subject to tight controls to prevent them being markedly more generous than their colleagues.

Of course, in situations of this kind a variety of tactics are adopted to try to increase the scope for discretionary liberality. Budgets are sometimes exceeded and the excess expenditures used to justify increases for subsequent years. And from situations of this kind innovations may emerge as a result of the skill of administrators in persuading committees to commit large sums to untried policies, but in general it seems to be the case that the constraints imposed by advance budgeting may take the place of legal restrictions in limiting discretionary behaviour.

There is a number of characteristics of British central government financing that contribute to the situation in which budgetary considerations are not normally part of the frame of reference of low-level decision-makers. First, by contrast with local government, central government budgets are not balanced accounts. Second, the sums of money involved are very large so that it is impossible to relate most individual decisions to global expenditure. Third, very many expenditures, particularly in the social security field, are based upon legally established entitlements, so that the main sources of variation from estimated expenditures are a consequence of factors out of control of the departments (demographic changes, sickness rates, unemployment rates etc.). Accordingly at this level auditing is not so much a process of ensuring that expenditures are confined to estimates, as a search for deviations from rules or norms. Supplementary Benefits Commission officers are not therefore conscious of budgetary limits; their main constraint if they seek to interpret their discretionary powers liberally is that they may be identified as deviating radically from their colleagues.

In such a system the rationing process is inherent in the rules. 'Normal allowances' are determined by statute, the politicians have decided to ration money for the poor by setting their 'normal' needs allowance at so low a level that they are forced to acknowledge that 'exceptional circumstances' may require additional payments. It is, in theory, still open to the individual SBC officer to interpret this in such a way that he, for example, decides that everyone in receipt of social security payments ought to get £10 extra for clothing each year. In practice he makes 'exceptional grants', with the general guidance of the Codes, to a limited number of people, confined by a vague view of what is reasonable in relation to the decisions other people make. In the long run slow modifications may occur in such a rationing process through changing views of what constitutes reasonable behaviour. Thus new recruits to the department may decide to adopt a slightly more generous approach and will thus contribute to a gradual revision of the 'norm'. More radical modifications will tend to be established by policy revisions of the kind described above in relation to 'excessive rents' where outside pressure led to a less restrictive kind of procedure. If a radical revision of the whole rationing policy is ruled out at the political level—for example, if there were no possibility of securing a basic allowance, that would rule out the need for discretionary additions—then outside pressure groups will tend to depend either upon finding sympathisers within the system in order to secure more liberal practices or upon putting continued pressure for the revision of allowances made to individuals. Changes of government rarely lead to actual changes in the framework of rules but they may lead to changes in the psychological climate in which officials operate, and thus have significant indirect effects.

Basically, then, the difference between the two kinds of rationing processes discussed above is that with the first kind the rationing process is quite explicit so that securing change depends primarily upon influencing the budgeting process, while the second kind of process involves much more subtle and perhaps complex controls on the allocation process and may not even be recognised as a rationing process by those responsible for it. Accordingly modifying such a process in relation to individual cases may be fairly easy but securing a radical revision of it involves influencing central political decisions about the distribution of incomes within a society. Discretion will survive in this case so long as politicians insist upon a rigorous rationing of resources for the poor whilst at the same time remaining unable to settle upon any hard criteria upon which to base such rationing. In other words, discretion becomes inevitable at the point where a demand for rationing interlocks with an inability to specify rules upon which such a process can be based.

The above account provides an outline of the way in which the delegation of decision-making responsibilities to subordinate officials arises. There is, however, also a number of more specific points, related to the general argument developed above, which must be mentioned in an explanation of the sources of 'discretion'.

It is essential to bear in mind that human variability makes the formulation of clear-cut administrative rules very difficult. Here the administrator is faced by the problem that tends to make generalisation in the social sciences very difficult. Not only are patterns of human behaviour very diverse, but they are continually subject to change. The cohabitation issue discussed earlier provides an example of the difficulty of framing rules in the face of a diversity of kinds of sexual relationships and changing concepts of marriage. But, in a similar way 'needs' are not simply definable in material terms; the social context may also be important. Thus, holidays for deprived children raise a number of discretionary issues for SBC officers, child care officers and education authorities. Even if the basic costs of the holidays are met by charities, other kinds of expenses have to be met if the children are not to be continually reminded of their own deprivation.

Issues of this kind, stemming from the diversity of individual needs, raise problems which Olive Stevenson has described as[13] 'problems of individualisation within a bureaucratic system.' They arise, she says, 'from the tension between what the theologian Tillich has called "creative" and "proportional justice"; the former concerned with the unique needs of individuals, the latter with ideas of equity—fair shares for all.'

In an effort to reduce the extent of discretionary additions to the allowances of pensioners and the long-term sick, the Ministry of Social Security Act provided for a special 'long-term addition' to all their allowances. This addition was 9s per week, and has subsequently been raised to 50p. When the Bill was debated by the Lords,[14] Lord Ilford pointed out that a 'long-term addition' of 9s could hardly be expected to eliminate discretionary additions which were then averaging 9s 6d per week. What has in fact happened is that the long-term addition has reduced the sensitivity of the system's response to special needs, since a very fit and active pensioner will get the 50p like everyone else but an unfit one will have his special needs—for special foods, help with laundry, extra heating etc.—offset against the 50p so that his allowance will only be increased by the extent to which his extra needs are calculated to exceed 50p a week. The scope of discretion has been reduced at the cost of sensitivity to diverse needs.

It has been stressed that a particularly salient characteristic of discretionary decision-making systems is that the core issues which face officials involve value judgements. Simon argues that the value elements in decision hierarchies should be the province of politicians.[15] (See Chapter 10 for a further discussion of this point.)

It is difficult to quarrel with this prescription, which corresponds well with a common view of the role of politics. But in practice politicians find it very difficult to make critical ethical decisions. At the end of the fifties some political scientists proclaimed the 'end of ideology'.[16] Their view has been shown to be ludicrous by the emergence into political conflict of interests which lay dormant or suppressed at that time, yet the suggestion that the most powerful protagonists on the legislative front in both Britain and the United States tend to evade ideological conflict is still largely true. Accordingly much legislation involves leaving important value or ethical issues unresolved.

The characteristic legislative situation is one in which a government tries to produce an Act which reconciles conflicting interests. Thus, for example, the Race Relations Act's clauses dealing with employment[17] are an attempt to protect racial minorities without disturbing the traditional prerogatives of employers or unions, hence its emphasis upon conciliation and its use of joint consultation machinery wherever possible. Similarly our social security legislation tries to reconcile the development of a universalistic system to meet all needs with a traditional attitude to the poor which regards them as undeserving unless they can produce unambiguous evidence to the contrary, but really at the margin leaves it to the officials dealing with individual cases to effect the reconciliation.

It is important to point out that the process of compromise between the political parties, and between government and the pressure groups, which tends to lead to the evasion of ideological or ethical issues is accompanied also by compromise between politicians and civil servants. There is no clear evidence that the general run of civil servants fight to maintain discretionary powers, but we do know that professionals fight hard to maintain their autonomy. It seems likely that, from time to time, politicians will be persuaded by their advisers that it is better to leave certain matters to 'the men on the ground'. Certainly, the author has observed local authority officials prepared to defend their freedom to exercise their judgement in the face of intervention from council committees. At this level one finds a number of 'semi-professions' jealous of their prerogatives. Thus the Cullingworth Committee[18] found that the 'grading' of tenants by housing visitors, in order to allocate them to houses of differing qualities, was defended as 'good housing management'.

The fact that some public servants will strive to maintain their discretionary prerogatives raises another significant issue. There is a substantial amount of evidence from industrial sociology on the advantages to be gained from allowing workers autonomy.[19] To give the worker some measure of control over his working life is seen as advantageous not only as an end in itself, but also as a contributory factor in the achievement of high productivity. It is also stressed as important where the quality of the product matters.

As an end in itself 'industrial democracy' must surely involve some conflict with 'political democracy' if it is to be sought in the public service. But it is not particularly relevant to follow that line of argument here; rather it is necessary to look at the more mundane question, is the fact that people operate more effectively if given a measure of autonomy an argument for granting civil servants discretionary powers?

The difficulty in dealing very satisfactorily with this point stems from two facts: (1) that it is never possible to eliminate all behaviour akin to discretion, and (2) many attempts to cut out discretion involve the adoption of rules which are, for a variety of reasons, evaded. The first of these points may be illustrated by reference to factors such as speed and helpfulness. Clerks with no discretionary freedom to speak of can nevertheless have a major impact upon the quality of service given to the public simply on account of the importance of the willingness with which they perform their alloted tasks. In some respects individuals with no significant discretionary freedom create an area of freedom for themselves by manipulating the little power they have to make the public wait or struggle with form filling and so on.

Similarly the studies by Blau[20] and Francis and Stone[21] on the reactions of public servants to rules suggest that discretion is exercised, even if illegitimately, in bending rules to either improve the service to the public or to meet their own personal needs. As Jacobs argues,[22] 'it is possible for an organisation to conform little or not at all to the conditions of bureaucracy, while maintaining an image of complete adherence to bureaucratic ideals.'

Thus, it may be suggested that an attempt to improve the service given to the public by a government department by eliminating discretion may run into difficulties (1) because civil servants will give a poorer service and (2) because they may try to create new areas of discretion unofficially. These problems may arise regardless of whether the rules themselves raise difficulties.

The most obvious way to control discretion is to formulate rules which cut down its operation to a minimum.[23] The discussion of how discretion arises has shown why this is often not a very practical possibility. Furthermore, as has been shown, the absence of rules, which is the defining characteristic of discretion, also limits the scope of the legal control of discretion. However this has not stopped constitutional lawyers regarding tribunals as the principal means of controlling discretion.[24] There is, of course, a number of useful functions which tribunals perform in relation to discretionary decisions. First of all, they ensure that the decisions taken are within the scope of the statutorily granted discretionary power and are made in a procedurally correct manner. Beyond this their main function is to secure a second look at particular decisions, which means merely that discretion is exercised for a second time by an independent group of people, thereby, so long as the tribunal can only vary the decision in the appellant's favour, increasing his chance of getting what he wants. The ultimate decision, whether it involves the upholding of, or the revision of, the original decision, is legitimated by a 'legal' process, but to pretend that this involves anything more than a repeat of the discretionary decision-making process is misleading.

Tribunal decision-making is sometimes justified as a technique involving the 'community' in the decision, in the same way as decision-making by a lay-magistracy is legitimated. But it makes more sense to say that the decisions taken by tribunals are a function of their membership. A typical tribunal in British government consists of a chairman,[25] who may have legal training, who is chosen by a secret process which tends to throw up upper-middle-class people active in voluntary organisations, and two other people who are generally a small businessman and a minor trade union official respectively. To describe an appeal to such a group as in any sense an appeal to 'representatives of the community' stretches the concepts of 'representative' and 'community' so far as to drain almost all meaning from them.

Having thus derided the appeal tribunal as a means of bringing 'community values' into play to control discretionary behaviour, it is appropriate to look at two other ways of doing this which have been suggested. One of these consists in pushing the onus for controversial decisions onto politicians. It has already been suggested that in their approach to legislation politicians seem often to evade value decisions. However it is generally considered that in various ways political figures should be involved in exceptional decisions, and in practice the extent to which this happens is generally more a function of pressure of work than a matter of principle. The parliamentary question and other more informal techniques of putting pressure on ministers provides an important source of control on administrative discretion[26] but its impact is rather random and arbitrary, and biased in favour of the middle-class person who will use this avenue for complaint.

One interesting aspect of the use made of political control of discretion is that it is regarded in Britain, in contrast to the United States so it seems, as in some respects prejudicial to 'good' administration. The Supplementary Benefits Commission was set up to stand between the administration of relief and the politicians, and thus to restrict political scrutiny of day-to-day decisions. Similarly in local government, where political involvement in personal decision-making is more likely because of the smaller scale, there is a general attempt to eliminate what is regarded as political 'interference'.

This, typically British, view involves treating elected politicians not so much as the sole arbiters of the public interest but as one element in a balanced system. The Maud[27] committee on the management of local government defended the traditional prerogatives of local authority officials and suggested that politicians should lay down general policies but keep out of day-to-day decision-making. A similar line was taken by the Cullingworth committee[28] on council house allocation, who, in stressing the need for all authorities to develop impartial 'points' systems, seemed insensitive to the extent to which special cases arise in day-to-day housing management. Politicians are seen as people who interfere in day-to-day administration on behalf of people for whom they want to do favours, rather than as a last court of appeal. The writer's observation, as a participant, of the working of a local authority housing committee suggests that this is not an unreasonable judgement on the kind of decision-making involved; yet it is a curious comment on our kind of democracy that we have so little confidence in the use of politicians as the ultimate check on discretion.

The other way of bringing community values into play in the exercise of administrative discretion is suggested by Simon:[29] 'Since the administrative agency must of necessity make many value judgements, it must be responsive to community values, far beyond those that are explicitly enacted into law.'

But what are those 'community values' to which the administrator is supposed to be responsive? It has already been pointed out that value decisions are often left to the administrator because of the inability of the political system to resolve conflict. So the administrator, earnestly hunting for relevant 'community values', will find only conflicting values. If, nevertheless, he thinks he perceives a solution to his dilemma it may be that he is responding to the values of a dominant group, or middle-class values, or even majority values. He may thus settle upon a particular approach to decision-making in conformity with his own values, and try to legitimise his position by reference to alleged community values.

The above discussion seems to suggest a total rejection of Friedrich's notion of 'administrative responsibility'[30] (see pages 170–1); this is not the case. Certainly the administrator can, and should, be conscious of the various viewpoints and interests current in the community; the argument is that he cannot readily move beyond the politicians' dilemma. Sensitivity to 'community values' may help him to avoid doing certain things, but it does not necessarily provide the answers to the problems which face him when he exercises discretion.

The Gulbenkian report[31] on community work provides an interesting discussion of ways in which community workers may find that responsiveness to 'community values' involves conflict with what they consider to be the overriding values inherent in their task. The notion that there are values to which they should be accountable and that these values may be different from those held by the people with whom they are working raises ethical questions which the Gulbenkian committee could only talk around and certainly not solve. They conclude,[32]

Community workers and their employing organisations have a responsibility to make conscious decisions about social changes and cultural values they wish to encourage, and what are the ethical constraints and imperatives in influencing people so as to bring about social change and what constitutes desirable social change. Self awareness and understanding of value assumptions is obviously an important element in training for community work.

The political naivety and the paternalistic assumptions underlying this prescription could be the subject of another essay; however, the point of quoting this here is to show that as an alternative to the idea of expecting people with discretionary powers to be subject to 'community values' some attempts are made, particularly in writings on social work, to suggest the need for a specific professoinal value system to guide decision-making

In a similar way, Kaufman[33] in a study of forest rangers in the

United States Forest Service suggests that the inculcation of a code of values through lengthy training serves as a means of controlling decision-making in the absence of rules. But there are several reasons why such a solution to the problem of control of discretion is not often applicable.

The Forest Service has a fairly clear objective, the maintenance of publicly controlled forests in the United States. In possessing this objective it is in some respects in conflict with those elements in American political life which are opposed to public enterprise. Its continued existence depends upon maintaining the integrity of its general goals and fighting off challenges to its activities. It will be argued in the next chapter that the assumption found in so much American literature on organisations that unification around a central goal (as suggested for example in Simon, Smithburg and Thompson's statement on values,[34] 'The organization's objective is the central value that members must accept if the organization is to succeed') is a characteristic of most public organisations is grossly misleading and often in fact entirely incorrect.

Most government agencies are multifunctional, and have built into them both conflicts about priorities between functions and conflicts about the values applicable to the performance of specific functions. The Supplementary Benefits Commission is not a unified agency committed to a certain clear-cut conception of its role, on the contrary it has already been suggested that there are currently a number of alternative principles upon which decisions may be based. Similarly, Keith-Lucas[35] has shown how it is impossible to discern anything approaching value-consensus in that part of the social work profession largely responsible for the Aid to Dependent Children programme in the United States.

In general, the notion of a 'profession' as a body of people performing a common task and sharing common values is a misleading one since value-consensus is all too rarely found. Furthermore, such value-consensus as may exist is likely to be chiefly centred around the protection of the professional group rather than linked to a particular concept of service to the public. Indeed, most studies of professionals in public administration have, as will be seen in Chapter 8, been concerned not so much with the imposition of professional values in administrative tasks as with the attempts of professionals to preserve their integrity from the power of the organisation.

Furthermore, where it is the case that a particular form of

discretion can be controlled by the inculcation of values, the problem lies in answering the question: Who should do the inculcating? People who would like to ensure by this means that Supplementary Benefits Commission officers are responsive to their own liberal or radical values should remember that competing with them to influence these officers are people who publish articles entitled 'The Truth about the Welfare Rackets'.[36]

Another problem facing anyone attempting to influence the behaviour of officials lies in the fact that the processes by which a new employee is socialised may involve, more than anything else, the acceptance of standards laid down not by his superiors but by his peers. It is pertinent to quote what J. Q. Wilson wrote on this point about policemen:[37]

> The policeman is neither a bureaucrat nor a professional, but a member of a *craft*. As with most crafts, his has no body of generalised, written knowledge nor a set of detailed prescriptions as to how to behave — it has, in short, neither theory nor rules. Learning in the craft is by apprenticeship, but on the job and not in the academy. The principal group from which the apprentice wins (or fails to win) respect are his colleagues on the job, not fellow members of a discipline or attentive superiors....

Undoubtedly, an absence of extensive training may make peer-group influence more significant, and it should be pointed out here that many civil servants have but scanty training for exercising discretionary tasks. One reason for this, as far as the SBC is concerned, is that wastage is so high that expensive training would be uneconomical. However, Blau has suggested another reason why peer-group influence may be important; this is that[38] 'Friendly relations with colleagues are a source of social support which helps reduce the anxieties and insecurities that arise in the work situation.' He showed that social support reduced the impact of 'reality shock' upon workers in a public welfare agency as they discovered some of the more unpleasant aspects of providing relief for uncongenial clients.

However, the existence of standards imposed from above, and inculcated through training, serves a valuable purpose within an organisation even if those standards are not readily accepted. For, while individual acts of discretion cannot be related to standards of behaviour, the pattern of acts by an individual can be studied and he can be checked if his behaviour deviates markedly from those standards. It has already been suggested, for example, that racial discrimination which cannot be discerned in a single discretionary act can be recognised in a number of such acts. Equally, extremely generous or extremely mean interpretations of SBC instructions can be identified.

The overriding argument of this chapter has been that there are severe limits to the extent to which discretion can be eliminated by rule formulation. Legal and political controls over discretion have been seen to involve simply substituting another kind of discretion for administrative discretion, a kind that is more accessible for some people but equally arbitrary and often more final. The control of discretion by ethical codes has also been shown to be impracticable, largely because discretion arises in the first place because of ethical conflicts which are hard to resolve. Without wishing to provide a misleadingly simple conclusion to this argument it can, however, be said that if each of these so-called checks on discretion can be found operating together they may contribute to providing some safeguards to the individual who is subject to such decisions. Rules confine the scope of discretion, appeals and complaints secure the maximum scrutiny of decisions, and the presence of explicit 'professional' standards, even if they are not always adhered to, provides some basis either for checking deviant officials or, if the standards are unacceptable, attacking the whole system.

But the underlying purpose of this chapter has been to suggest that at least some forms of discretion are inevitable in administration; they will be found as a consequence of the complexity of social life, the ethical conflicts endemic within society, and the inability of political processes to handle all such conflicts. The way discretion develops within a particular department will then be a function not only of the statutory framework but also of the social pressures upon the department from outside and of the social characteristics of the people within the department whose discretionary decisions will be required. To understand the dynamics of discretionary behaviour we have, as Selznick says, to analyse an organisation 'as an institution', 'a natural product of social needs and pressures—a responsive, adaptive organism.'[39]

Organisational Goals

The concept of 'goals' is very widely used in the literature on organisations; yet it is rarely defined and is used in a variety of ways which will often not stand up to close examination. Few writers are prepared to make their usages clear, and very few are ready to acknowledge that, whatever their particular usage, the imputation of goals is highly problematic. Perrow describes this weakness as follows:[1]

Social scientists have produced a rich body of knowledge about many aspects of large-scale organisations, yet there are comparatively few studies of the goals of these organisations. For a full understanding of organisations and the behaviour of their personnel, analysis of organisational goals would seem to be critical. Two things have impeded such analysis. Studies of morale, turnover, informal organisation, communication, supervisory practices, etc., have been guided by an over-rationalistic point of view wherein goals are taken for granted, and the most effective ordering of resources and personnel is seen as the only problematical issue. Fostering this view is the lack of an adequate distinction between types of goals. Without such clarification it is difficult to determine what the goals are and what would be acceptable evidence for the existence of a particular goal and for a change in goals.

This deficiency in organisational studies is made the more serious by the fact that very often the possession of goals is treated as a defining feature of formal organisations. Blau and Scott, for example, suggest that formal organisations can be distinguished from other kinds of social organisations inasmuch as[2] 'they have been formally established for the explicit purpose of achieving certain goals'. And, while discussions of 'goal displacement' and 'succession of goals'[3] are included in their book, they nowhere examine their usage of the concept of goal and take it for granted

that there are recognisable goals present to experience such trans-
formations.

In the same way Mouzelis defines formal organisation[4] 'as a
form of social grouping which is established in a more or less
purposive manner for the attainment of a specific goal'. He recognises that individual goals may conflict with organisational goals
but sees no problem in making this distinction, despite the fact
that he is uneasy about the formal/informal dichotomy[5] which is
closely linked with this distinction. As was suggested in Chapter 3,
it is the problematical nature of 'goals' within organisations that
tends to make a rigid use of the formal/informal dichotomy unworkable.

Albrow has shown that this tendency to treat goals as given and
non-problematic but nevertheless a defining characteristic of formal
organisations involves in practice an identification of sociology
with those forms of organisation theory developed to help managers to meet their objectives. He suggests that the definition of
organisations in terms of goal-orientation[6] 'is not a definition of
real organisations but of a hypothetical or idealised situation to
which a theorist concerned with improvements and future states
might wish them to tend. Such ideal formulations are invaluable
in the context of organisation theory but a bias results if sociologists employ them uncritically as defining existing situations.'

It is certainly the case that many sociologists have taken managerial objectives as the only relevant 'goals' for the organisations
they have studied. Some acknowledge this openly, but many, as
Albrow suggests, do it implicitly while still pretending to be
engaged on 'value-free' sociology. In some cases this particular
bias is obscured because, like Blau and Scott, the sociologist
avoids defining goals, but other writers reach a similar point of
view by way of misleading definitions. Before proceeding to look
at the problems associated with the use of the concept of 'goal'
with reference to public administration it will be helpful to look
at some of these misleading definitions.[7]

The most straightforward approach to this issue is to seek to
define goals by reference to written statements of organisational
objectives. This may obviously be an important source of information on this subject, but of course statements of this kind do not
always exist. Furthermore, where they do exist, they may be
statements provided as part of a public relations exercise rather
than as true statements of purpose. Finally, where they are in-

tended as statements of purpose, they may nevertheless not be accepted by all members of the organisations. In particular, they may not be widely accepted because they are regarded as out of date.

This leads to a second approach to goal definition, in terms of objectives specified when the organisation was founded. Such an approach is implied by Barnard's account of the emergence of co-operative activity as a basic source of the complex organisation (see page 22). Albrow attacks such approaches to the definition of goals as involving an unhistorical myth. He argues:[8]

These accounts are altogether too like the social contract theory of the origins of the state and society. At some point of time, never specified, individuals conceive an objective with uncommon un-animity and clarity to live an organized social life.... Their formulation of rules and goals is in fact a long and tortuous progress. It is rarely possible to indicate a point of time at which they begin. If organizations have founders, and nearly always the 'foundation' amounts to the reorganization of existing organizational elements, it is rare for them to have the slightest conception of how the organization is to develop.

Perhaps the best-known approach to goal definition is that involving attribution of organisational goals over and above the goals set out by any individuals. At its simplest this means that students of organisations impute 'goals' on the basis of their observations of organisational behaviour, a process which implies subjective judgements about purpose and discrimination between kinds of activities observed. Obviously this process very easily leads to, in practice, acceptance of the goals of dominant elements in the organisation. But additionally it may lead to reification, the acceptance of the idea that the organisation has[9] 'an existence and behaviour independent of the behavour of its members'. This particular pitfall characterises the approach of Parsons to this issue.[10] For him, 'a formal organisation in the present sense is a mechanism by which goals somehow important to the society, or to various subsystems of it, are implemented and to some degree defined.'

It is important to emphasise at this stage that the arguments set out above are all concerned with showing the difficulties involved in treating orientation towards specific goals as a defining characteristic of formal organisations, and not with attacking the use of the concept of 'goals'. These two things are easily confused because the crucial over-riding argument here is that goals are unclear and the subject of controversy; therefore, while it will be maintained later in the chapter that the study of 'goals' or goal-oriented behaviour involves considerable difficulties, the concepts will nevertheless be used to some effect. The point here is that the concept of goals is too difficult to be used in a simple definition of organisations. In recognition of this Albrow offers a definition of organisations which acknowledges 'goals' as problematical:[11] 'organizations are social units where individuals are conscious of their membership and legitimise their co-operative activities primarily by reference to the attainment of impersonal goals rather than to moral standards.'

But it may be objected that heavy weather is being unnecessarily made of this discussion because the goals of public administration are clear; because the civil service pursues, in the words of Etzioni,[12] 'goals set by the government'. There are several reasons why this is not the case. In the first place the civil service is a part of the government, with a policy-making role in its own right. In the second place, as was shown in the last chapter, government often does not lay down clear goals so that the implementation of 'policy' becomes in many respects a continuing process of interpretation and modification of goals. And in the third place, even where 'goals' are apparently clearly set out in Acts of Parliament they may still be replaced, in practice, by other goals more important to individual civil servants.

Perrow provides an approach to this subject that makes considerable sense in these terms, when he distinguishes between 'official' and 'operating' goals:[13]

Official goals are purposely vague and general and do not indicate two major factors which influence organizational behaviour: the host of decisions that must be made among alternative ways of achieving official goals and the priority of multiple goals, and the many unofficial goals pursued by groups within the organisation. The concept of 'operative goals' will be used to cover these aspects. Operative goals designate the ends sought through the actual operating policies of the organization; they tell us what the organization actually is trying to do, regardless of what the official goals say are the aims.

'Official goals' in Perrow's sense are unusable as defining characteristics of an organisation, they define only what spokesmen

D

for the organisation say it is trying to do. They are postulated as part of a legitimisation process, the most characteristic forms of which are, in public administration, the speeches made by a minister in introducing a new Act of Parliament. At best, statements of official goals are too general to tell us much about organisational activities, at worst they are deliberately misleading. Unfortunately, however, Perrow's concept of 'operative goals' is not much clearer because their discovery depends upon the imputations of the observer.

Given then that it is not advisable, and very often not possible, to talk about organisational goals, does this mean that the concept of goals can be used only with reference to individual objectives? Is it always the case that, when talking about goals in connection with the study of organisations, it is only possible to talk about the goals of individuals? The answer is that the concept of goals can be used with reference to organisations, if it is acknowledged (1) that its usage must be separated from any inference about 'ends' as distinct from 'means', and (2) that its use implies the existence of either consensus or dominance, or both.

In the discussions of the definition of organisations in terms of goals which have been considered above, there is an underlying equation of 'goals' with 'ends'. If, as has been suggested, goals cannot normally be ascribed to organisations then particular kinds of behaviour which are seen as purposive, or goal-oriented, cannot be distinguished as either directed to the attainment of ends or to the attainment of what are considered merely means to other ends. This throws a slightly different light upon the phenomenon that is normally defined as 'goal displacement', which Blau and Scott express in the following way,[14] 'in the course of adopting means to attain organisational goals the means may become ends in themselves that displace the original goals.' In the terms used here this particular means/ends distinction becomes pretty valueless and it is perhaps better to follow Simon[15] and see goals as specific positions on 'means-ends chains'.

Furthermore, in equating 'goal displacement' with bureaupathology, (the diversion of organisations from seeking to achieve socially valued ends)[16] Merton has misled sociologists into treating behaviour which does not directly contribute to the attainment of specific goals as in no way relevant to the attainment of those goals. This point is well taken up by Gross, who argues:[17]

The paradox may be stated as follows: an organisation must do more than give attention to goal attainment in order to attain its goals. A useful approach is that suggested by the Parsonian functional imperatives. Whether or not one is prepared to agree that these and no other imperatives exist, they do represent an attempt ... to state a set of conditions necessary for system survival. As such they apply directly to organisations. It is noteworthy that only one of the system imperatives is goal attainment. The names given to the other imperatives are adaption, integration, and pattern maintenance and tension management. The import of these categories is that a good part of any system's energies must be given over to activities that do not contribute in any direct sense to goal attainment but rather are concerned essentially with maintaining the system itself.

We need not be led by Gross or by Parsons into the trap of reification; it is sufficient to acknowledge that the point is being successfully made that activities within a complex organisation may knit together for the attainment of specific objectives, in ways that crude notions of how means may become ends do not take into account. The message of Michels'[18] 'iron law of oligarchy' is not that bureaucratisation must be avoided—ends will never be attained that way—but that ways must be sought to harness a complex organisation to maximise the attainment of ends. The successful running of an organisation with a complex purpose depends upon many activities which may seem very unrelated to that purpose. The people responsible for maintaining the stability and the security of the organisation may well lose sight of any wider objectives; nevertheless they may still have a vital contribution to make, a contribution which others who are much more conscious of a need to aim for specific goals cannot do without. As Roche and Sachs argue with reference to personality types in political movements[19]

Both the bureaucrat and the enthusiast supply a movement with vital components. Each by himself works badly; left alone, the bureaucrat simply goes in concentric circles around his precious organization, while the enthusiast rushes unsheathed from one ideological orgasm to another. Consequently, a healthy vital social movement needs both, and profits from their complementary assets.

Thus, the argument here about the relationship between 'goals' on the one hand and 'ends' and 'means' on the other has two parts. The first part of the argument is that groups within organisations may coalesce around 'goals' of various kinds, and that it is therefore misleading to categorise them as either 'ends' or 'means'. The second part of the argument is more subtle: it is that groups, who at one level of analysis may be seen to be seeking different goals (particularly if attempts are made to break down behaviour into 'ends oriented' or 'means oriented'), may find that their different behavours fit together to enable them to attain objectives that they could not attain separately. In this sense Gross[20] writes of 'output' and 'support' goals, and in prescriptions for executive behaviour, from Barnard[21] to Selznick[22] and beyond, the coordination of such behaviour is seen as the key task for the successful executive.

The difficulty with the line of argument developed in the last paragraph is that it seems to involve slipping back into one of the errors pointed out earlier in the chapter. If disparate activities, undertaken by individuals who acknowledge differing personal goals, nevertheless fit together to contribute to the achievement of some more general objective, can one say that the organisation has a 'goal' without indulging in reification? There are really two possibilities here. It may be that, to adopt a physical analogy, the result of a situation in which a number of different forces pull in different directions is movement in a direction related to but not specifically intended by the people who imposed any particular force. Specific social acts produce effects very different from those intended by the actors; when these acts occur within an organisational context, it is misleading of the sociologist to provide an explanation of their consequences in terms of over-riding organisation goals.

The other possible way to explain the shape of particular patterns of activity which fit together to lead to the attainment of specific 'goals' is to suggest that some of the actors involved are successful in giving their own goals primacy, Fox's approach to this issue is to suggest that organisations can be conceptualised as 'coalitions of stakeholders'. He defines stakeholders[23] 'as individuals or groups who depend on the organisation for the realisation of their goals and on whom, in turn, the organisation is dependent for its continuance'. He points out that stakeholders include management, employees, consumers, creditors and a whole range of people who have an interest in the organisation's activities. The control of an organisation involves the coordination of the interests of the various stakeholders[24] 'to ensure that the organisation can continue to offer the minimum inducements for continued participation by each of the interests.'

The implication here is that specific interest groups are successful in achieving a situation in which those who might disagree with their 'goals' can be persuaded or coerced into accepting a situation in which they devote themselves to aiming for personal goals which do not interfere with the 'goals' which the dominant group set for the organisation.

In order to do this the aspirant 'controllers' of the organisation may well have to make concessions, if only in order to provide resources or activities to satisfy the personal goals of other 'stakeholders'. This process of securing stakeholder support may prove difficult and may lead to changes in the nature or activities of the organisation, of a kind unwelcome to those attempting to control it, a phenomenon which other sociologists have called 'goal displacement'. In some cases the distinction made above between controlling and noncontrolling stakeholders may, of course, be invalid since concessions may be made of a kind which properly speaking disperse control or shift control from one group to another. The concept of 'goal' must no more be used to infer a clear-cut situation in which one group does, and always will, impose its objectives than it must be used to infer consensus.

To deal fully with this difficult subject would require an exploration of some of the wider problems of the explanation of 'order' within societies, a topic beyond the scope of this book. Certainly as far as public administration is concerned the success or failure of politicians in imposing goals upon public bureaucracies and in preventing the distortion of those goals needs to be considered in relation to the more general question of public acceptance of particular kinds of social order.

Another theorist who approaches the subject of organisational goals in terms of constraints upon individuals is Simon.[25] He provides a useful account of the way in which constraints operate to provide organisational mechanisms to structure the choices open to individuals, but he does not effectively relate his analysis of the importance of constraints to the wider question of dominance within organisations.

Simon points out that in general one cannot regard goal selection as a process in which constraints can be disregarded:[26] '... it is doubtful whether decisions are generally directed toward achieving *a* goal. It is easier and clearer, to view decisions as being concerned with discovering courses of action that satisfy a whole set of constraints. It is this set, and not any one of its members, that is most accurately viewed as the goal of the action.' And so, with regard to organisational decisions:[27]

> ... we observe that many, if not most, of the constraints that define a satisfactory course of action are associated with an organizational role and hence only indirectly with the personal motives of the individual who assumes that role. In this situation it is convenient to use the phrase organisation goal to refer to constraints, or sets of constraints, imposed by the organizational role, which has only this indirect relation to the motives of the decision makers.

Finally, to conclude this discussion of theoretical approaches to the concept of goals, it is appropriate to refer to some practical suggestions for the identification of goals which are in general consistent with the points that have been made. Subject to the general reservation that his approach evades the questions of legitimation and acceptance, Gross's suggestions for the study of 'goals' are worthy of note:[28]

> Two kinds of evidence are necessary before one can confidently assert that a goal is present: *intentions* and *activities*. By 'intentions' we understand what, in the participants' view, the organization is trying to do. That is, what they believe the goals of the organization to be, what they feel are its aims or the direction in which it is moving as an organization. Intentions will involve verbal statements or inferences that may be made from symbolic acts, gestures and other types of meaningful acts. By 'activities' we understand what persons in the organization are in fact *observed to be doing*, how they are spending their time, how resources are being allotted.

The position taken up, therefore, in the remainder of this chapter will be that it is useful to use the concept of organisational goals in order to discuss behaviour in a context in which men strive to act in purposive ways, but that before using such a concept it is most necessary to be aware how readily its use can mislead. In particular, the use of the concept of goals is associated with three particular pitfalls: reification; the introduction, wittingly or unwittingly, of assumptions about the presence of consensus; and a tendency to imply that organisational objectives are, or ought to be, constant over time.

Having said this it is now appropriate to go on to look at some useful studies of the setting, modification and alteration of goals, forearmed with the recognition that many of these studies start with misleading assumptions about the extent to which unambiguous goals are a characteristic of formal organisations. It will be found that approaches of this kind are similar in type to assumptions, discussed in Chapter 3, that the formal structures of organisations can be treated as firm and fixed so that informal 'deviations' from them can be traced. In some cases these are useful simplifying assumptions for organisational studies, but when they are built into the theory they become as misleading as economists' assumptions about 'perfect competition'.

Mention has already been made of the classic contribution to the study of the subversion of goals by subordinate members of organisations, Merton's discussion of 'goal displacement'. Merton's argument is that in the bureaucratic organisation in which conformity and obedience to rules is considered most important to ensure accuracy and predictability,[29] 'Adherence to the rules, originally conceived as a means, becomes transformed into an end-in-itself; there occurs the familiar process of *displacement of goals* whereby "an instrumental value becomes a terminal value".'

Merton's analysis stresses the impact of the organisational situation on the personality. He suggests ways in which the elevation of 'means' to over-riding importance transforms not only the extent to which the organisation is oriented towards 'ends' but also the personalities of the officials involved; in the long run, these two facets of the situation reinforce each other. Other writers have suggested ways in which goals are subverted not as part of a process in which personality changes are occurring but, on the contrary, because individuals are seeking to protect their personalities from the pressure of the organisation. The conflict here between 'bureaucratic personality' theorists on the one hand and theorists like Crozier who stress this other point of view is discussed in Chapter 7.

There have been a number of important studies of pressures upon organisational goals from their environments. Clearly this is a topic of importance for public administration in the light of the fact that such organisations operate in a political context. There are obviously situations in which the political masters of public organisations seek, through legitimate political channels, to impose new goals upon such organisations or to change old ones. This book is not concerned with these 'legislative' processes. But there are also other situations in which the objectives or goals of legislators are specifically subverted by the pressures which administrative agencies experience when they seek to put new policies into practice. These may be described as examples of 'goal displacement', and deserve particular attention.

The kind of goal displacement which occurs in public administration is particularly associated in this way with new policies, with innovations which attract controversy. Burton Clark has suggested an approach to this topic which locates the problems of innovating organisations in value insecurity.[30] Goal change is related by Clark to the possession of 'precarious values'. He suggests that values tend to be precarious when they are undefined, when the people involved in implementing them have positions which are not fully 'legitimised', and when they are 'unacceptable to a "host" population'. These three points merit more detailed examination.

Clark himself expands his first point in the following way:[31] 'Values are *undefined* when they are not embodied in existing goals and standards of committed groups. They lack specific normative reference and no one knows what various symbols really mean.' Examples of this phenomenon were provided in the previous chapter where it was suggested that discretionary powers are often left to officials because politicians are unprepared to face up to value issues. Inasmuch, therefore, as politicians have a general desire to liberalise a particular aspect of administration but are unwilling or unable to spell this out unambiguously in legislation they render it likely that their aspirations to change values will be negated by prevailing community values.

A failure to define values clearly may be just a consequence of a failure to think through a particular problem properly, but it is very much more likely to stem from a situation in which Clark's third point is relevant, where values are the subject of controversy and are unacceptable to part or all of what Clark calls a 'host population'. If this is the case, legislators may well foresee difficulties if they create a situation in which goals are too clearly defined. They then face a problem which Gross[32] has called the achievement of a 'balance' between clarity and vagueness, using a physical analogy which sounds satisfactory until one tries to work out where such a 'balance' can be achieved, in which case it may be suspected that sometimes a point of balance does not really exist. Donnison has portrayed the dilemmas associated with this issue rather well:[33]

Discretion, vagueness, and unexplicitness are only tolerable and useful if their limits are reasonably clear and their implications restricted in scope. Objectives which are too precisely defined tend to be restrictive if cautious, or disruptive if radical. But objectives which are too vague tend to destroy a sense of purpose and provide no foundation upon which to establish proper standards of performance.

There has been a number of studies of ventures undertaken as part of the New Deal programme in the United States which provide evidence on the way in which idealistic social experiments can be undermined by a failure to face up to the crucial value issues involved. Selznick's *TVA and the Grass Roots*[34] is perhaps the best known of these studies. In the Tennessee Valley Authority the 'grass roots' doctrine functioned not so much as a true commitment to community democracy but as a protective 'ideology' in an attempt to assure, at one and the same time, TVA's critics on the left that the experiment was democratic and its critics on the right that local interest groups were not being disregarded. In practice the grass roots doctrine largely surrendered control over the TVA agricultural programme to the interest groups controlled by the larger and more prosperous farmers in the area.

Banfield[35] has described a similar confusion over values which had a devastating impact upon a farm resettlement programme. Those in charge of this venture were quite unable to resolve the conflict between a need to justify the venture in economic terms as an experiment in land reclamation and a desire to create a democratically run collective farm. In hovering between the two it failed to satisfy those of its critics who were always on the lookout for examples of 'creeping communism' to condemn, but it utterly betrayed the members of the settlement and engendered irresponsible behaviour on their part by failing to grant real community control.

The recent history of the United States is full of examples of this kind, social experiments which have failed because the political system demands a continuing process of compromise. Federal government administrators move out with missionary zeal to implement a new social reform programme, only to find that they have to protect themselves from a Congress[36] always eager to cut their budget and close down their programme, and that, in order to do anything effective in the field, they are required to compromise with state, county and city governments.[37] It is little wonder that it is easy to find examples from the field of American government and administration of ambiguous goals, distorted goals and displaced goals. It is surprising, therefore, that American students of administration have been so ready to treat goals as if they are straightforward, easily discerned, phenomena.[38]

The greater degree of centralisation present in British government, the absence of a real separation between executive and legislative and of local government autonomy, obviously cuts down the extent to which governments are unwilling to give administrative bodies clear-cut goals. However there are many examples of situations in which policy goals are distorted or undermined by compromises with powerful pressure groups. The intentions of policies have been seriously distorted in fields like health, education, transport and the provision of pensions by compromises which policy-makers have found it necessary to make with various interest groups. Sometimes, moreover, administrators play an important role in persuading politicians to make value compromises with arguments about administrative burdens and problems. For example, proposals to ensure that recipients of supplementary pensions were made fully aware of the way in which their allowances were calculated, so that they would know whether they had been granted an allowance to which they were entitled, were rejected by the Minister solely on the grounds that the department was overburdened with administrative tasks.[39] This was one example of a number of ways in which a policy change aiming at providing a certain kind of benefit as of right was undermined.

It is also important to point out here a new kind of development in British administration, which has been widely hailed as being more democratic but could well be subject to exactly the problems of goal displacement which faced the American New Deal experiments, that is those policies which involve forms of community participation such as the Community Development Projects[40] and the 1968 Town and Country Planning Act.[41] The first danger that faces such initiatives is that participation will in practice be confined to a few, or that some of the participants will prove more successful than others because they are more powerful, or skilful, or just more vociferous than others.[42] The second kind of danger is that the doctrine of participation will merely provide a smoke-screen for planners whose actions will be as arbitrary as before but more difficult to oppose because they have been 'legitimated'. In the words of Dennis:[43]

It must be stressed ... that participation means something more than knowledge fed to a decision-maker for him to examine or neglect according to the play of his own interests and energies, and use or discard as he sees fit. It also connotes control of the decision-maker to ensure that the values which are incorporated in any scheme are those of the people affected by it.

The concepts of 'community' and 'participation' are both highly ambiguous; the combination of circumstances in which both local authorities and middle-class-dominated pressure groups are very ready to present themselves as spokesmen for 'the community', and, on the other hand, deprived groups are slow to organise and find it difficult to penetrate the corridors of power, creates a situation in which the ostensible goals of community participation policies are continually under threat and could be subverted almost without the fact being noticed. The author and Ruth Issacharoff have published an account of one such public initiative which has suffered in precisely this way,[44] though in this case, Clark's second point is also very significant in that the position assigned by the government to the community relations 'movement' largely denied it full legitimacy.

Clark writes of situations in which[45] 'Social values tend to be precarious when the position of functionaries is not fully legitimated', that 'in specific organisations or in the general society, values may be precarious because of the weak position of custodians in the social structure.' The community relations movement was created as part of a government programme to ameliorate race relations. Given the extent of prejudice and discrimination in British society it is to be expected that any organisations faced with this task would be in a weak position. But the government made the situation of those working in community relations particularly weak in three different ways. It decided that community relations work should be run by quasi-independent bodies with government funds but with no guarantee of direct government support. Thus it refused to place the considerable institutionalised power possessed by a centralised system of government behind the movement. Next, it decided that the key organisations in community relations, the local committees, should be coalitions, in which local authorities should play a major part, of[46] 'all the main religious bodies and political parties and as many as possible of the various local organizations, both statutory and voluntary'. In this way it determined that the local committees would always have to compromise with, and would probably be dominated by, the powerful white organisations in their areas. Finally, the government's own actions in other areas of race rela- tions—its introduction of restrictive and in some respects harsh immigration regulations, its tardy and inadequate response to the need for antidiscriminatory legislation, and its failure to clamp down upon discriminatory behaviour by some local authorities— tended to give succour to the values the community relations movement was supposed to oppose.

It will be very clear from this example that where values are precarious because of the social conflict surrounding them, then politicians will tend to compound the difficulties of those whom they select to translate them into organisational goals, not only by giving them an unclear mandate, but also by putting them in a position in which they find it hard to achieve 'legitimacy'. This leads directly to a situation in which organisations in such posi- tions gravitate towards safe and noncontroversial activities. In the case of the adult education schools which Clark studied[47] this involved sacrificing academic ideals and responding to consumer demand. In general, in situations of this kind, organisational security begins to be put before any movement towards contro- versial, and hence disruptive, goals and, in the long run, original goals (or the goals that might have been postulated had the organisation been prepared to pause to try to formulate them) are forgotten. Marris and Rein said of some of the projects which . preceded the Poverty Program in the United States: [84]

> Once the projects began to put their programmes into effect, their actions were more than ever shaped by the means to hand. They were under pressure to produce results, and reluctant, at the outset, to run too great a risk of failure: so they accomplished first the programmes which came easiest—a summer camp, vacation jobs for high school students, training courses for well qualified applicants, holiday tasks for college volunteers—rather than those which mattered most. Sometimes they even appropriated to their sponsor- ship activities already in being. And in developing their plans, they went after new money, rather than new ideas. The organizations soon acquired an interest in their own survival, growth and influence which upset their original agenda.

Earlier in this chapter it was suggested that the Americans have had to face the goal-displacement problem in a particularly acute form because their institutional structure demands an extreme and continuing sensitivity to political pressure. The natural response to this situation has been the development of what has been called 'cooperative strategy', bringing into the decision-making processes those parties who would otherwise be able to affect the political security of an organisation. Thompson and McEwan[49] provide a useful analysis of the various kinds of cooperative strategy, which they see as differing in respect of the stage at which the outsider enters into the decision process. They further suggest[50] 'that the potential power of an outsider increases the earlier he enters into the decision process.'

The first kind of cooperative strategy Thompson and McEwan outline is 'bargaining', which refers to[51] 'the negotiation of an agreement for the exchange of goods or services between two or more organisations'. Bargaining tends to be concerned with resources rather than explicitly with goals but[52] 'to the extent that bargaining sets a limit on the amount of resources available or the ways they may be employed it effectively sets limits on choice of goals.... To the extent that the second party's support is necessary he is in a position to exercise a veto over final choice of alternative goals, and hence takes part in the decision.'

The second kind of cooperative strategy is called 'co-optation' by Thompson and McEwan and is more or less Selznick's concept of 'informal co-optation' (see pages 29–30):[53]

Co-optation involves a greater degree of compromise with outside parties. It involves inroads on the process of deciding goals; not only must the final choice be acceptable to the co-opted party or organization, but to the extent that co-optation is effective it places the representative of an 'outsider' in a position to determine the occasion for a goal decision, to participate in analyzing the existing situation, to suggest alternatives, and to take part in the deliberation of consequences.

Thompson and McEwan go on to show how the adoption of co-optation renders it probable that an organisation will adopt a consensual approach to the formulation of policies:[54]

Co-optation is an important social device for increasing the likelihood that organizations related to one another in complicated ways will in fact find compatible goals. By thus reducing the possibilities of antithetical actions by two or more organizations, co-optation aids in the integration of the heterogeneous parts of a complex society. By the same token, co-optation further limits the opportunity for one organization to choose its goals arbitrarily or unilaterally.

Thompson and McEwan discuss 'coalition' as their third kind of cooperative strategy, and as[55] 'the ultimate or extreme form of environmental conditioning of organizational goals' involving a situation in which 'two or more organizations act as one with respect to certain goals'. So this is a situation in which a joint commitment from different organisations is deemed necessary for goal attainment and in which, therefore, a high degree of consensus has to be reached.

Conditioned by necessity, in the way that has been described, attempts have been made in the United States to develop theories of community organisation, involving cooperative strategies, to solve problems of deprivation and discrimination.[56] Such theorising has naturally come under fire because it involves the assumption that an essentially consensual strategy can solve problems which are rooted in conflicts of interest. Accordingly Morris and Rein[57] have argued that while strategies of this kind may be appropriate where coordination goals are being aimed at, they are not appropriate where goals of change are sought. They suggest that where goals of change are sought organisations are engaged on a strategy of what they describe as 'individual rationality' as opposed to the 'co-operative rationality' which is involved if it is considered that there are problems which differing organisations are prepared to work together to solve. Morris and Rein then go on to suggest a simple model of the relationship between types of strategy and types of structure, in which cells 1 and 4 represent goals, and cells 2 and 3 potential kinds of goals displacements.

	Type of Structure	
	Federated	Simple
Type of Strategy		
Cooperative rationality	1 Integration	2 Ritualism
Individual rationality	3 Survival	4 Change

They suggest that an organisation which has a simple structure, which does not attempt to secure the cooperation of other interests, will be merely going through 'rituals' if its aim is to secure community consensus upon some particular object. On the other hand an organisation which has, by co-optation or coalition, secured the support of other organisations will soon be fighting for its survival if it tries to seek goals involving community change. The maximum kind of cooperative strategy open to a change-oriented organisation is bargaining, and even that carries with it severe risks.

The obvious conclusion to be drawn from this analysis, a conclusion that many Americans drew from the failure of the Poverty Programme, is that since the American institutional structure more or less requires that any government agency pursues a cooperative strategy such organisations cannot be expected to be very effective change agents. In such a situation, change must be forced upon governments by independent bodies—a conclusion that is not very encouraging to minority groups committed to working within the normal pressure-group channels.

In Britain, on the other hand, where it is easier for agencies of change to operate without a cooperative strategy, some of the problems of urban redevelopment, for example, have not assumed so acute a form. The checks on urban renewal which have been so significant in Chicago[58] have not existed to hamper the activities of British municipal authorities. But democratic politics is not only concerned with the ends of administration; it may also be concerned with the means, and accordingly the 'daddy knows best' approach to administration which has characterised the central and local government agencies concerned with social engineering has increasingly come under fire in recent years.[59] In other words the cry for participation is a demand for the development of cooperative rationality in areas where hitherto individual rationality has prevailed.

Some comments have already been made about the consequences of mistaking partial or unequal participation for something more comprehensive, equally it has to be recognised that participation does not mean exactly the same thing as consensus. Britain seems to have an unhappy knack of picking up American ideas about five years after they have been proved to be failures. The 'Community Relations' idea is a most striking example of this. If 'participation' is not to produce goal displacement in change agencies, a great deal of care needs to be exercised in defining the over-riding interests involved, the kinds of participation which are legitimate, and the procedures to be adopted to prevent deadlock.

This discussion of goal displacement has served to make clear two important general points which are central to the purpose of this book. The first of these concerns the use of the concept of 'goal' in relation to public administration. It may be that securing 'participation' or preserving 'consensus' ('one nation') is just as much a goal of a particular government as securing change. It may be, too, since the world is changing all the while, that the 'goal' of a particular government is to check, change or to come to terms with it. In other words the approach adopted by many sociologists of treating goals as 'ends', and seeing goal displacement as a process in which 'means' are substituted for 'ends', involves an abstraction from a reality that is very much more complex. 'Goals' can be made a useful concept for the study of public administration only if the student is prepared to abstract a particular phase in the history of the process of government and view it as temporarily a distinct entity. But to see the whole process of public administration in a country as a series of goal-attainment processes cannot realistically be a statement about behaviour directed towards long-run ends, but only a description of a situation in which many people are in various places on a large number of small means-ends chains, some of which other people have provided for them, which they may or may not acknowledge and may or may not freely accept, others of which they have provided for themselves.

The second point that emerges from the discussion of goals is that it makes no sense to see politics as providing the 'goals' of administration in any straightforward way if in practice the goal attainment processes in which administrators are involved are under continual threat from outside groups. If means can be goals just as much as ends then politicians are as likely to want to be concerned with means as with ends, and value issues are likely to arise in connection with either. It follows from the difficulties which occur over the use of the language of goals in public administration that the task of distinguishing administration from politics, which will be discussed later in the book, will prove equally difficult.

6

Authority

A substantial number of writers have dealt with authority within
organisations; inevitably, therefore, a wide range of definitions of
authority has been used. Different approaches to the definition of
authority, and of two closely related concepts—influence and
power—derive often from different ideological assumptions about
the nature of social control. At one extreme are found writers
whose emphasis is primarily upon the coercive aspects of control,
writers who see the power to use sanctions as all important for the
explanation of compliance. At the other extreme are those who
emphasise the consensual nature of social relationships, and who
see acceptance and commitment as the key factors in the explanation of compliance. Yet writers at both extremes tend to use the
concept of authority in explaining compliance.

Arguments of this kind, deriving essentially from deeply held
preconceptions about compliance, are particularly liable to arise
because of the methodological problems that confront the social
scientist who tries to explain why one man obeys another. There
is an obvious case for saying, when faced with this kind of issue,
that all the social scientist can conclude is that in certain specified
kinds of situations men tend to obey other men. But to do this is
to refuse to try to get to grips with one of the most significant
problems that faces those who seek to understand human behaviour, what has been described as 'the problem of authority'.[1]
Such an understanding is necessary if the sociologist is to say
anything useful about the viability of patterns of social organisation which seek to minimise the authority relationship, or about
ways in which authority may be exerted or combated.

The difficulty in explaining compliance is particularly associated
with the fact that, even when authority relationships are formally
prescribed within organisations, they frequently deviate from such
a formal pattern, a fact that is sufficiently widely observed to have

been given popular currency in such expressions as 'the power behind the throne', 'éminence grise' and 'the tail wags the dog'. It is particularly difficult for the social scientist to study such behaviour on account of the fact that the actors involved in such relationships are likely, according to their interests, to try to either conceal or exaggerate the true facts of the situation. Furthermore, actors involved in either formal or informal compliance relationships are likely, again according to their needs, to either over- or under-exaggerate the degree of voluntarism exercised in such relationships. In social relationships we practise continual but varying deception both of other people and of ourselves as to the amount of independence we have from the control of others, sometimes claiming to be in bond when we are free, sometimes claiming to be free when we are really subject to compulsion. Similarly, as the controllers or would-be controllers of the activities of other people, we also tend to give an impression of the relationship distorted in one direction or the other, according to our needs and those of the situation.

Thus the social scientist who seeks to study authority relationships finds himself examining an aspect of social life where the subjects of his study will be likely to be deeply committed, emotionally as well as socially, to presenting a distorted view of their relationships with other people. And inevitably, forced to choose between several alternative distortions of a particular situation, the social scientist will find it difficult to avoid accepting an interpretation of reality congenial to his own ideological predispositions. To give a crude example, if management say, 'We are one big happy family,' while the workers say, 'We are exploited,' and if both sides contrive, as they very often will, to prevent the researcher probing their relationships too deeply; then if he is determined to go home and write up something, the sociologist will be left to the mercy of his own ideology. This is, of course, slightly exaggerated cynicism, but it is probably a desirable starting point for the discussion of such an emotionally and ideologically charged subject as authority.

It is important to explain the concept authority in relation to 'power' and 'influence'; with power resting upon an individual's ability to force another individual to do his will, while influence implies a situation in which an individual willingly obeys or follows another.

The normal situation within an administrative organisation is one in which subordinate obeys superior, and nobody gives a thought to the question of whether he is really submitting to superior power or willingly accepting influence. But in order to understand the full implications of the normal situation, to delineate its boundaries and to explain why authority is accepted so readily so often and yet rejected in some situations, it is necessary to probe more deeply into the explanation of the phenomenon.

In Chapter 8 of their textbook, *Public Administration*, Simon, Smithburg and Thompson,[2] having discussed very briefly what they call the 'traditional' approach to authority as a legal concept defined in terms of legitimacy, proceed to treat authority as a psychological phenomenon. They say[3] 'we shall be concerned with the fact that under certain circumstances people *do* accept the commands and decisions of others, rather than the fact that a legal system imposes upon them the *duty* to do so.' They suggest that this acceptance of authority occurs in two kinds of situations, when the individual carries out a proposal without considering its merits and when he carries out a proposal even though he is convinced it is wrong. They recognise that there are limits to this acceptance of authority, using here the concept of 'area of acceptance' developed by Simon in his *Administrative Behavior*.[4]

Simon, Smithburg and Thompson go on to develop four categories of authority, defined in terms of the reasons for the acceptance of authority. Three of these 'types of authority' fall clearly into the category of 'influence' suggested above:

1 Authority of confidence, based particularly on expertise or 'functional status'.

2 Authority of identification, based upon the notion of group loyalty.

3 Authority of legitimacy, which Simon, Smithburg and Thompson say people accept because 'they feel they *ought* to go along with the "rules of the game." '[5]

The fourth of Simon, Smithburg and Thompson's 'types of authority', on the other hand, involves recognition of the institutionalised power aspect of authority: they call it the 'authority of sanctions'. Yet significantly they suggest it is less important for the explanation of the acceptance of authority than legitimacy. This view derives partly from the fact that they assume that, because sanctions are rarely used in organisational situations, they are insignificant. Thus they see the threat of sanctions as of minimal importance and do not deal with the possibility that powerless individuals accept authority because they know that if they came into conflict with those who wield sanctions they could not win. Furthermore Simon, Smithburg and Thompson's view of the unimportance of sanctions fails to acknowledge that within an organisation the withdrawal of future benefits—for example, promotions—may be a significant sanction that is commonly used, or at least believed to be commonly used, and thus far more important than punishment, which takes the form of the removal of current privileges. As Fox puts it,[6] 'Every sanction has its positive and negative aspects. Financial rewards, promotion prospects, praise and approval, transfers to more desired work, and any other form of gratification are positive but also have a negative aspect in that they embody a conditional clause threatening their withdrawal or withholding if the required behaviour is not forthcoming.'

In the work of Simon, Smithburg and Thompson, there is a tendency to equate authority with influence and to put forward a consensual view of organisational compliance which underemphasises the impact of power. Their theory is primarily a psychological one, with but a limited attempt being made to relate what are essentially interpersonal aspects of organisational roles to the wider context of the organisation as a whole or to the organisation's position in a wider society.

R. V. Presthus goes much further than Simon, Smithburg and Thompson in trying to analyse authority as a special phenomenon arising out of a relationship between interpersonal relationships in organisations, and organisational and social roles. It is therefore worthwhile to quote his definitions of authority, influence and power:[7]

Authority can be defined as the capacity to evoke compliance in others on the basis of formal position and of any psychological inducements, rewards, or sanctions that may accompany formal position. The capacity to evoke compliance without relying upon formal role or the sanctions at its disposal may be called *influence*. When formal position is not necessarily involved, but when extensive sanctions are available, we are concerned with *power*. The definitions turn upon formal position or role because this point of reference best suits the conditions of large-scale organisation. The sanctioned control of organised resources through formal position is probably the major source of power in modern society. Authority, power and influence are usually interlaced in operating situations.

Thus Presthus defines authority in terms of formal position. Yet he goes on to suggest a view of organisational authority in which psychological elements play just as significant a part as they do in the theories of Simon, Smithburg and Thompson. He does this by suggesting that authority must be defined[8] 'as a transactional process, characterized by active, reciprocal interrelationships in which the values, training and perceptions of members play a crucial role in defining and validating the authority of organizational leaders.' Presthus describes the various processes by which authority is 'legitimated', and uses that concept in a wider sense than is usual in the social sciences. He suggests that legitimation[9] rests upon four bases: technical expertise; formal role or position in the organisation's hierarchy; rapport or the capacity of leaders to meet individual needs for recognition, security, and pleasant working relations; and finally, legitimation through a generalised deference towards authority.

Superficially it may appear that Presthus' four types of legitimation can be equated with Simon, Smithburg and Thompson's four types of authority. But to do this would fail to do justice to Presthus' very much more subtle approach. Thus, the latter writers mix a power category in with their three categories of influence. However, the category in Presthus' theory that Peabody[10] (who does try to assimilate the two theories) equates with 'authority of sanctions', legitimation by 'formal role', is based upon a tendency to invest formal positions with an aura of importance. Similarly, people do not necessarily take notice of experts because they are experts; there are social processes leading to the legitimation of experts which may be very necessary before experts will have much influence.

Presthus' notion of the importance of generalised deference to authority is also an important one for the full understanding of the means by which organisational authority is underwritten by individual personality factors.

Presthus offers here, then, a much less naive approach to organisational harmony than that offered by Simon, Smithburg and Thompson, recognising how psychological devices can be brought into play to support organisational authority. Interestingly enough in a more recent book the third of the latter trio, V. A. Thompson,[11] has examined how persons in formal authority positions seek to make themselves more secure by the use of such devices, which he names 'ideological' and 'dramaturgical' approaches to the protection of the positions of heads of formal organisations. The ideological approach involves in particular the elaboration of theories about the importance of leadership. He argues,[12] 'the tendency of leadership studies has been to associate heroic, charismatic traits with persons in superordinate positions; and, consequently, these studies have served an ideological purpose in helping to keep attention focused on individuals and not on the institutional structures that underly their difficulties and frustrations.' Similarly Thompson sees the development of human relations or 'managerial social psychology' as involving a similar focus upon securing compliance for managers to divert attention from questions about the dispensability of management.

The dramaturgical approach defined by Thompson involves the creation of impressions of managerial importance by the use of what are often called status symbols: size of office, thickness of carpet, protection by secretaries and so on. These devices are essentially concerned with the translation of formal authority into influence.

Presthus' concern is to show how those in authority acquire influence, and to suggest that if this does not happen, their positions will be in danger. Bierstedt, on the other hand, is much more concerned not to confuse sociological and psychological explanations of authority.

Bierstedt firmly rejects theories that equate authority with influence in any form.[13] For him, authority is definitely institutionalised power, and the particularly interesting aspects of his essay on this topic are concerned with the discussion of how society bestows authority upon certain roles:[14]

In this process several things happen. In the first place, informal procedures and patterns of interaction come to be standardised as statuses. It is the institutionalisation of procedures into norms and roles into statuses which results in the formal organisation of the association. Norms and statuses then constitute the structure of the association; they are its organisation. More particularly, the role of leader, which one or several members of the group have been playing, comes to be institutionalised in one or several statuses to which authority is now attached in accordance with the norms. These roles become statuses in order that the stability of the association may be assured and its continuity guaranteed.

Thus authority is attached to positions and not to specific persons, and an authority system is built up that has majority, though not necessarily universal, social support. Any challenge to authority positions within that system is likely to be seen as a challenge to the majority and to the system with which they are identified. Thus Bierstedt argues that[15] 'authority is always delegated. Its ultimate source is the power of the majority.' But the significant point is that for Bierstedt a majority support for those in authority may not necessarily exist within a particular organisation; his is a much wider view of social support than that put forward by Simon, Smithburg and Thompson since the majority that sustains an organisation may be found in the society as a whole.

Yet, while Bierstedt's view is not entirely a consensual one, even he exaggerates the extent to which authority, if not exactly influence, is nevertheless of necessity a widely accepted phenomenon. His view is built upon a general assumption that (1) power is evenly distributed between individuals in a society as a whole, and (2) upon denial of the notion that an organisation may itself contribute to making the balance of social power unequal. Certainly when subordinate B is in conflict with superior A, their conflict can be seen in terms of generalised social expectations of their roles, but if B has been wronged, he cannot depend upon the 'majority' re-examining the relevant 'social contract' in order to decide whether to support him in righting that wrong. Rather, the outcome of such a conflict will depend upon the immediate resources of power that B can muster to combat the institutional power of A. Bierstedt is under no illusions about the importance of power in sustaining authority, yet his argument leads to apparent naivety, particularly evident in his essay on the sociology of majorities, about how easily such power can be taken away.

In the above discussion, three theories have been examined in which there seems to be a link between the extent to which authority is equated with influence and the extent to which consensus is emphasised as a characteristic of organisational compliance. Simon, Smithburg and Thompson are so anxious to emphasise the consensual element in organisational behaviour that their use of the concept of authority is muddled, and leads inevitably to a more complete equation of authority with influence than is justifiable. Presthus, on the other hand, achieves a clever contrast between authority and influence by showing how formal authority may be bolstered up by influence, a point he develops much more fully in his book, *The Organizational Society*,[16] in particular relation to what he calls 'generalized deference to authority'. Finally, Bierstedt conveys very clearly the notion of authority as institutionalised power by reference to the relationship between authority and society.

Two recent contributors to the debate about authority, Buckley[17] and Fox,[18] interestingly revert to a definition of authority which equates it with influence but, unlike Simon, Smithburg and Thompson, suggest that power rather than authority is often of key importance in the explanation of organisational compliance. For them, 'apathetic conformity' is a key characteristic of much organisational behaviour. In adopting this approach they both stress ways in which mixtures of authority and power contribute to the maintenance of organisational control, and are able to deal with issues overlooked by Bierstedt because of his stress upon majorities.

Buckley points out that people in subordinate positions may have a variety of attitudes to power structures. He argues that[19] 'there is a wide gap between large-scale, participative, informed consent ... on the one hand, and overt opposition ... on the other' and that many people may comply without either a commitment to obey or a consciousness of coercion. If a minority accept 'authority', the majority may find that they have little alternative but to comply, so that[20] 'a social structure may be "legitimized" or "institutionalized" only from the point of view of a small minority of members of the system.' Buckley goes on, 'As a general proposition, we are forced to allow that, inasmuch as power and authority are relational concepts, what may be a system of authority to some actors may be a system of power to others.'

Fox[21] throws light upon some of the complications inherent in compliance relationships by making use of Merton's distinction[22] between deviants who reject socially prescribed means of attaining 'culture goals', but acknowledge the legitimacy of those goals, and deviants who reject the goals too. Within organisations there will be many individuals who neither totally accept authority, nor totally reject it. Many organisational employees will not have to be coerced into compliance, rather they will passively accept the status quo while feeling considerable discontent about many aspects of the system. When conflicts arise within the organisation, those who control it will compete with the active malcontents for the allegiance of this large apathetic group.

Having dealt very fully with the use that has been made of, and the insights gained from, the concept of authority and its two related concepts, influence and power, it is necessary now to introduce the work of another theorist who has contributed to extending the understanding of organisational authority, Etzioni. Curiously enough, however, while doing this he does in fact explicitly reject the use of the concept of authority.

Etzioni's contribution to this subject is found in his *A Comparative Analysis of Complex Organizations*.[23] Etzioni rejects the concept of authority because of its equation with legitimate power, arguing that he is interested in the bases of compliance, a phenomenon related to individual needs and not necessarily to legitimacy. He thus supports the view of those students of authority who define it as institutionalised power, but considers it more important to direct his attention to types of compliance and thus to take up a position not so very far away from that taken by Simon, Smithburg and Thompson in their analysis of types of authority. Which once again demonstrates how confusing it can be to try to compare different approaches in terms of the concepts used!

According to Etzioni:[24]

Compliance refers both to a relation in which an actor behaves in accordance with a directive supported by another person's power and to the orientation of the subject to the power applied. There are three kinds of power coercive, remunerative, and normative; and three kinds of involvement alienative, calculative and moral.

Although these types of power and types of involvement together make nine possible types of compliance, Etzioni is primarily concerned with what he calls the three 'congruent types': 'coercive' compliance, involving coercive power and alienative involvement, 'utilitarian' compliance, involving remunerative power and calculative involvement, and 'normative' compliance involving normative power and moral involvement. He argues that[25]

Congruent types are more effective than the incongruent types. Organizations are under pressure to be effective. Hence to the degree that the environment of the organization allows, organizations tend to shift their compliance structure from incongruent to congruent types and organizations which have congruent compliant structure tend to resist factors pushing them toward incongruent compliance structures.

The study of public administration in non-totalitarian countries is concerned with organisations which are often balanced awkwardly between Etzioni's utilitarian and normative types of compliance, a complication which Etzioni recognises but rather brushes aside in his definition of utilitarian organisations:[26] '... organizations in which remuneration is the major means of control over lower participants and calculative involvement (i.e. mild alienation to mild commitment) characterizes the orientation of the large majority of lower participants.'

By contrast, compliance in the kinds of organisations Etzioni describes as normative is based[27] 'principally on internalization of directives accepted as legitimate. Leadership, rituals, manipulation of social and prestige symbols, and resocialization are among the more important techniques of control used.'

The tendency for many organisations to have compliance structures which do not fall neatly into Etzioni's categories has been clearly recognised in industrial sociology: as Fox points out,[28] 'jobs located towards the top of the hierarchy provide scope for wider and deeper aspirations than do jobs located towards the bottom.' Accordingly,[29] 'positions at the top seem likely to offer the possibility of a high degree of normative agreement; positions at the bottom a high degree of normative conflict.'

The presence in public administration of a large number of people in middle positions, the strength of whose allegiance to the organisations is not at all clear, may present those in controlling positions with particular difficulties in maintaining the right balance between what Etzioni calls remunerative and normative power.

Etzioni provides a useful further classification of different types of power, clearly relevant to the problem already discussed in this chapter, when he makes a distinction between 'power derived from office' ('authority', in the terms used earlier) and personal power (almost the same as 'influence' in the previous discussion). The following diagrams set out this relationship:

A Typology of Elites[30]

	Power derived from office	
Personal power	+	−
+	Formal Leaders	Informal Leaders
−	Officers	Non-elite

Types of Elites and Activities Controlled [31]

	Informal Leaders	Formal Leaders	Officers
Instrumental activities	x	xx	xxx
Expressive activities	xxx	xx	x

x = least likely   xx = more likely   xxx = most likely

These concepts of 'instrumental' and 'expressive activities' are taken by Etzioni from Parsons, who argued that 'every activity must solve four basic functional problems: it must fulfill two instrumental needs of input and allocation, and two expressive needs of social and normative integration.'[32]

Etzioni argues, supported by a great deal of evidence from industrial sociology, that the division of instrumental and expressive activities between formal and informal leadership particularly tends to occur in the utilitarian organisation, and in the coercive one. The normative organisation, on the other hand, tends to enjoy much greater commitment to formal leadership, and will be likely to break up if such commitment is absent. Presumably, the public administrative organisation, which could not normally break up in such a situation, would tend to swing in the utilitarian direction in the event of changes in the attitudes of subordinates to those in command. In this kind of situation, senior officials are likely to have recourse to the psychological devices outlined by Thompson (see pages 109–10) and may be slow to recognise the need to adjust control policies to take account of the changed situation. For example, the high wastage and grave dissatisfaction over incomes and hours in the nursing profession today may be symptomatic of just such a failure of the hospital service to come to terms with a shift in the nature of compliance.

Thus Etzioni offers some insights into the relationship between authority and influence, even though he largely avoids the use of these terms, and thereby he provides a link between the study of authority and psychological studies of leadership. Leaders secure willing support, therefore leaders are sought to transform subordinates into followers.

Traditionally, the search for leaders has been a search for people with specific, often 'heroic', traits. In the words of Bavelas:[33]

Early notions about leadership dealt with it almost entirely in terms of personal abilities. Leadership was explicitly associated with special powers. An outstanding leader was credited not only with extensions of the normal abilities possessed by most men but with extraordinary powers such as the ability to read men's minds, to tell the future, to compel obedience hypnotically. These powers were often thought of as gifts from a god, as conditional loans from a devil, or as the result of some accidental supernatural circumstance attending conception, birth or early childhood. Today, claims of supernatural powers are made more rarely, but they are not entirely unknown. Of course, milder claims – tirelessness, infallibility of intuition, lightning-quick powers of decision – are made in one form or another by many outstandingly successful men.

The notion of leaders as men who are considered by their followers to possess striking traits is contained in Weber's concept of charismatic authority.[34] Leadership by people of this kind is called for only in exceptional situations and, even in those situations, the spell of the charismatic leader may well vanish if he is unable to take decisions, or to find someone to help him take decisions, in order to translate the dedication of his followers into effective action. In less dramatic situations, therefore, it is rash to assume that leadership selection can be based upon a search for the possessors of 'heroic' traits.

Nevertheless, under the influence of concepts of leadership of this kind, a great deal of attention has been given to the search for leadership traits, even if the traits sought have been of a more prosaic kind. In general the search for leadership traits has not been very successful; Bavelas provides the following account of the more positive findings:[35]

On various tests, persons who are leaders tend to be brighter, tend to be better adjusted psychologically, and tend to display better judgment. Studies that have concentrated on the social behaviour of leaders show that they 'interact' more than nonleaders. They tend to give more information, ask for more information, and to take the lead in summing up or interpreting a situation.

These studies add up to little more than the not very surprising discoveries that leaders need to be at least of reasonable intelligence, self-confidence, sociability, personal attractiveness and so on. Interestingly some studies of leadership also suggest that leaders who stand out too markedly from their followers tend to be distrusted.

However, even the modest findings of the trait studies have come under attack because of their lack of attention either to situations or to variations in group membership. Pigors argues,[36]

'It is nonsense to talk of leadership in the abstract since no one can just lead without having a goal. Leadership is always *in* some sphere of interest, and *toward* some objective goal seen by leader and follower.'

Accordingly Gibb suggests that the correct approach to the study of leadership traits is as follows:[37]

> The traits of leadership are any or all of those personality traits which in any particular situation, enable an individual to (i) contribute significantly to group locomotion in the direction of a recognised goal, and (ii) be perceived as doing so by fellow group members.... Different people want different things of leadership. Patterns of behavior which constitute effective leader behavior in one group may not be effective in another. As group goals change, leadership needs change and different forms of leader behavior are demanded.

There are several different points that need to be disentangled here. First, there are differences in task. Cartwright and Zander refer to an attempt by Krech and Crutchfield to list different 'functions' of leadership in which fourteen such functions are suggested:[38] 'They propose that a leader serves to some degree as an executive, planner, policy-maker, expert, external group representative, controller of internal relationships, purveyor of rewards and punishments, arbitrator, exemplar, group symbol, surrogate for individual responsibility, ideologist, father figure or scapegoat.'

Second, there are differences between groups. There are markedly different definitions of leader and follower roles in different cultures, as studies by Richardson[39] and Miller[40] have shown. Moreover even within one culture there may be subcultural variations in response to authority situations. The personality structures of group members may also be relevant. For example, Lewin's[41] theory about the superiority of democratic styles of leadership has been shown not to hold with groups whose members have 'authoritarian personalities'.

Third, as Etzioni has suggested, individuals may expect a very different kind of leadership according to whether their orientation to the organisation is 'calculative' or 'moral', and may also require both 'instrumental' and 'expressive' leadership—very different kinds of leadership which it may be impossible to find combined in the same person. Somewhat similarly, Korten[42] has suggested that individuals may more effectively be led by authoritarian leaders when faced by what they recognise as serious and ambiguous problems, yet be less ready to accept this sort of leadership style in other situations.

So far it has been suggested that there may be grave difficulties involved in trying to achieve any equation between leadership qualities and authority situations, suggesting that to devise effective selection devices one must know not only a great deal about the tasks for which leadership is required, but also have information about the cultural context of the situation, about the personalities of the potential followers, and about the orientation of the followers to their work tasks.

This subject is made even more complicated by the institutional framework within which superordinate officials are required to operate. To begin with subordinates will have views about the processes by which their superiors are selected and accordingly, since acceptance is vital for leadership, may undermine the effectiveness of a superior simply because they do not accept the legitimacy of the selection process. For example, in Britain junior civil servants tend to have strong views about the importance of seniority for promotion. Hence they will tend to be hostile to any new superior who does not seem to them to have put in the service to merit a senior position. If he is promoted from among their own ranks, in particular, they may have very strong views about his suitability for a leadership position which will undermine any respect they might have had for a superior officer. Significantly too, such views may well influence the promotee's assessment of himself, and undermine his position in that way.

This last point leads on to yet another complication in the search for leadership qualities, this is that the individual's own assessment of his social situation may markedly influence his behaviour. Success gives the personality an enormous boost, and individuals often discover leadership qualities in themselves when they are called upon to lead. Equally, and this is particularly true of authoritiarian groups, individuals experience patterns of deference when they acquire positions of authority that make their tasks very much easier than might be expected from any assessment of their personality prior to selection. This, too, follows from the earlier point about subordinates' views on the legitimacy of selection processes. As Gibb suggests,[43] 'In some instances it may be said that prestige within a group is acquired by virtue of a certain status in an institution which embraces that group, as in the case of a parish priest. In such a case the assumption of a leadership role is made easier ...'

In general the study of leadership has been carried out by social psychologists, typically experimenting with small groups of volunteers outside complex organisational structures. Researchers of this kind have paid comparatively little attention to what Fiedler has called[44] 'position power' and tend to exaggerate the importance of interpersonal influence. Given, then, that it is very difficult to select leaders for bureaucratic organisations, it may well be asked whether this really matters. Bureaucratic organisations have two characteristics which lend credence to this point of view. One of these is the fact discussed earlier that it may often be expected that members will accept the general principles of the authority system developed by the organisation. The other is the fact that within complex organisations interpersonal relations are highly routinised.

Bavelas argues that within organisations many areas of decision-making are covered by rules and procedures, and that management consists of anticipating new situations so as to structure areas of choice. He suggests that:[45]

The trend of management has been to remove as many of its decisions as possible from the area of hunch and intuition to that of rational calculation. More and more, organisations are choosing to depend less on the peculiar abilities of rare individuals, and to depend instead on the orderly processes of research and analysis. The occasions and opportunities for personal leadership in the old sense still exist, but they are becoming increasingly rare and circumscribed.

Within a complex organisation, the individual's responsibilities are often very clearly defined, and he will be well aware of the limit of his own discretionary freedom. In the extreme case, as has been suggested by Crozier's study of bureaucracy in France,[46] relationships are so regularised that the authority relationship itself becomes almost meaningless, the only members of the organisation with any power in relation to their fellows being those at the very top and those experts whose help is needed when normal routine breaks down. This is of course a rather exceptional example, yet other studies, such as Blau's[47] study of a federal law-enforcement agency in the United States, show how superior/subordinate relations can become highly formal, being either very restricted interactions or, again, relationships that only become problematical in exceptional situations.

Both Blau and Crozier suggest that supervisors will try to avoid conflict with subordinates with whom they are frequently involved in face-to-face relations. For example, supervisors will avoid taking unpopular decisions and will refer controversial matters to their immediate superiors so that their roles can be reduced to ones in which they merely convey decisions to their subordinates. Or they will use bureaucratic devices, such as performance statistics, to avoid making personal judgements about their subordinates' work, so that they can say, 'Your record is not good,' rather than 'I think your work is of a low standard'. In this way, procedures provide a means of escape from situations which might have otherwise called for qualities of leadership.

In many public organisations superior officers find that the extent to which they actually need to assume responsibilities for the 'leadership' of subordinates is determined not only by the extent to which subordinates' tasks are predetermined but also by the extent of subordinates' commitment to the organisation and to their task. So it is important to mention that persons selected for positions of authority in public administration are not merely picked to supervise, they are also selected to perform complex tasks themselves. Indeed, as is exemplified by the almost total disregard of selection and training for the management function in the British higher civil service until very recently,[48] in many cases the supervisory role is regarded as an unimportant aspect of the task of the senior official.

There is another significant aspect to this task differentiation. This is that it seems likely that in so far as the superior official has responsibilities as an expert, by virtue of either training or experience, for particular aspects of the organisation's task, it makes it easier for him to exercise authority in respect of matters covered by his own expertise. This is what is involved in what Simon, Smithburg and Thompson call the 'authority of confidence'. To a recognised expert the psychological issues associated with leadership are unimportant; as Presthus and Thompson have suggested, the need to establish an aura of authority does not exist where expertise is readily recognised.

The comments that have been made about the irrelevance of leadership for supervisory or managerial tasks in a public agency deal very largely with the middle ranks in such an organisation. It may well be, however, that leadership qualities are required in those who occupy the top positions in an organisation, those who have risen beyond the protective framework provided by the hierarchical structure. Thus Crozier,[49] having drawn attention to the lack of need for leadership in the middle ranks of the French bureaucratic system, suggests that the French civil service has been structured to provide for an imaginative and dynamic elite who are above the rigid system they control.

Katz and Kahn[50] suggest four reasons why leadership is needed at the head of organisations, because of 'the incompleteness of organizational design', 'changing environmental conditions', 'the internal dynamics of organization' and 'the nature of membership in organizations'.

'The incompleteness of organizational design' is a reminder that one of the serious mistakes that students of organisations make is to regard them as finished entities with completely developed formal structures. This fallacy was examined in Chapter 3; here it is important to reiterate that organisations are subject to a continual process of elaboration. Senior officials have a key role to play, both on account of a need to develop the organisation and also because they may be required to limit or control structural changes initiated, sometimes almost by accident, by subordinates.

Katz and Kahn's reference to 'changing environmental conditions' also emphasises that public organisations are engaged in a continuous relationship with the general public, and that this is a significant source of change. Indeed, it is necessary to go beyond Katz and Kahn's functionalist proposition since many public departments have, amongst their responsibilities, a need not only to respond to change but also to initiate change.

It naturally follows that organisations which are in a state of change will produce problems of 'internal dynamics' for their senior officials. Arbitrating between conflicting elements within an organisation and shifting personnel between sections are typical tasks in this category which may call for leadership qualities.

Katz and Kahn's fourth reason for the need for leadership in complex organisations refers to the obvious fact that people do not fit into organisations in the neat way that those who control them would like them to. Thus the most effective control of an organisation demands 'expressive' leadership, another name for 'good human relations' or 'skilful man manipulation'.

In his *Leadership in Administration*,[51] Selznick brings together these various reasons for needing organisational leadership. He argues that creative leadership is needed to give direction to an

E

organisation whilst maintaining support both from the organisation's staff and from forces in its environment. He sees as equal failures the idealistic executive who cannot secure this kind of support, and the executive who is so enmeshed in his organisational and social environment that he succumbs to the conservative forces which can so readily prevent organisational innovation. Clearly Selznick's 'leader' must be both an instrumental and expressive leader within his organisation and a politician in his dealings with his environment—functions that may be difficult to combine.

A considerable amount of attention has been given to the distinction between 'expressive' and 'instrumental' leadership. In a summary of studies of leadership, Cartwright and Zander argue,[52] 'It appears that most group objectives can be subsumed under one of two headings: (a) the achievement of some specific group goal and (b) the maintenance or strengthening of the group itself.' They then go on to suggest that different kinds of leadership are required for these two kinds of objectives:[53]

Everyday experience in groups provides many examples of instances where members make group maintenance their major concern to the detriment of work to be done, or where too much interest in task achievement leads to insufficient attention to group maintenance. Managers and administrators who, for some reason, must perform both types of functions often report that a recurring problem for them is to find a proper balance between these two types of requirements.

There are several reasons why these two types of leadership are not easily combined by the same individuals.

Etzioni argues that individuals who seek to combine 'instrumental' and 'expressive' leadership will tend to experience conflicts. He says,[54]

To a limited degree an instrumental leader can exercise expressive leadership without commanding the rare talents of a 'great man'. A foreman can have a beer with his men or go bowling with them without corrupting his authority. But sooner or later the relation between his expressive and instrumental commitments will come into question. When management increases its demands, the foreman must decide whether to circumvent the new demands, thus keeping his 'popularity' with the workers, or impose them, which is likely to alienate the workers and undermines whatever expressive leadership he has attained.

An important aspect of Etzioni's theory is his stress on the low commitments to the organisation of rank-and-file workers, whose compliance is of the 'utilitarian' kind. For a group of workers of this kind a supervisor will find it difficult to play an expressive leadership role simply because such a role will tend to have been pre-empted by an individual thrown up from within the subordinate group. Etzioni goes on to argue that leaders of normative organisations do not face this problem and can effectively combine 'expressive' and 'instrumental' leadership. It has already been suggested that the public department is often an unstable mixture of 'utilitarian' and 'normative' organisation. Thus any single section within such a department may contain individuals who differ markedly in the strength of their attachment to the organisation. In such a situation, office cliques may form, some centred around unofficial 'expressive' leaders while others are more effectively attached to the official 'leadership'. These competing loyalties may be an important source of conflict within a department.

Another problem provoked by the need for different kinds of leadership within organisations is that successful bureaucratic careers involve a progression upward through a hierarchy in which different leadership roles are required in different positions. This is a specific example of the more general point made earlier that relevant leadership traits are conditional upon situation.

But there are further problems here as far as the development of 'instrumental' leadership is concerned: that is that promotion, job rotation and the complexity of bureaucratic roles all combine to make it difficult for successful officials to develop the close face-to-face relationships with their subordinates which are necessary for the establishment of expressive leadership. The problem is well summarised by Gibb in a passage making particular reference to leadership in voluntary organisations but which is also applicable to expressive leadership in a public department:[55]

Formal organization, particularly in large groups, involves not only a differentiation of role and function but also, and inevitably, differential degrees of participation in the affairs of the group. There emerges not a leader and his group, but a leader, an administrative staff (or bureaucracy), and a group of relatively inactive members. Bureaucratic organization changes significantly the relation between a formal leader and his group. The leader of a large bureaucratic organisation cannot be so representative in his behavior as can the informal leader of a smaller primary group. His very position in the bureaucracy gives him a different perspective and, of course, the longer he occupies this office the more different that perspective is likely to be, since he has access to new kinds of knowledge and is subject to extra-group pressures.

The other function of leadership, which Selznick refers to, involves dealing with the environment of the organisation, a function that may be called political in the widest sense, and which recognisably involves politics in a narrow sense as far as public administration is concerned.

Brown has attacked the Fulton committee for a tendency to ignore the political tasks of civil servants in their enthusiasm for developing 'management'. He argues:[56]

It would have been more realistic for the Fulton Committee to accept that political needs rule out any fundamental change in the top management of central departments, except perhaps in special fields like defence and management services which are protected from detailed parliamentary review by security considerations or by sheer lack of political content. Otherwise, the more important a field of administration is, the less likely that the administrative technologists working on it will be left in peace.

Selznick describes the situation in which an organisation sees its goals as clearly set and its concerns as purely internal as a 'retreat to technology'. He illustrates this phenomenon most effectively with some military examples:[57]

The retreat to technology is associated with the difficulty in integrating political and military strategy. When military commanders – or diplomats – attempt to define a sphere of 'purely military' decisions, this is congenial to the creation of secure boundaries within which known principles can be applied; and it abets the avoidance of responsibility for decisions that cut across those boundaries. More important, the idea that there is a division of labour – some people charged with political decisions, others with military ones – opens the way to the evasion of responsibility even within the more narrow fields. When either political or military decisions are especially difficult, dealing with vague and unpredictable elements, it is convenient to allow the decisions to be made on other grounds.

Leadership in administration entails political sensitivity; impeccable instrumental and expressive leadership is valueless without an ability to make an effective impact upon the environment. So, in Selznick's words,[58] 'The executive becomes a statesman as he makes the transition from administrative management to institutional leadership.'

It has been suggested in this chapter that authority should be defined as institutionalised power. This approach is particularly appropriate to public administration, as those who exercise authority in a government bureaucracy do so with the full weight of the government behind them. The unwilling subordinate finds himself in conflict with a very powerful apparatus. It is significant that civil servants in Britain have no contractual rights with regard to their pay, conditions of service, security of tenure and pensions; theoretically they are servants of the Crown and subject only to the Royal prerogative.

Yet this aspect of public authority must not be exaggerated. In a democratic country, whatever the actual terms of service of its employees, the government is always conscious of the extent of public scrutiny of its treatment of its servants. It will therefore recognise the need to be a model employer, and for justice to be seen to be done when it takes disciplinary action.

Thus those in the top positions in a public bureaucracy are always aware of the need to substitute 'influence' for 'authority' wherever possible. This is more particularly true of their dealings with their more senior subordinates, who will perform their responsible tasks more effectively if they are committed to what they are doing and feel free to use their initiative. Above all in dealings with professionals the use of arbitrary authority can prove to be a most destructive weapon.

In his comparative study of organisations, Etzioni never deals very effectively with the governmental institution; in company with the school and the hospital it seems to fall awkwardly between the 'utilitarian' and the 'normative' organisation. However, it can be suggested that public bureaucracies tend to be utilitarian organisations but ones to which many employees feel a greater degree of commitment than do junior employees in the business firm. But as far as professionals and senior administrators are concerned the administrative organisation comes close to Etzioni's normative type. It may be suggested that public bureaucracies go through phases during which their normative attractiveness increases followed by periods of consolidation when their more committed employees experience disillusion. Thus Merton[59] has discussed the impact of the New Deal in the United States upon committed intellectuals who were drawn into public administration. These people were initially deeply committed to the agencies that they joined, but in due course found government work rather frustrating and disillusioning.

A great deal of attention has been paid to the search for leadership traits and the study of leadership within organisations. But the most significant finding from such studies has been that leadership qualities are situational and not easily identified. There has been a tendency to confuse authority with leadership. This confusion has been partly a linguistic one, but has also partly been a consequence of the fact that persons in senior positions within organisations can often exercise authority effectively without apparently possessing any special 'leadership' qualities. Indeed it may be suggested that in some respects bureaucratisation makes leadership unnecessary. However, a number of situations have been outlined where this does not seem to be the case. Three different kinds of leadership seem to be required: 'expressive', 'instrumental' and 'political'. The degrees to which these different kinds of leadership are required varies for different organisational roles. In general, 'expressive' leadership may be a valuable attribute in a low-level supervisor, who can avoid responsibility for unpopular 'instrumental' decisions but may have a vital role to play in securing effective work from subordinates. 'Instrumental' leadership, by contrast, may be particularly required of middle-ranking officials who have special responsibilities for the functioning of the bureaucratic machine. Finally, at the very top, qualities of political leadership, in the widest sense of the word 'political', are needed to provide for a dynamic relationship between the organisation and its public.

7

Bureaucracy and Personality

The administrative organisation has typically a complex structure of a kind which many writers have described as 'bureaucratic'. In Chapter 2 it was suggested that, for many writers, bureaucracy implies something more than a complex organisation. For them, bureaucracies are characterised as rigid and slow, with effective action hampered by red tape. Although the main arguments on this topic are concerned with the inherent limitations of elaborate formal procedures, several writers have sought to show that bureaucratic rigidity is in some respects a consequence either of the impact of working in a rule-bound context upon the personalities of individuals, or of a tendency for bureaucracies to recruit people with inflexible personalities.

The impact of the demands of complex organisations upon individuals has been a theme developed in several popular American sociological tracts.[1] The picture of the independent frontiersman trapped in the bureaucratic organisation is an American equivalent of the happy peasant forced to work in the 'dark satanic mills' as portrayed in some views of the industrial revolution in Britain. It involves a nostalgia for an idealised past which contains sufficient of a germ of truth to appear plausible while, at the same time, it distorts analysis of present realities by oversimplifying them.

In the study of public bureaucracy, the 'organisation personality' theory links up with another theme which has had a place in popular mythology for many centuries, a theme which several European novelists[2] have developed most effectively, the portrayal of the clerk in public service as an individual whose life becomes dominated by the complex rules which he is required to follow in his dealings with the public.

Merton,[3] in a pioneering essay on organisational sociology, took up this theme and attempted to explain the conditions under which 'bureaucratic personalities' are likely to be found. His essay is therefore the starting point for this chapter.

It is important to recognise the links between this theme and the topics of authority and formal organisation discussed earlier. The position of those in authority is markedly simplified if subordinates are submissive individuals conditioned to following their superiors uncritically, and much of the literature on authority suggests that many subordinates will be of this kind. Moreover the implication of much managerial training is that the successful operation of a system of authority will depend upon creating bureaucratic personalities. (This is implicit in Simon, Smithburg and Thompson's approach to the concept of authority—see pages 107–8.) On the other hand some of the more sophisticated writers in this field have recognised that there are severe dangers in creating over-submissive subordinates, and that, as was shown in Chapter 3, there are advantages to be gained from having bureaucrats who are unwilling to be excessively bound by formal rules. Moreover, subordinates will resist over-formalisation, and so it may be said that they will try to avoid becoming bureaucratic personalities.

In his essay, Merton takes issue with Weber because, in his analysis, 'the positive attainments and functions of bureaucratic organization are emphasized and the internal stresses and strains of such structures are almost wholly neglected.'[4] He contrasts this with the popular emphasis upon the imperfections of bureaucracy. Drawing on other studies that have suggested that individual personalities are moulded by social roles he argues in the following way:[5]

(1) An effective bureaucracy demands reliability of response and strict devotion to regulations. (2) Such devotion to the rules leads to their transformation into absolutes; they are no longer conceived as relative to a set of purposes. (3) This interferes with ready adaption under special conditions not clearly envisaged by those who drew up the general rules. (4) Thus, the very elements which conduce toward efficiency in general produce inefficiency in specific instances. Full realization of the inadequacy is seldom attained by members of the group who have not divorced themselves from the meanings which the rules have for them. These rules in time become symbolic in cast, rather than strictly utilitarian.

Merton argues that bureaucrats are likely to show particular attachment to rules that protect the internal system of social relationships, enhance their status by enabling them to take on the status of the organisation and protect them from conflict with clients by emphasising impersonality. Because of their function in providing security, rules of this kind are particularly likely to be transformed into 'absolutes'.

Merton's essay is applied to bureaucratic organisations in general, but there are reasons why it may be particularly applicable to public administration.

First, public servants are placed in a particularly difficult position *vis-à-vis* their clients. They may be putting into practice political decisions with which they disagree; they are facing a public who cannot normally go elsewhere if their demands are unsatisfied, as they often can with private enterprise; and the justice of their acts is open to public scrutiny, by politicians and sometimes by courts of law. They are thus under particular pressure to ensure that their acts are in conformity with rules. Rules are bound to play a big part in their working lives.

Second, the careers of public servants are normally organised very much along the lines of Weber's bureaucratic model. Indeed, in this respect at least, state bureaucracies often come very close to Weber's 'ideal type'. The need for fairness in selection and promotion, because of the need for the public service to be able to withstand criticism, leads to the development of highly regularised career structures. It tends to be very difficult to justify dramatic or unconventional promotions, and therefore civil service careers are oriented towards what F. M. Marx has called 'the economics of small chances'. Marx explains this expression in the following way:[6]

In the first place, the ideology of service itself minimises the unabashed display of consuming ambition. In some respects, indeed, service is its own reward. Moreover, the mass conditions to which personnel policy and procedure must be addressed in large-scale organisations cry out for recognition of the normal rather than the exceptional. Meteoric rise of the outstandingly able individual is therefore discouraged quite in the same way as favouritism and disregard of rules are discouraged. Advancement, if it is not to attract suspicious or unfriendly eyes, must generally stay in line with the 'normal'. Exceptions call for too much explaining. All this tends to make rewards for accomplishment something that comes in small packages at fairly long intervals.

Such a career structure obviously puts an onus upon conformity, and will tend to create a situation in which if a public servant becomes conspicuous for disregarding rules it will be more likely to hamper than enhance his career.

Marx's book is interesting in particularly developing the picture of the civil servant as a bureaucratic personality on account of the factors discussed above. He therefore characterises the civil service as 'the settled life'[7] in which security is valued above high rewards. He says, 'the merit bureaucracy is not the place for those who want to make money, to rise fast, to venture far, or to stand on their own.' Marx concedes that senior civil servants are usually required to be of a reasonably high calibre, but suggests that those who compete for entry will be mostly the 'solid—as contrasted with the brilliant but restive, for instance'.

Marx goes on to suggest that the career structure he describes in this way reinforces the pressure for uniformity within a government bureaucracy which arises from the political need for equity and consistency. Thus he claims, 'When the common rule and the common mind combine, the natural consequence is a narrowness of perspective—a weakness more aggravating than mediocrity in administrative performance.'

Marx suggests, then, that the 'bureaucratic personality' will be both a product of the fact that only certain types of people choose to join the civil service, or indeed the fact that selection procedures may pick out certain types of people, and a product of the bureaucratic environment. The two influences upon personality operate to reinforce each other. In the same way, Merton recognises this interaction as a key problem for research. He asks:[8]

To what extent are particular personality types selected and modified by the various bureaucracies (private enterprise, public service, the quasi-legal political machine, religious orders)? Inasmuch as ascendency and submission are held to be traits of personality, despite their variability in different stimulus situations, do bureaucracies select personalities of particularly submissive or ascendent tendencies? And since various studies have shown that these traits can be modified, does participation in bureaucratic office tend to increase ascendent tendencies? Do various systems of recruitment (e.g. patronage, open competition involving specialised knowledge or general mental capacity, practical experience) select different personality types?

There is, therefore, a number of related issues to consider here: (1) to what extent certain types of people choose to embark on bureaucratic careers, (2) the impact of selection processes in selecting certain types from amongst those who seek to enter bureaucratic careers, (3) the extent to which personalities who do not fit the organisational environment drop out in the course of their careers, and (4) the extent to which success or failure in climbing a career ladder is associated with personality characteristics.

A study of the attitudes of undergraduates competing for entry into the administrative class of the British civil service has suggested that students are deterred by an image of the work of higher civil servants as involving dull routine work in a big impersonal organisation.[9] Whether or not this is a realistic image does not concern us here; the point is, however, that this image must be expected to deter certain kinds of students, leaving as candidates for the civil service a group to whom the bureaucratic situation appears more acceptable.

Whatever the truth behind such a bureacratic image it may prove very difficult to get rid of it; moreover, inasmuch as such an image restricts the field of recruitment, it will tend to operate as a self-fulfilling prophecy by providing recruits who are likely to adopt a way of life that will conform to that image.

As far as civil service recruitment is concerned, it is important to point out that the normal choice for a graduate these days is not so much a choice between bureaucratic employment and non-bureaucratic employment as a choice between different types of bureaucratic employment. The student who thinks he can avoid this situation easily in a world dominated by large bureaucracies is deluding himself, a fact of which increasing numbers of students are becoming aware. It may be suggested that the contrast between an education for 'freedom', an education process in which students are taught to be contemptuous of the big bureaucracies, and the reality of the bureaucratic situation most students must face once they leave university is an important cause of current student unrest, with the comparatively nonauthoritarian university organisation being made the scapegoat for the hard world outside.

While there is little hard evidence on the point, psychologists have suggested that there is a tendency for selectors to choose persons who seem like themselves, probably on the basis of an assumption, which they may not always recognise they are making, that since they are successful in the organisation other people like themselves are likely to be successful too. However, selection procedures are normally a little more sophisticated than mere uncontrolled interviews, and the British Civil Service Department uses outsiders to help with interviews, so it may be unwise to suggest anything more than that selection procedures are some-times likely to favour potential conformists. Chapman adds an interesting gloss on this by suggesting that any tendency towards 'playing safe' in selection may be enhanced by doubts about the validity of some of the more informal procedures.[10]

It is also not possible to say much about wastage. Once again, if an organisation makes considerable demands upon the person-ality it is likely that those who find it difficult to respond to those demands will drop out, often at an early point in their career. Clearly it may be dangerous to ascribe wastage to the impact of organisational demands on the personality without much evidence on what such a situation involves, but equally it is dangerous to ascribe wastage merely to such things as pay, opportunities and so on. Moreover, although wastage is obviously a loss as far as outlay on training is concerned and may well be a sign of inade-quate selection processes, it may be a positive gain to the organisa-tion to dispose of persons who could prove to be highly disruptive. But it may be undesirable to lose disruptive people if disruption could have been a positive force in improving the organisation.

Clearly, at this point, the discussion is making little progress since two alternative possibilities are becoming apparent, on neither of which is there much clear evidence. On the one hand it may be that organisational nonconformists will tend to be merely disruptive elements, while, on the other hand, it can be argued that disruptive elements are precisely what organisations need to prevent them becoming too highly bureaucratised. This leads on to the fourth point made above, that success in climbing a bureaucratic career ladder may depend upon the possession of certain personality characteristics, and it is on this last point that there is the maximum scope for doubt about the bureaucratic personality theory. In discussing this issue it is fruitful to have a look first at a theoretical approach to the concept of the bureaucratic personality developed by R. V. Presthus in his book, *The Organizational Society*.

Presthus suggests that the impact upon the individual of his socialisation in early life affects his success in the organisational context, with the conformist individual finding the organisation's environment more congenial than the less highly socialised. Presthus argues:[11]

If social structure is critical in molding individual behavior and personality, the big organization can usefully be conceived as a small society whose characteristics of specialization, hierarchy and authority have a similar influence upon its members. The mechanism that society employs to inculcate its values may also be seen at work within the organization. The organization, in a word, socializes its members in a way similar to that of society. It co-opts the learned deference to authority inculcated by institutions such as the family and the church.

Presthus suggests that three types of organisation members may be found:[12]

1 Upward-mobiles: authoritarian conformists who succeed on account of their ready acceptance of the bureaucratic situation.

2 Indifferents: 'the uncommitted majority who see their jobs as mere instruments to obtain off-work satisfaction'.

3 Ambivalents: 'a small, perpetually disturbed minority who can neither renounce their claims for status and power nor play the disciplined role that would enable them to cash in such claims'.

The difficulty with Presthus' theory is that his picture of the upward-mobile tends to correspond with the rigid personality structure seen as the 'authoritarian personality' by other writers, and he does indeed draw on the studies of the authoritarian personality to support his own theory. Yet others have conceived of this type of person as an individual incapable of rising beyond the bottom ranks of an organisation because of his inability to take decisions on his own. Argyris,[13] moreover, has developed a theory diametrically opposed to that of Presthus in that he suggests that individuals, socialised to accept responsibilities and stand on their own feet, are thwarted by roles in bureaucratic organisations which deny them scope to use their initiative and subject them to a childlike dependency; hence he suggests that rigid and dependent personalities fit most readily into subordinate roles.

Presthus' rejoinder at this point would presumably be to argue that the people who fit most readily into subordinate roles are the ones who are most likely to be selected for promotion as they will please their superiors. This may be the case in some circumstances, but is it to be concluded that all the efforts that are made to identify potential for promotion in the civil service and in other large organisations achieve no more than the identification of rigid conformists. Can one conclude, too, that, when Argyris argues[14] that one way out for dissatisfied individuals is to seek to win advancement in the organisation, that this is merely woolly optimism? It has become fashionable to deny that organisations offer any scope for the enterprising individual just as it has become fashionable to believe that bureaucracies have rigid formal structures; in many ways Presthus' theory is just W. H. Whyte's *The Organisation Man* dressed up in the language of social psychology, while the concrete evidence for the case is just as absent. The evidence available on the formalisation of bureaucracies, as has already been shown, suggests that such organisations are by no means as rigid as is popularly believed. In this respect then, inasmuch as the bureaucratic personality theory is so closely associated with the idea of formalism, it must be suspect too. At least it may be suggested that while there is some evidence that junior organisation roles require or may produce organisational personalities, it seems less plausible to suggest that success in moving up an organisation's promotion ladder will depend on similar qualities. Moreover, most bureaucratic organisations contrive to avoid the rigidity associated with trying to identify potential top men by their performance in menial roles by bringing in talented recruits well above the bottom of the ladder. Inasmuch as there is some substance in the bureaucratic personality theory it provides a strong argument against what is often seen as 'democratising' recruitment, by making everyone start at or near the bottom and leaving the talented to climb the long promotion ladder by establishing their claims to high position by means of honest toil in lowly positions.

Presthus takes up very clearly the position that conformity is necessary for organisational success. Argyris suggests by contrast that the upward-mobile in the organisation will be an individual who refuses to settle down in the subordinate role demanded of him and will, therefore, be something of a nonconformist. If it is accepted that, as many students of organisational behaviour have suggested, the low-level employee comes under considerable pressure to conform in various ways,[15] then it is reasonable to postulate that individuals may seek a variety of escape routes depending upon intelligence, personality and upon the alternatives open to them.

Levinson[16] has suggested that there are four possibilities open to the organisation member who comes under pressure to conform: personality change, resignation, 'apathetic conformity' (the reaction of Presthus' indifferent) or the gain of sufficient power to change the organisation. The present discussion is primarily concerned with Levinson's fourth alternative, and the difficulty is that he does not provide an answer to the basic question—how does the deviant attain power without becoming a conformer? The only alternatives to the pessimistic conclusion that he does not succeed, lie in arguing that in the theorising of Presthus and others on this point both the human personality and the bureaucratic organisation are treated as very much more monolithic than they are in reality.

The argument here as far as the individual is concerned is that in a complex society men occupy a variety of roles. They are not just 'bureaucratic personalities' or 'indifferents'. Outside work they may be husbands, fathers, club-members, team-captains and so on, and may be expected to present themselves in different ways in these different roles.[17] Is it not, therefore, plausible to suggest that at work they may play diverse roles too, and that they may be able to play parts that do not involve the total investment of their personalities in single relationships with the authority structure of the organisation? If adaptability and originality are required for advancement, as well as conformity, may it not be that the following simple, almost trite, propositions make the best sense: that success will depend upon being not too conformist and not too nonconformist, that the ambitious 'deviant' will have to make decisions about where to compromise and where not to, and that individuals will satisfy their superiors in respect of some roles they play but will succeed in keeping others protected from close scrutiny.

But naturally such complex individual strategies will be made easier if the organisation is also not a monolithic entity. And on this it has already been shown that a large government department will be far from a simple unified organisation. At all levels in an organisation, as Dalton has shown (see discussion in Chapter 3, especially pages 47–57), there are likely to be factions, and conflicts of both a personal and an ideological kind are likely to be rife in a public department. Thus individuals are not faced by a simple choice between conformity and deviance, but rather with choices between differing groups demanding differing kinds and levels of conformity.

Much of the theory on the relationship between the socialising pressures of the work situation and the individual personality is based upon studies of manual workers in factories. At their level, the organisational pressures are much more monolithic than they are at middle management levels. Equally, in this discussion it may be reasonable to suggest that the bureaucratic personality theory is more likely to apply to the low-level clerk in a government department than to the man with major administrative and managerial responsibilities.

Argyris' main interest was in the study of the behaviour of industrial workers, and his theory is a contribution to the large body of literature on what other writers have described as 'alienation'. If this theory is applied to the clerk in the government department, it seems very plausible to suggest that the alienated worker in this context will have a significant outlet for some of his frustrated feelings, in that he may often be in a position to vent his feelings against, and exercise power over, members of the public. Unlike industrial workers, many bottom-level bureaucrats have other people, members of the public, in what may be called a position 'subordinate' to them. Some evidence on this point is provided in a study by Blau of a public welfare agency[18] in which he shows that agents who were not well integrated in the agency were most likely to behave bureaucratically and with hostility towards clients.

In a similar way the rigidity which is seen as a characteristic of the bureaucratic personality has been regarded by a number of writers as a mode of self-protection for the individual whose integration in and commitment to the organisation is severely limited. For example, A. K. Davis'[19] study of the American navy suggests that formalism can function to protect people from taking responsibilities, an orientation he particularly associates with the attitude of the conscript to the armed services. Similarly Gouldner[20] points out that many rules serve to protect subordinates from insecurity inherent in their low-status positions.

In examining bureaucratic rigidity, Crozier gives a very interesting twist to the theory of the bureaucratic personality by suggesting that the bureaucratic situation, far from being a situation in which the personality is manipulated, is in fact one in which individuals are able to avoid total involvement and thus can protect the integrity of their own personalities. He argues that[21]

Resistance to participation, and preference for centralized authority and the stability and rigidity of a bureaucratic system of organization, by preserving for each member a minimum of autonomy and individual discretion, proceed from the same values which peasants, craftsmen and noblemen embodied in the delicate balance of human relations that characterized the *art de vivre* of traditional France. In a certain way, a bureaucratic system of organization provides a combination of the values of a traditional *ascriptive* society and those of a modern *achievement-oriented* society.

This is a very interesting line of argument which suggests that it may make more sense to talk about 'bureaucratic behaviour' than about the 'bureaucratic personality', and to suggest that there are a number of reasons why alienated members of large organisations may be expected to adopt such forms of behaviour. It is much easier to establish the existence of bureaucratic behaviour than it is to establish the psychological mechanisms that lie behind such behaviour. Furthermore this is another example of a situation in which it is roles rather than personalities that should be considered. All the concrete evidence that can be quoted merely establishes the existence of 'bureaucratic behaviour'. One important reason for the absence of evidence on the impact of the bureaucratic situation upon the personality is that it would be very difficult to secure such evidence. First, it would require a very long-term study of a group of employees, while academics, for obvious career reasons, prefer to undertake studies that give relatively quick results. Second, one would need to distinguish the effects of ageing from the impact of the organisational role. Third, one also really needs to be able to show that role habituation in a bureaucracy has certain special effects distinguishable from any similar phenomena in other areas of life. And finally, one would need a group of subjects whose work roles varied very little over a long period.

There are many roles, even at relatively low levels in organisations, which may not be highly bureaucratised. Thus Presthus suggests that professionals and experts of all kinds may not fit neatly into the bureaucratic situation, and even Merton, in another essay,[22] has suggested that intellectuals may occupy significantly peripheral roles in public organisations.

Modern public administration calls for the employment of experts in very large numbers; it also needs to create specialists from the ordinary recruits in its own ranks, and to give professional or semiprofessional responsibilities to a high proportion of the staff of administrative agencies. Indeed, it has been argued that it is unrealistic to attempt to identify the specifically bureaucratic role, since[23] 'role specialization is the hallmark of a bureaucracy'.

It is generally acknowledged, then, that the concept of the

bureaucratic personality would not normally be applicable to professionals and that this is true largely because their commitment to the organisation is less total than the nonprofessionals'. This freedom from strong organisational ties derives partly from the tendency for professionals to possess marketable skills which they can, and probably will in the course of a career, take elsewhere, and partly from the discretionary freedom which they are granted on account of their expertise.

There is also a variety of organisational roles which are open to differential interpretation. In particular, individuals may choose to interpret their roles in professional or in nonprofessional ways.

The whole subject of specialist or professional roles, and the drawbacks that may go with them in terms of lack of organisational power, will be considered in the next chapter.

It is important to bring together the main lines of argument in this chapter. The starting point was the theory of the 'bureaucratic personality', and it was noted that Merton was attempting to analyse sociologically the widely accepted stereotype of the bureaucratic official. To describe the picture of the bureaucratic official as a stereotype is to illuminate the overriding reason why the bureaucratic personality theory runs into such difficulties. On the most superficial level the public official's role is difficult to distinguish from the role played by a very high proportion of the employed persons in a modern complex society. At this level we are all 'bureaucratic personalities', in which case there is nothing very special about the role of the public servant. On the other hand, if an attempt is made to analyse roles more deeply it will be found that distinctions can be made both between the many different roles in a public bureaucracy, and also between alternative adjustments to formally similar roles. The bureaucratic personality theory is both too specific, in trying to single out certain kinds of organisational roles in a context in which most people are organisational employees, and too general in implying the existence of uniformity of roles in organisations where such uniformity does not exist.

There is a secondary criticism of the theory which can be made that suggests that there is a tendency to assume that the existence of 'bureaucratic behaviour' is evidence of the existence of 'bureaucratic personality', when in practice such behaviour may be a means of protecting the individual from total involvement in his work situation.

It must be admitted of the 'bureaucratic personality theory' (1) that it has been widely observed that certain kinds of people seek, or are more successful in, certain work roles, (2) there is some evidence for the view that individuals are moulded by their work roles, and (3) that government bureaucracies tend to be rather formalised and routinised organisations for the personnel for whom points (1) and (2) are likely to be applicable. More evidence is therefore needed to establish to what extent, and in what ways, these points are applicable to government agencies, bearing in mind the wide variety of both roles and role interpretations available to individuals in them.

8

Expertise and Professionalism

This chapter will deal with three interrelated topics which have been given considerable attention in discussions of public administration in recent years. The first of these topics has been one that has particularly interested British students of public administration; the relative importance of, and relations between, specialists and generalists in the public service. The second topic, the relations between staff and line, is not the first topic disguised by other terminology since it is a mistake to assume that 'staff' are always specialists and 'line' always generalists. The first pair of concepts refers to kinds of qualifications, the second to organisational roles. The second pair has been given particular attention by organisation theorists, and their use is particularly associated with the study of industrial enterprises. The third topic is concerned with the extent and nature of professionalism in administrative organisations. The study of professions has been the particular concern of sociologists, who have been interested in two aspects of this subject, professions as distinctive elements in the social structures of complex industrial societies with special power and status, and the potentiality for conflict between professional organisation and bureaucratic organisation.

The concept of the generalist administrator is in many respects a peculiarly British one. A comparative examination of the relative importance of generalists and specialists in Britain, Australia, France, Western Germany, Sweden and the United States found that[1]

None of the other countries have anything like our Administrative Class, generalists in functions and generalists in background. Recruitment to the higher Civil Service on the basis of an entirely non-vocational education is rare. It is true that in most continental European countries there are administrators who are not specialists – professionals in our sense and who, in the European context, can be described as all-purpose administrators. In each case, however, they have legal training directed to their work (administration in administrative law countries has a higher legal content than in Britain)…. Most foreign civil servants would therefore be surprised at our preoccupation with the rival merits of generalists and specialists. All of them can be regarded as specialists of one kind or another, their knowledge and training related to the kind of work they do.

The notion of 'generalists in background' derives from the nineteenth-century approach to the recruitment of higher civil servants which involved an attempt to select the most able young men available on the assumption that such people would be those who could do best in competitive tests based upon the education provided in the universities and public schools. At the time the British higher civil service was set up, it was by no means clear what specialisms, if any, were required for the administration of government. In any case, even though a few farsighted people[2] were prepared to acknowledge the growing relevance of economics and statistics, it was quite clear that few who were regarded at that time as 'the ablest and most ambitious youths'[3] were likely to study such subjects. The argument developed by Macaulay, therefore, to justify a dependence on the products of the university system of the time was that[4]

Whether the English system of education be good or bad is not now the question. Perhaps I may think that too much time is given to the ancient languages and to the abstract sciences. But what then? Whatever be the languages – whatever be the sciences, which it is, in any age or country, the fashion to teach, those who become the greatest proficients in those languages and those sciences will generally be the flower of the youth – the most astute – the most industrious – the most ambitious of honourable distinctions.

Subsequent apologists for the generalist tradition in the British civil service have gone beyond Macaulay's position in seeking to rationalise the case for the recruitment of the generalist with a 'liberal' education by reference to what they see as the specific abilities or virtues inculcated by such education.[5] This is a view for which there is no real evidence and which has very naturally come under fire from those prepared to argue for education in manifestly relevant subjects. Under this kind of attack the traditionalists have naturally fallen back upon the argument developed by Macaulay.

The traditional generalist/specialist division in the British civil service was one between members of the administrative class, recruited in their early twenties with nonvocational degrees, given little formal training and moved regularly from job to job, and members of the large numbers of specialist classes, recruited to perform specific jobs on the basis of their educational, professional or technical qualifications.

In recent years the exclusion of people from the specialist classes in the British civil service from most of its highest ranks has been a growing source of dissatisfaction to many people. Two lines of attack have been open on this issue. On the one hand it is argued that it is inconsistent with the Macaulay doctrine of selecting the 'best people' to exclude scientists and professionals from consideration for senior offices, regardless of their specific expertise. On the other hand it is claimed that people with specific expertise should occupy the key decision-making roles in government departments concerned with their speciality. These two alternative lines of argument suggest a new form which the specialist/generalist argument is beginning to take.

The Fulton Committee appeared to take the latter of these two alternative views. They argued:[6]

Frequent moves from job to job within the Service or within a department give 'generalist' administrators proficiency in operating the government machine, and in serving Ministers and Parliament. But many lack the fully developed professionalism that their work now demands. They do not develop adequate knowledge in depth in any one aspect of the department's work and frequently not even in the general area of activity in which the department operates. Often they are required to give advice on subjects they do not sufficiently understand or to take decisions whose significance they do not fully grasp. This has serious consequences. It can lead to bad policy-making; it prevents a fundamental evaluation of the policies being administered; it often leads to the adoption of inefficient methods for implementing these policies – methods which are sometimes baffling to those outside the Service who are affected by them; and it obstructs the establishment of fruitful contacts with sources of expert advice both inside and outside the Service.

The fuller professionalism now required from all administrators ... in turn calls for new principles to be applied to their selection, training and deployment. It must be accepted that for the administrator to be expert in running the government machine is not in itself enough. He must in future also have or acquire the basic concepts and knowledge, whether social, economic, industrial or financial, relevant to his area of administration and appropriate to his level of responsibility. He must have a real understanding of, and familiarity with, the principles, techniques and trends of development in the subject-matter of the field in which he is operating.

This position, so far from proposing the opening up of the generalist career structure for specialists, does in fact involve the transformation of the generalist stream into specialist streams. But in so doing the Fulton Committee inevitably came into conflict with the defenders of the traditional system. One of their proposals for the introduction of specialisms involved the development of new recruitment principles favouring the graduate in 'relevant' subjects. This came under fire from a minority of the Committee itself and was rejected by the government. Stripped of this provision the whole notion of the development of specialisms was put in jeopardy as the amount of training provided within the civil service is, and is likely to remain, insufficient to take the place of three or more years' university education in a specific discipline.

But the Fulton Committee weakened its own case for the development of specialisation in the various subjects of government activity by calling for the same individuals to develop another kind of specialism—in the management of public departments. This adds yet another dimension to the confusion and conflict surrounding the specialist/generalist distinction.

To the American student of administration the concept of the 'generalist' does not signify so much a man without specific qualifications as a man trained in 'administration' or 'management', rather than in some other expertise less totally relevant for the administrative task. Gross, in a discussion of the generalist/specialist distinction, makes the following points on the expertise of the generalist:[7]

... the generalist administrator may be something of a specialist in administration. He may be a specialist in handling one or more of the specialized tools of administration. This is not the same, it should be added, as being a professional production engineer, accountant or job analyst; in the former instance the expertise relates rather to the use of experts in these technical fields. The administrator may also be something of a specialist in the more general arts of governance. Expertise of this sort may come from broad experience in a variety of administrative posts, from study and learning and even from research and theory. In this sense, becoming a generalist may itself be a form of intense specialization.

Clearly, if being a generalist involves a specific expertise for which specific aptitudes may be required and for which specific training is appropriate, then these requirements may be in conflict with any requirement that the administrator should be the master of the subject matter of his department. Ridley describes these two alternative concepts of the expertise needed by the administrator as the 'how' and the 'what' of administration.[8] He suggests that the mastery of the former is the main concern of American administrative science textbooks, while the 'what' of administration has been the main preoccupation of the British administrative class. This is an over-simplification which obscures yet another important facet of the administrative task as far as senior civil servants are concerned. This other facet is the political one, so that political skill must be added to the qualifications that have already been suggested as necessary for the 'perfect' top administrator.

The Fulton Committee attacked the British higher civil service for being masters of neither the 'what' nor the 'how' of administration, of having neither the specialist expertise to enable them to cope with the subject matter of administrative tasks nor the managerial expertise to run their departments efficiently.

It is obviously rather unfair to accuse civil servants of failing to possess two characteristics which in any case they would find it difficult to combine. Any restructuring of the civil service in an effort to meet both criticisms therefore raises in an acute form a problem which the system already faces, the problem of integrating different roles in an effective way. This is an issue of the integration of 'staff' and 'line', to be considered later in the chapter. But the most telling criticism of Fulton's attack on the civil service is that it pays little attention to the political roles played by top civil servants. This line of criticism of Fulton has been most effectively developed by R. G. S. Brown[9] who has pointed out the crucial role administrators play as mediators between experts, within their departments, and politicians. Many writers have suggested that one of the weaknesses of British government has been a tendency to under-use experts.[10] But the way to increase the use of experts does not necessarily lie by way of sweeping away generalist administrators. On the contrary, if the trend toward 'technocracy',[11] towards a situation in which people find it increasingly difficult to control administrators through either their elected representative or by other more direct means, is not to be accelerated by influxes of experts, then 'mediators' of this kind may be of increasing importance.

This is not to say, of course, that men who have studied classics or history at Oxford or Cambridge are necessarily the best people to play this role, or that men whose initial training is in some relevant expertise are necessarily incapacitated from playing it, but that it is a distinct and important role which needs to be played by *someone* in a democratic political system. Indeed many other administrative systems, including British local government, meet the similar problem of providing for effective communicating and coordinating roles in a somewhat different form because the people who reach top administrative positions get there by way of success in specialist positions.

But there is another sense in which senior administrators need to be able to play political roles, too. Perhaps one of the reasons why British civil servants have been disinclined to look across the Atlantic for advice on the 'how' of administration is that they recognise that American administrative science may not be able to teach them very much about how to 'run' their department. Furthermore, much of the literature that parades as administrative science draws heavily upon research and theorising in relation to the problems of industrial management. The administrative problems that face civil servants concerned with integrating the activities of senior subordinates engaged on, for example, preparing economic forecasts or the budget of a large and complex department, cannot sensibly be compared with the problems facing the management of a factory producing a single product. It is therefore suggested that even 'management' for a senior civil servant is very much a political task too, a complex matter of being able to operate effectively in a situation of internal politics of a highly difficult kind. Understandably, therefore, any civil servant who goes looking for the 'principles' of administration upon which he can base his decision-making may well conclude that his intuitive 'art' is preferable to the things he finds in many textbooks.[12] In this sense he, like a craftsman, possesses an expertise that is founded upon experience and understanding of a non-intellectual kind rather than upon possession of a body of formally established knowledge.

The generalist is expected to be master of what may be described as the content of the area of policy-making for which he is responsible. He is also expected to be a good manager. Yet, on top of all this, as a civil servant he has to possess political skills; to be able to translate the advice he gets from experts into political terms that have meaning for his 'masters', to be able to translate, too, the politicians' requirements into practical policies, and to be able to handle all the pressures upon him from the public, from pressure groups and from his own colleagues. If he is only master of the political skills he is playing an important and often under-rated part in the machinery of government. The problem is, if the political role is taken to be the key one, how can he play this part effectively and yet maintain a coherent and productive relationship with those to whom managerial and expert roles are delegated? Too much of the discussion about the reform of the British civil service in recent years seems to involve the postulation of a need to search for a superman, who can combine all the roles suggested above. Insufficient attention has been given to the alternative approach to civil service reform that involves seeking better ways to divide up and then coordinate the different roles.

Further examination of the relations between specialists and generalists requires consideration of the various roles they play and thus of the issues which have been subsumed under the heading, relations between line and staff.

Blau and Scott describe the staff/line distinction as follows:[13]

The distinction between staff and line is one that has long informed the study of formal organizations. Line organization places emphasis on differences in rank, and its members have authority over production processes. Staff organization directs attention to specialization, and its members usually function in a research and advisory capacity. In short, line officials possess formal authority, whereas staff members furnish specialized and technical advice to the appropriate line officials in the organizational hierarchy.

It is clear that this distinction is one that has been developed in the course of studies of fairly stable industrial organisations where there is a straightforward production task being performed. In such a situation, staff functions will include research to try to improve the product, accounting and other management services to try to improve the organisation, personnel management and so on. Some writers distinguish here between 'staff' functions and 'auxiliary' functions:[14] 'auxiliary units are supposed to assist the line organizations by performing certain common tasks for them, while the staff units are supposed to assist the chief executive by performing certain tasks for him that he could not otherwise delegate to the line units.' In other words, some tasks of this kind are fairly routine, including such mundane things as the maintenance of buildings and the organisation of canteens, while others involve giving expert help with decision-making processes. This discussion is primarily concerned with the latter kind of staff rather than those who perform auxiliary functions.

The line/staff distinction is one that does not translate very easily from the industrial context into general organisation theory. Etzioni[15] has tried to apply it in a meaningful way to organisations such as universities and hospitals with odd results stemming from the fact that the people who at first glance appear to fit into the 'line' category are the nonprofessional administrators who have in fact to be designated 'staff' to make sense of the concept. Simon, Smithburg and Thompson show that the distinction can be equally misleading when applied to public administration.[16]

Why then has the distinction been brought into this discussion? There are two reasons for this, one of them is that, merely because it has been widely used in discussions of administration and management, there has grown up a certain mythology about it which contributes to behaviour in organisations. The other reason is that it helps to draw attention to the fact that there are problems involved in integrating, within an organisation, people who perform different kinds of functions; as such it is no more and no less misleading than the specialist/generalist distinction but draws attention to roles instead of attributes.

The first of these two points can be disposed of fairly briefly. Simon, Smithburg and Thompson provide a valuable discussion of the reasons why the 'myths' surrounding the staff/line distinction are preserved.[17] To put their case very simply, the use of the distinction helps to allay some of the anxieties surrounding problems of status and responsibility in an organisation. If the organisation structure can be expressed, or perceived, as a neat pyramid with staff functions clearly hived off as involving advisory responsibilities to specific people in the line hierarchy, this may provide a sense of security for some people, particularly people in the 'line' hierarchy who feel insecure. Indeed V. A. Thompson[18] has gone so far as to suggest that hierarchical systems are preserved to protect the authority of redundant line 'managers' who are unnecessary links in bureaucracies where specialists are really the all-important people. Such a view involves largely disregarding the coordinating, or other political functions, of nonspecialists which were discussed earlier. However, his point may be taken, that what he calls the[19] 'monistic theory of responsibility' with which the staff/line distinction is associated, provides an ideological device to protect certain 'line' prerogatives, while bearing little relation to modern organisational realities.

The Fulton Committee's management consultancy group distinguished[20] 'four aspects which make up the total management task of the Civil Service: (a) formulation of policy under political direction, (b) creating the "machinery" for implementation of policy, (c) operation of the administrative machine, (d) accountability to Parliament and the Public'. It is, of course, the tasks which come under the heading (c) which can most readily be compared with the tasks carried out in a simple industrial enterprise. It is appropriate, therefore, to examine first the applicability of the concepts of staff and line in relation to these tasks but, before doing this, it is important to make clear that such tasks should not necessarily be regarded as typical of public administration or even in any sense 'central' concerns of government. To do so would be to subscribe to the misleading notion of public administration which sees it as the implementation of policies and, therefore, as a process quite distinct from politics. This is a notion which is criticised in Chapter 10. In other words, just because activities of this kind can most readily be equated with activities which are regarded as 'line' ones in industry there is no need to subscribe to one of the myths described by Simon, Smithburg and Thompson,[21] that 'line' activity is somehow 'more important' than other organisational activities.

Typical examples of administrative machinery that operates permanently and can be seen as independent of the policy-making process are activities which could be largely hived off from the central administrative system to function in semi-autonomous agencies, such as the collection of taxes, the payment of social security benefits and the provision of employment services. In Chapter 4, aspects of the administration of the supplementary

benefits system have already been discussed; it is convenient therefore to look at this part of the administrative machine to see how
the line/staff model can be used to describe it and to identify
points of tension.

In the lower levels of the Supplementary Benefits Commission
hierarchy, all the characteristics of the line model are present even
though, at the time of writing, this hierarchy is becoming more
complicated as a result of the integration of National Insurance
benefits and supplementary benefits as the responsibility of a single
department. This change does not affect the general points which
will be made below. A comparatively straightforward 'pyramid'
diagram of the line hierarchy could be provided taking in the
distinct levels of headquarters, the regional offices and the local
offices. Moreover, procedure is sufficiently routinised at the lower
levels that this hierarchy could be chopped off below headquarters
or regional level, at least as far as communications are concerned,
and still continue to operate for some time in much the same way
as the industrial units in a factory can continue to operate without
communications from management. The local office is therefore a
comparatively coherent unit.

In the local office the routine processes of assessment of individual need and payment of benefits are organised in a simple
hierarchic structure containing about four or five levels. But even
here there are certain tasks which it has been found most appropriate to make the responsibility of specialists. For example, there
are officers known as 'liable relative officers' who are responsible
for attempts to secure contributions from the husbands of deserted
wives and the fathers of illegitimate children. There are also often
officers who specialise in the investigation of suspected fraud, and
officers whose job it is to help or coerce unemployed men back
into work. By the standards of highly trained professionals these
officials are but partial or embryonic specialists, yet the emergence
of specific responsibilities and areas of competence of this kind
starts to raise some of the problems which industrial sociologists
have identified as conflicts of interest between staff and line.

Managerial issues associated with the role of the liable relative
officer in a supplementary benefits office include: What amount of
staff time should be devoted to this special function? To what
extent should the treatment of a woman's material needs come
under the control of an officer concerned with securing contributions from legally responsible men? Accordingly friction may

arise between officials with the normal responsibilities for payments and specialists of this kind. These conflicts may be individual disputes about power and autonomy, but may also involve ethical and policy issues. A simple segregation of what are seen as special responsibilities in this way starts to complicate organisational functioning and may bring up fairly fundamental issues which make them significant for something more than the 'operation of the administrative machine'.

These examples involve individuals who are drawn from the ranks of what may be described as line officials to perform specific functions for a limited period of time. Much greater problems might arise if any of the four following conditions applied: they were engaged on specialist duties for such a period of time that they became regarded as ill-equipped to move on to other duties; they occupied ranks which placed them on different career ladders to their line colleagues; they were members of a separate hierarchy (so that, in effect, one had to go to the top of the ladder to find a superior held in common with their 'line' colleagues); or they regarded themselves as members of a profession with standards independent of the organisation employing them.

The operation of the general principle of rotation of promising staff between duties, which occurs in the middle and higher ranks of the British civil service, creates a situation in which individuals are suspicious of tasks which seem to involve the development of any form of specialisation. Such positions are feared—whether rightly or wrongly is rarely clear—as potential blind-alleys where individuals will be stuck unnoticed by their superiors and insufficiently qualified for advancement. Exceptionally the opposite kind of belief develops about specialisms: that the individuals who secure them will have special opportunities to win the attention of their superiors. In such cases specialists will suffer not so much because they feel that their superiors have pushed them into a corner, but because their peers will be suspicious of them and will not want to present them with opportunities to 'stand out from the crowd'.

In the example quoted of specialisms in a local office within the supplementary benefits system, the posts involved could be occupied by specialists on a different career ladder. The liable relative officer and the fraud officer could, for example, be lawyers, while attention to the employment problems of individuals could be in the hands of a social worker. In practice, such specialists are only found at a fairly high level in the headquarters hierarchy and operate in a largely advisory capacity. Despite the general complaints of the specialists about their status, the phenomenon of the detached specialist who operates in a context in which he is generally separated from a hierarchy of his own specialism is not widely found outside the policy-making levels of the civil service. The departments that make heavy use of specialists have generally either:

1 Units in which specialists predominate, with the nonprofessionals providing subsidiary roles, so that the line/staff phenomenon is found in the 'upside-down' form described by Etzioni,[22] or

2 Parallel hierarchies in which administrators and specialists are found in separate but side-by-side structures[23] with the specialists subject to overall control by a professional who is accorded high status (exceptionally this may be a status equivalent to a permanent secretary, as is the case with the Chief Medical Officer in the Department of Health).

The Fulton proposals for a uniform grading system throughout the civil service may in the long run increase the likelihood that persons with different specialisms work side by side. It will be interesting to see whether this simplified structure masks a situation in which individuals with different specialisms are in effect in different career streams. If this does become the case then line/staff conflicts could be exacerbated by a situation in which competition for advancement between individuals with different specialisms is not prevented as it is now by the presence of quite separate career patterns within each of which there are fairly predictable opportunities and a strong emphasis on seniority. It might be useful to look at local government for evidence on the problems associated with the presence of specialists and nonspecialists, with partly distinct and partly common tasks, on a common career ladder dominated by one group (in this case the specialists). Work in the town clerk's department of a local authority calls for the use of some legal specialists, who probably are only engaged on truly legal work for part of their time. Yet a high proportion of the people who reach the top positions in this branch of local government are solicitors.[24] This is, then, a situation in which individuals belong to a common hierarchy, have functions that are partially separate on account of differing expertise, but tend to have radically different career prospects. It is often assumed that such situations are preferable[25] to the other sort of problem of this kind which besets local government where people in different specialist departments are required to work together, a situation which calls for a great deal of coordination at the top. It is suggested here that each system of organisation for combining specialisms with each other or with tasks that don't involve rigorous specialisation involves problems. It would be valuable to see some research being done on the advantages and disadvantages of the various methods of tackling this issue. Management textbooks are full of prescriptions on this subject, some of them written by practical men who feel that they have found the best approach, but actual research has been rare in industry and almost totally absent in public administration.

An important issue in recent British controversies about public administration has been the justifiability of lay control over departments or divisions of experts. Earlier in the chapter the general nature of the case for and against generalists was discussed but now there are a number of points to be made about the roles involved, points that are often forgotten in the heated discussions which arise because of the animus expressed by some people against government by 'amateurs'. In Britain the debate on this issue has in fact been dominated by a concern with the political role of civil servants. Since the concern here is with the management of activities at the level the Fulton Committee distinguished as the 'operation of the administrative machine', it is of value to have a look at an attack upon the traditional stress on the importance of line management made by an American administrative theorist with a strong interest in public administration, Victor Thompson.

Thompson's thesis is as follows, that there is, in modern bureaucracy:[26]

... a growing gap between the right to decide, which is authority, and the power to do, which is specialized ability. This gap is growing because technological change, with resulting increase in specialization, occurs at a faster rate than the change in cultural definitions of hierarchical roles. This situation produces tensions and strains the willingness to co-operate. Much bureaucratic behavior can be understood as a reaction to these tensions. In short, *the most symptomatic characteristic of modern bureaucracy is the growing imbalance between ability and authority.*

Thompson argues that line managers use a variety of devices to protect their authority and that accordingly the effective use of specialists is undermined. Specialists tend to be forced to use informal channels of communication to solve problems, and, since informal decision-making tends to require consensus in order to challenge the formal structure, efficiency is sacrificed to agreement.

It is not clear to what extent Thompson is attacking lay control of specialist activities and to what extent he is simply drawing attention to a problem endemic to the complex organisation. Inasmuch as he infers the former there are a number of weaknesses in his position. If he is attacking the notion of hierarchy altogether then he himself provides evidence for the main difficulty here—that in the absence of hierarchy, group decision-making is required and this means the obtaining of consensus. Whatever the democratic arguments for decision-making by consensus, whatever the benefits it provides to the morale of the participants, it makes little sense to argue that the best possible decision will emerge from the random interplay of a number of experts of different kinds operating as an informal group, unable to fully understand each other and needing to reach arbitrary conclusions by making concessions to each other or by delegating responsibilities to the most forceful or congenial member of the group.

The alternative to an entirely unstructured approach to decision-making involves elevating some member of a group to a leadership role. If the group is a number of experts—say an architect, a surveyor, an accountant and a lawyer planning a new housing project (a rough approximation to what actually happens in English local government)—then such a leader will be the possessor of normally *only one* of the several relevant sets of expertise. Will he be selected on the basis of personality qualities? Or will one particular expertise be regarded as the one which should be given most attention? In either case biases may be developed in the decision-making process which make it, as far as the representatives of the unfavoured specialisms are concerned, an inefficient process in just the same sense as it would be under a lay leader. Even if the specialisms involved in a situation of this kind are comparatively similar, the continuing rapid growth of knowledge is a threat to communication and understanding, a point that is only too clear in those areas of government where economists or physical scientists are involved.

Once there is in existence a hierarchical system, with an indivi-

F

dual or individuals drawn from a group of specialists with responsibilities for organisation and coordination, further problems
develop out of the fact that the individual specialist who assumes
administrative responsibilities can rapidly lose touch with his subject.

Gross[27] provides a valuable discussion of some of the problems
of role conflict for the specialist who becomes an administrator.
He suggests that while, in the early stages of a professional's career,
he is concerned with gaining advancement and increased responsibilities by improving his professional ability, he finds that as he
advances he begins to acquire administrative responsibilities. He
thus begins to experience role conflict and competition between
professional work and administrative work for his time and attention. He also finds he has to assume responsibilities for which his
professional training has not in any way prepared him.

If the professional who finds himself in this position continues
to advance, his dilemma increases because his administrative
burden increases and he finds it more and more difficult to keep
in touch with his speciality:[28]

> The administrator may feel that he is being torn to pieces. Many
> years of training, his professional loyalties and ambitions, his
> intellectual predilections, all push him towards a continuation of the
> professional career which he has so arduously built up in his
> younger years. Yet in most cases this can only be done at the cost of
> sacrificing leisure, health, family life or administrative performance.

Finally the upward-mobile professional may reach the very top
of his career ladder where he acquires the biggest increment of
administrative responsibility of all, and becomes, for example, a
Medical Officer of Health or Director-General of Research. At such
a level it becomes quite impossible for people like him[29] 'to give
adequate attention to professional literature, conferences, writing
or research. Their "inside work" increasingly involves relations
with other managers rather than specialists. In addition, there is an
increasing preoccupation with external relations.'

Gross goes on to discuss the development of specialist roles
which are high in rank and prestige as an alternative to dissipating
specialist skills by turning them into administrators, but he argues
that such people inevitably are in some respects administrators if
they are involved in decision-making problems.

This whole discussion should not be interpreted as necessarily a defence of the 'generalist' administrator. Of course Thompson is right about the conflict between 'specialists' and people with top decision-making responsibilities; where he is wrong is in inferring that this particular problem can necessarily be solved by an attack on the status and power of generalist line administrators. It is a more intractable problem than that, a problem that grows with the increasing complexity of the tasks of modern government.

The discussion of line/staff relations so far has been largely confined to but one of the four tasks the Fulton Committee listed as amongst the management functions performed within the British civil service, the 'operation of the administrative machine'. Even though the local office of the Supplementary Benefits Commission is unconcerned with the first task listed by Fulton, 'formulation of policy under political direction'—at this level policies are passively accepted from above—the two other tasks, the creation of 'machinery for implementation of policy' and 'accountability to Parliament and the Public', though not seen as a central concern in a local office, have a considerable impact upon its day-to-day working. Activities concerned with the creation or at least the improvement of 'the administrative machinery' are of a kind which are close to the concept of staff functions described by the students of management. In the Supplementary Benefits Commission's offices they can be seen as recognisably management functions which are delegated to people who specialise in them, at least temporarily. Teams of officials concerned with inspection and auditing visit local offices in rotation. These officials may be comparatively low in rank but they report to more senior people at the regional offices or headquarters, so they are an adjunct to the executive hierarchy. Similarly the training of staff is also taken partly out of the hands of local management and put in the hands of headquarters or regional staff who specialise in it. All these people are not specialists in the sense that they possess an expertise differentiating them from their colleagues in the local offices, but they do have specialised functions separated from the machinery concerned with the day-to-day administration of the service. Their functions are concerned with maintenance and improvement of the administrative machinery. Where the actual creation of new administrative machinery is involved there will be a similar interference by headquarters with the day-to-day work of local offices, with a similar use of special staff to help initiate experiments and innovation. The most salient example of 'staff'

organisation in this area is the 'organisation and methods' teams
sent out from the Treasury to have a look at the administrative
machinery in the departments of government.

The basic point here is that if one looks at the organisation of a
department from the ground level, as has been done by taking a
'local office' perspective, one may perceive that, surrounding the
simple hierarchy in which the typical official is placed, there are a
number of different staff roles. But if one looks at this same
hierarchy from above, the neat staff/line distinction is not so clear.
One sees instead an elaborate network of people, all of broadly
similar expertise, members of the nonspecialist ranks of the service
with no members of specialist classes mixed in with them, who
perform a variety of functions all of which are necessary for the
running of the machine. The machine is, after all, a network of
people whose tasks interlock, not a mechanical device whose
maintenance and repair can be seen as quite distinct from its
functioning as a productive device.

Much the same can be said about the tasks of civil service
management which Fulton described as 'accountability to Parliament and the Public'. Dealing with the question and complaints of
Members of Parliament is the responsibility of fairly senior staff
in a government department, but it makes little sense to treat these
responsibilities as quite independent of the day-to-day running of
the administrative machine. On the contrary, Parliamentary control devices, however inadequate they may sometimes be, are a
part of the control structure of a government department. These
phenomena are forever in the background as individual civil
servants go about their daily tasks, and when a member of the
public does complain to an MP, not only does that complaint
travel down the hierarchy to the source of the trouble but it may
also have wider implications for practices and procedures elsewhere in the department. The general public often sees government
departments covering up and refusing to acknowledge malprac-
tices. It is a mistake to assume from this that nothing has happened
within the departments in such cases.[30]

In the same way, direct appeals and complaints from members
of the public have an impact upon the administration of departments and, although it may be sometimes convenient to give a
specific officer or group of officers responsibility for the administration of appeal or complaints machinery, it would be misleading

to portray this as a process which can be realistically distinguished from day-to-day department management.

The same cannot be so readily said for the last function mentioned by Fulton, 'the formulation of policy'. This may seem a rather strange thing to say about the management of a government department, that while political accountability cannot be distinguished from day-to-day management, the formulation of policy may be. Traditionally, the formulation of policy has been the responsibility of the administrative class of the British civil service, who have had to combine this function with the overall management of the administrative machine and with dealing with the issues which arise from day-to-day political accountability. One of the most significant criticisms of the traditional system was that, in the course of trying to combine policy-making with their other responsibilities, the administrative class paid insufficient attention to this vital task.

The Fulton Committee made the following comment on the problem:[31]

At present policy-making, especially long-term policy thinking and planning, is the responsibility of officers over-burdened with more immediate demands arising from the parliamentary and public responsibilities of Ministers. The operation of existing policies, and the detailed preparation of legislation with the associated negotiations and discussions, frequently crowd out demands that appear less immediate. Civil servants, particularly members of the Administrative Class, have to spend a great deal of their time preparing explanatory briefs, answers to Parliamentary Questions, and Ministers' cases. Generally this work involves the assembly of information to explain to others (civil servants, outside bodies and so on) the policies of the department, how they are operating, and how they apply in particular cases. Almost invariably there are urgent deadlines to be met in this kind of work. In this press of daily business, long-term policy-planning and research tend to take second place.

Others have dealt more harshly with this aspect of the functioning of the civil service, linking this problem with an over-riding passivity and attachment to the status quo, attributable perhaps to bureaucratic inertia, perhaps to the amateurism of civil servants, perhaps to the social class interests of the administrators. For Opie,[32] 'A great defect of the present system is therefore that means become elevated into ends in themselves, that achieving the goals of policy becomes less important than maintaining past policies. The policy-makers in a ministry come only too easily to regard the ministry's policies as their own.' Nicholson similarly attributes to the civil service a general passivity[33] and resistance to new ideas, and a Fabian pamphlet on the reform of the civil service commented on a[34] 'tendency for civil servants to be too negative in their approach, concentrating on procedure and the day to day dispatch of paper rather than on the substance of problems, and being too ready to seek compromises'.

In recent years there has been a number of attempts to inject into the upper ranks of the civil service people who can provide a contribution towards policy planning. One such example has been the introduction of economists into government departments. There has been an Economic Advisor in the Treasury since the 1940s, and economists have been recruited to the Treasury and some other departments in increasing numbers since that time.[35] Thus, during the years of Conservative rule between 1951 and 1964, economists grew in numbers and importance in the machinery of government.[36] Yet most of these economists found that they suffered from the disadvantages that industrial sociologists have found[37] 'staff' personnel often suffer from—lack of status, inability to influence the 'line' hierarchy and lack of authority in critical areas of decision-making.

When Labour came to power in 1964 the new government sought to overcome this problem in two ways, by a dramatic increase in the numbers of economists—and particularly of high-powered people who were put in senior positions with direct lines to ministers—and by setting up an economic planning department heavily staffed by economists, the Department of Economic Affairs. Brown sees these new developments as the beginning of a new era of importance for economists. He argues,[38] 'The central position of economists could be deduced *a priori* from the status and quality of senior economists in the policy-making structure', and, having given an account of the high-powered people who were appointed, he concludes, 'It is impossible to believe that men of such reputation and standing would allow an administrator to intervene between them (or economic staff reporting to them) and the Prime Minister, Chancellor or Minister concerned'.

Others have been less sanguine about this development. Brittan[39] and Opie,[40] two of the 'irregular' recruits of this period, have both reported their disillusionment about the difficulties of securing the information to develop policies and the influence to get those policies adopted in the face of the established administrative class machine. The staff/line problem is more all-pervading than was imagined, and it is not simply a case of experts being able to push amateurs on one side. Furthermore, in the field of economic policy-making the critical problem which faced economists who were committed to policy planning was that economic crises required short-term expedients which the career administrators were experienced at providing.

Perhaps the most interesting aspect of the Labour government's experiment in the field of economic planning, from the point of view of a discussion of methods of organisation, was the fact that a new department was set up to undertake the task, the Department of Economic Affairs (DEA). This created a situation in which the economic experts were provided with a very senior minister of their own and were not forced to work within the Treasury hierarchy. Brittan suggests that this was a serious mistake, an attempt to solve policy dilemmas by an administrative change. He argues,[41]

There is no art in giving the balance of payments priority and leaving it to the man down the corridor to make a fuss about growth and employment. Equally there is no art in giving expansion the maximum priority, if you do not have the responsibility for the balance of payments and sterling. The art is to find a way of managing demand and the balance of payments which will combine satisfactory expansion with price stability and external solvency. It is difficult to think of a worse way of achieving this than the artificially fostered ministerial rivalries of Labour's early years.

Against this view it can be argued that it is better to put the locus of conflict in the Cabinet, where it is bound to bring such issues to political attention, than to bury them within the civil service. There is a great deal of evidence that the DEA's demise stemmed largely from a failure of political nerve, and in particular from a failure to come to terms with a short-term economic problem, as Brittan himself documents.[42] Inasmuch as this was the case it is not altogether reasonable to attack the DEA experiment on organisational grounds. This seems to be the view of Opie:[43]

The division into two, with a Ministry of Expansion (as it were) to press the case for, and policies to promote, economic growth, and a Treasury to look after the short-term management of the economy (including the level of employment and the balance of payments) seems a very sensible one in principle. It has the major advantage that disagreements are fought out *between* two ministries rather than *within* one, and hence can if necessary be sent all the way up to Cabinet level. Disagreements thus become public, and must be resolved where they belong, on the laps of ministers. They can't be patched up or papered over, somewhere down the line.

But in the context of the payments deficit of 1964 and the succession of exchange crises that followed, the balance of power increasingly tilted towards those responsible for the urgent, the short-term, the reserves and the external value of sterling. This was not so, right at the start, while the elemental force of the first First Secretary of State for Economic Affairs held sway. But withing six months even he had started to dismantle the external defences, by announcing the 5 per cent cut in the Temporary Import Charge. . . .

From then on it was downhill all the way for the DEA, a decline that was accelerated by the eventual departure of George Brown. It is beyond the scope of this book to speculate about the relative importance of economic factors, political personalities and organisational structures in this particular piece of history of the machinery of government. The purpose of referring to it here is to stress that in the light of the known problems of integrating experts with a longer-than-traditional view of economic policy-making into the machinery of government, it made considerable sense as an experiment.

The Fulton Committee, on the other hand, produced proposals for the development of policy planning in government departments which seem to run straight up against the staff/line problem. They propose the setting up of Planning Units within departments to be staffed by comparatively young civil servants. They argue that:[44] 'Thus some of the most able, vigorous and suitably qualified young civil servants will be able to have an early and direct impact on top policy-making. . . .' They consider that the heads of such Units should also be comparatively young. They would be Senior Policy Advisers with direct and unrestricted access to their respective ministers. The Fulton Committee go on,[45]

We have considered what the status of the Senior Policy Adviser needs to be if he is to fulfil most effectively the role described. Much will depend on the way the Minister wishes to organise his top-level advice. . . . We do not wish to make specific recommendations about the Senior Policy Adviser's rank, provided that it is clearly under-stood that he should have the status commensurate with his being the Minister's main adviser on long-term policy questions and on their implications for the day-to-day policy decisions that have to be taken.

The 'irregulars' imported into the civil service by the Labour government enjoyed positions of this kind, and had in addition the advantage of being quasi-political appointees with political sympathies with their ministers, yet when it came to the point where the government had to choose between long-term and short-term considerations they lost out. Of course there should be more planning, more long-term thinking, in British government, but there are grounds for suspecting that there will be many disillusioned young men in the Planning Units recommended by Fulton, who will find that they face considerable disadvantages on account of their positions in the organisational structures of their departments.

Earlier in this chapter it was suggested that the generalist/specialist distinction, which has so preoccupied recent British students of administration, has little significance in the context of United States government. There another related issue has been given a great deal of attention, the phenomenon of professionalisation. The American concern has not been with generalist control over specialists, but rather with the power of specialists and the conflicts they may experience between loyalty to their profession and loyalty to the organisation which is employing them. Much of the literature tends to present professionalism as a 'good' thing, a source of work satisfaction for the individual and a guarantee of integrity to those the professional serves, and bureaucracy as a 'bad' thing, imposing hierarchical control in a capricious way that undermines both autonomy and standards. For example, Etzioni suggests,[46] 'the ultimate justification for a professional act is that it is, to the best of the professional's knowledge the right act,' while the 'ultimate justification of an administrative act ... is that it is in line with the organization's rules and regulations, and that it has been approved—directly or by implication—by a superior rank.'

In the following discussion it will be shown that the relationship between professional organisation and bureaucratic organisation is more complex that this, particularly as far as public administration is concerned. Furthermore, it will be suggested that in so far as there is conflict which may be crudely described as 'professionals versus bureaucracy' the ethical arguments are not nearly as one-sided as those who see organisational employment as a threat to freedom have tried to suggest.[47]

There is a considerable sociological literature on the attributes of professions, and there is disagreement as to what are the defining characteristics.

The core element in all definitions of a 'profession' is technical 'expertise',[48] 'based on systematic knowledge or doctrine acquired only through long prescribed training'. Linked with this is a protected monopoly of that expertise, a licensing system through which the State provides a guarantee that only people who have been through a process of training and acquired a certificate, granted by those other members of the profession who control it, shall be regarded as possessing the skill in question.

In order to secure this kind of state protection the aspiring profession will probably have to establish that it is able to control its members and guarantee a certain minimum of service. This leads us then to one of the most controversial aspects of the definition of a profession, its possession of an ethical code. At one extreme sociologists see ethical codes as part of a social contract which guarantees a high standard of service to the public, a pledge to protect the public from the potential abuses of a monopoly position:[49]

> The monopoly, enjoyed by a profession vis-à-vis clients and community is fraught with hazards. A monopoly can be abused; powers and privileges can be used to protect vested interests against the public weal. The professional group could peg the prices of its services at an unreasonably high level; it could restrict the numbers entering the occupation to create a scarcity of personnel; it could dilute the caliber of its performance without community awareness; and it could frustrate forces within the occupation pushing for socially beneficial changes in practices. Were such abuses to become conspicuous, widespread and permanent, the community would, of course, revoke the profession's monopoly. This extreme measure is normally unnecessary, because every profession has a *built-in regulative code* which compels ethical behavior on the part of its members.

But this is an extreme view, which takes a very sanguine position on the powers of society to control a profession and the profession's readiness to practice self-denial. How in practice can the standard of work of a professional group with a monopoly of a complex expertise be checked? How can the public revoke a profession's monopoly when it does not know whether or not by so doing it will put itself at the mercy of dangerous people? Doctors, for example, possess an expertise which places them in a very strong position to protect their professional prerogative without giving anything in return. Moreover the agreement which gives a profession independence and autonomy is not a 'social contract'—an agreement between a profession and the public—but a political concession secured by a powerful pressure group. Many such agreements were secured a long while ago, and are not likely to be re-negotiated.

Hence, perhaps the most significant characteristics of professional codes of ethics are not the clauses which provide protection to clients but the clauses which protect professionals from unfair competition with each other. In so far as they are concerned with standards of service, however, professional ethics tend not so much to control the content and quality of the service as to provide a guarantee that *a* service will be given. They define certain things that must *not* be done by professionals, they have little to say about what *should* be done. They are concerned with means and not with ends.

Reference has been made to the importance of 'autonomy' in defining a profession. Writers on this subject differ in the extent to which they emphasise 'autonomy'. Those professions which are of long standing in Europe and the United States are sometimes described as 'free professions' because they have been traditionally practised by self-employed men working under contract to individual clients. Law and medicine are perhaps the best examples of free professions. Bennion[50] confines his use of the concept of profession to those professions which, even if they are often practised within organisations, nevertheless have a 'foundation in private practice'. Most sociologists who have used the concept, however, are prepared to acknowledge that, although the growing extent to which professions are practised within organisations is transforming the nature of the phenomenon in some respects, the concept is still applicable to a profession which is not practised 'privately' if it is governed by an autonomous body. This means that the professional within an organisation is a member of a professional community extending beyond the bounds of that organisation and beyond its direct control.

Wilensky links the issue of professional autonomy with the question of ethics in outlining ways in which he considers that professionals are threatened by organisations. He points out that[51] 'organizations develop their own controls; bosses, not colleagues, rule—or at minimum, power is split among managers, professional experts, and lay boards of directors. The salaried professional often has neither exclusive nor final responsibility for his work; he must accept the ultimate authority of non-professionals in the assessment of both process and product.'

Then Wilensky goes on to argue that[52]

Bureaucracy enfeebles the service ideal more than it threatens professional autonomy. Both salaried *and* self-employed professionals are vulnerable to loss of autonomy when demand for service is low and dependence on powerful clients or bosses unreceptive to independent professional judgement is high. But where comfortable organizational routines take command, the salaried professional ... may lose sight of client needs more quickly than his solo brother.

But there is another side to this, that is a situation in which demand for service is high and the professional group itself is powerful. Such is the situation which the doctors have acquired for themselves within the National Health Service, where a professional commitment may be seen as a threat to policy within a public bureaucracy.[53] Thus the hostility of some doctors to the Abortion Act has influenced the effectiveness of that Act, yet doctors are protected from censure by the doctrine of professional freedom, a doctrine which they have the power to uphold.

If the professional has learnt his standards of performance and behaviour from other professionals, and has feelings of loyalty to and expectations of support from other professionals, then the impact of this upon the relationship between him and the organisation he works for will depend upon (1) the demands the organisation makes upon him, and (2) where the members of his professional reference group are located.

Although it is not denied that in very many cases public bureaucracies may make uncongenial demands or may impose undesirable restrictions on the professionals who work for them, it is important to bear in mind, before one starts getting paranoid about organisational power, that public employment also sometimes provides professionals with creative opportunities they might have difficulty in getting if they remained independent practitioners, a fact to which many British architects could surely testify. There are areas of public employment in which some kinds of professionals have been given a protected and privileged status together with resources greatly in excess of amounts they could obtain if they remained independent. Since the Second World War the experience of scientists in government research laboratories in both Britain[54] and the United States[55] has been of this kind. Furthermore, where this has occurred it has often been recognised that hierarchical forms of control are inappropriate and collegial decision-making structures have been developed.

There are thus in public administration situations in which, to quote Wilensky, organisations are 'infused with professionalism'. In such situations, Wilensky acknowledges,[56] 'the salaried professional may have more autonomy in his work than those self-employed professionals whose relatively low income forces them to scramble for many clients or who depend on the patronage of a few powerful clients.'

Goode[57] takes this argument a step further to suggest that it may be the case that bureaucratic power and professional power reinforce each other—to increase societal control over individual professionals, argues the 'functionist' Goode, but the opposite may also, and perhaps more plausibly, be argued.

If the professional employee is a member of a larger professional group within an organisation, not only will he be protected from lay control in some measure, but he may also find that his professional peers and his organisational peers are the same people. In other words his professional reference group will be within the organisation. Whether or not this situation affects his commitment to the organisation will, of course, depend upon the commitment of his peers. Loyalty to colleagues may contribute to loyalty to the organisation or may be loyalty to a dissident group.

Simon, Smithburg and Thompson provide, in the following passage, an account of some of the concomitants of professional attachment:[58]

The strength of professionalism as an influence upon behavior is due to the fact that the professional attitudes the employee brings to the job — produced by his prior training — are continually reinforced by his associations with other members of his professional group. Professionalism results, then, from the combined influence of prior training and association with an outside group — the profession.

In an organization made up entirely or primarily of one profession — for example, the professional staff of the United States Public

Health Service or the employees of a city police department – the professional loyalty reinforces the organization loyalty and makes for a closely knit group. Many organizational tasks require, however, the cooperation of several professions, and here the professional loyalties may compete with organizational loyalties.

Not only do some professionals working in organisations experience a conflict of loyalties but they may also have to take difficult decisions about the extent to which they want professional careers. Earlier in this chapter reference was made to Gross's discussion of the way in which the successful professional finds himself drawn into administrative roles. Clearly this is a process that some professionals may resist if they have a strong attachment to their specialisms and to the professional community. To take account of this, Gouldner[59] has attempted to develop a typology of organisational orientations based upon Merton's distinction[60] between 'cosmopolitans' and 'locals'. Merton developed this distinction in a study of patterns of community involvement in a small American town. Gouldner applied it in a study of the orientation towards their organisation of teachers in a liberal arts college. He defined cosmopolitans as[61] 'those low on loyalty to the employing organization, high on commitment to specialized role skills, and likely to use an outer reference group orientation'; while locals were 'high on loyalty to the employing organization, low on commitment to specialized role skills, and likely to use an inner reference group orientation'. Accordingly the locals tended to see their interests as closely tied up with the college, and were often keen to attain senior administrative roles; while the cosmopolitans looked outside to a wider professional community, seeking esteem from publications which enhanced their reputation in this community and being prepared to move to other colleges in pursuit of advancement.

This dichotomy can be applied particularly to those professionals who possess skills which they can use either inside or outside the public service. Individuals, like the 'irregulars' described by Brittan and Opie, who are recruited to help tackle specific government tasks or to assist a particular political party, particularly face this question of role choice and, together with it, a special dilemma. This dilemma has been highlighted by Merton in his essay on the role of the intellectual in public bureaucracy. Merton points out that[62]

... the intellectual commonly experiences a series of frustrations, once he becomes an integral part of a bureaucracy which is in some measure controlled by those who can neither live with him nor without him. The honeymoon of intellectuals and policy-makers is often nasty, brutish and short. This has an understandable sociological basis. The intellectual, before he enters upon his bureaucratic post, is wont to consider his intellectual problems in abstraction from the demands of specific other persons. He may feel that a problem is solved on its own merits. Once he finds himself in a bureaucracy, he discovers that the intellectual task itself is closely connected with social relations within the bureaucracy. His selection of problems for study must be guided by what he knows or thinks he knows of his client or prospective clients; his formulation of the problem, his analyses and reports must be geared to the same relationship to a client. In short, where he had previously experienced a sense of intellectual autonomy — whether real or spurious is for the moment unimportant — he now becomes aware of *visible control* over the nature and direction of his inquiries.

Merton suggests that this frustration leads to eventual withdrawal from public service. The intellectual is faced by two alternatives, both of which may be unpalatable: to adjust to the bureaucratic system, to orientate himself to operating in its political system and thus to achieve some measure of effectiveness by becoming an insider, a local, an organisation man (an approach to his role that tends to involve compromise and the suspension of some intellectual or academic standards); or to maintain his integrity and independence but inevitably, therefore, remain an outsider, an expert who experiences grave difficulty in securing attention for his point of view.

A British case study which illustrates this thesis is C. P. Snow's *Science and Government*,[63] in which he demonstrated that the acceptance or rejection of certain kinds of scientific advice in the thirties and during the Second World War depended very largely on the success of certain leading scientists in securing close personal relations with the holders of power.

Several attempts have been made to elaborate the local/cosmopolitan dichotomy, including a not very satisfactory one by Gouldner himself. One elaboration which is worthy of comment is in an article by L. Reissman,[64] which was written several years before Gouldner's article but is a logical development of this kind of dichotomy. Reissman's article is based upon an empirical study of bureaucrats, whom he divides into four types, as follows:

1 *Functional bureaucrats.* Individuals with a professional orientation to their work who are described as 'facing outward and away from the bureaucratic structure, whose future plans include doing research along lines of professional interests' and who entered the civil service for 'positive reasons' such as 'material gains' and the existence of 'unique opportunities'.

2 *Specialist bureaucrats.* Civil servants who also have a professional orientation but who feel more strongly identified with the bureaucracy and seek advancement within the service. These individuals, Reissman argues, normally entered the civil service for 'negative reasons', being forced in by an absence of other opportunities. The specialist bureaucrat is described as an 'ambivalent character' with 'a desire to "get ahead" in his profession, yet realizing that this must occur through the mechanism of the bureaucratic promotion system'.

3 *Service bureaucrats.* These are also described as ambivalent, 'oriented in terms of the bureaucratic structure' but seeking recognition from groups outside the bureaucracy; committed, in other words, to service to a particular group or groups in society and using the bureaucracy to achieve such a goal. These are the committed intellectuals whose dilemmas are so well diagnosed by Merton.

4 *Job bureaucrats.* Civil servants who are immersed in the structure, whose professional skills only provided an entrance qualification and helped to determine the nature of the work done. Job bureaucrats seek 'recognition along departmental rather than professional lines', they find satisfaction in technical aspects of their work, are 'rule oriented' and see their careers in terms of internal advancement.

The theories of Gouldner and Reissman tend to suggest that individual professionals have a great deal of freedom of role choice. This will not always be the case. As Reissman suggests by distinguishing between the 'positive reasons' of the 'functional bureaucrats' and the 'negative reasons' for joining the civil service of the 'specialist bureaucrats', personal market situations may play a big part in determining role orieintations. Young professionals may have opportunities to establish cosmopolitan careers for themselves but if they fail, for whatever reason, to seize such opportunities they may well face the situation in which the only prospects for self-advancement lie in becoming locals. Alternatively, in their middle years some professionals may find their hopes of organisational advancement frustrated and seek to turn outward again to the wider community. The achievement of either of these kinds of patterns will be highly dependent upon the state of demand for particular specialisms and the career structures provided by specific organisations.

However, lest the reader acquire an unbalanced view of the nature of this problem, it is important to reiterate that the local/ cosmopolitan dilemma only applies to some professionals. There are many examples in modern states in which public employment provides opportunities for professionals to practise their expertise in a highly protected environment. Thus Glaser demonstrated that, for a group of government-supported research scientists he studied, professional goals appeared entirely consistent with what were understood to be the organisation's goals. In such a context, he argued,[65] 'a local orientation helps to maintain the opportunity to pursue research and to have a career at a highly prestiged locale, both thoroughly consistent with the cosmopolitan orientation. In using the notion of dual orientation, we end up talking of organizational benefits, not problems.'

In the above discussion of professionals the concept has been largely confined to specialists in subjects other than administration. But what about administration itself: can this also be regarded as a profession? Undoubtedly, in a situation in which various forms of expertise are growing in importance, the administrator finds his role under attack in the manner adopted by V. A. Thompson in *Modern Organizations* and is likely therefore to claim, or seek to develop, a special expertise of his own. Administration passes the first 'test' of professionalism if it can prove to be a specialised discipline. It will be fairly clear from this book that the author believes that the rudiments for such a discipline do exist. But on the other hand it is quite obvious that many administrators operate successfully with no other relevant background than long experience. It is likely that in due course practitioners of public administration will require lengthy training in their own discipline, as opposed to the sketchy introduction to other people's disciplines which British higher civil servants get at present.

The second test of the presence of professionalism lies in whether or not the aspiring profession possesses autonomy. Brian Chapman has little hesitation in writing of a 'profession of government' distinguishable in these terms. He claims to show[66] 'the emergence of the civil service in Europe as a distinct profession, with most of the distinguishing features of the classical professions: self-recruitment, self-discipline, self-government, and sustained efforts to prevent outsiders interfering in its external affairs'. The main point here is emphasised later in his book:[67] 'The most striking point is the extent to which political and legislative influence has been eliminated. In the fields of discipline, promotion, training, and recruitment a group of officials is generally responsible, not an outside body.'

To show that in very many states civil services succeed in establishing a considerable measure of autonomy, in freeing much of their internal administration from interference by politicians, is not to establish the existence of a 'profession of government'. Where is the external community of equals to which the individual professional can appeal for support? This 'self-government' is merely domination of the organisation by its most senior members; there is no equality for lower-ranked 'professionals' and no external reference group to which they can look. Such community, such normative order, as does exist rests upon an acceptance of hierarchy not upon any sense of interdependence.

Finally, if public administration is to be regarded as a profession, it is appropriate to seek the presence of a code of professional ethics. There has been a long debate amongst students of public administration about the accountability of civil servants. Notable in this debate was the Finer/Friedrich controversy in which Finer[68] emphasised formal controls over civil servants while Friedrich[69] stressed the limitations of such controls and therefore emphasised the need for civil servants to be responsive to the public interest in general. Friedrich's position is very understandable in the light of the extreme difficulties involved in imposing direct control over civil servants, but leaving the interpretation of the public interest open in this way provides enormous scope for bias, particularly bias towards the status quo.

Friedrich's concept of an ethic of responsibility is one sort of approach to an ethic for public servants, but it is not of the same kind as the typical professional ethic. The professional typically looks inwards to his interpretation of his expertise for guidance in decision-making, while that part of his ethic which is enforced by his professional community is concerned with general standards of behaviour or, as was said earlier, with 'means' rather than 'ends'. The administrator is involved in playing a part in political decisions, about the distribution of resources, about freedom, about relations with other countries and so on. Any ethic that dealt with matters of this kind would pre-empt democratic decision-making. In this context it is appropriate to point out that the rudiments of such an ethic have been seen by some to play an influential part in determining the behaviour of British higher civil servants. Chapman[70] has recently drawn attention to the importance of the Platonic ideal of guardianship of the community for past generations of members of the administrative class. He apparently sees this tradition as worthy of preservation, as a source of 'liberality' in the civil service. That is all very well but it is crucial to recognise that it is also a source of paternalism.

In a situation in which the administrative machine is growing increasingly difficult to control, and in which more and more occupational groups are seeking professional autonomy, it is tempting to see the best approach towards ensuring the maintenance of certain standards in administrative behaviour as lying in the direction of giving attention to the professional socialisation of administrators. As Albrow argues[71]: 'The professional official has achieved emancipation from the machine to follow the objectives of his professional conscience. It makes the content of that conscience of immediate concern to us all.'

The difficulty with following this course of action, if one's objective is to make civil servants somewhat more responsive to the popular will than Plato's guardians, is that a political struggle must inevitably materialise to influence the contents of administrators' consciences. The fundamental ethical issues which underlie this problem also form the basis for some of our most fundamental political conflicts; perhaps, therefore, the most satisfactory civil servants in a democratic state are ones without overactive consciences.

The establishment of general standards of behaviour on the part of public servants is, of course, highly desirable. On the other hand if the ultimate objective of professionalisation is autonomy to follow the dictates of conscience then this can never be an adequate substitute for political control over the civil service.

9

The Social Backgrounds
of Higher Civil Servants

As was shown in Chapter 1, classical discussions of bureaucracy
have been deeply concerned with the impact of the development
of complex administrative organisations upon public policy-making
but have often tended to imply that bureaucratisation is a process
that affects all kinds of organisations in exactly the same way.
Arguments have developed as to whether bureaucratisation increases or decreases efficiency, and there have been disagreements
about the extent to which power shifts into the hands of the
officials, but, as Lipset argues,[1] 'The justified concern with the
dangers of oligarchic or bureaucratic domination has, however,
led many persons to ignore the fact that it does make a difference
to society which set of bureaucrats controls its destiny.'

Bendix suggests in fact three important considerations on this
point. He argues:[2]

No large-scale organization is in fact 'technically rational' because
it must always involve,
(a) the social and ideological background of a diversity of persons,
which their formal positions within an administrative hierarchy cannot
obliterate;
(b) the institutional setting in which the organization must function
and its effect on the psychology of internal operation;
(c) the historical and psychological context in which people outside
the organization view its activities.

This chapter is primarily concerned with the first of these points;
the other points have been referred to elsewhere in the book.
However, it will be found that it is sometimes difficult to consider
the first point in isolation from the other two.

Considerable attention has been paid in Britain to the study of
the social backgrounds of civil servants, and in fact the contributions of British sociologists to the study of public administration

have been almost exclusively confined to this topic. It was significant that the only research task the Fulton Committee on the civil service asked a sociologist to perform was a head-counting exercise of this kind.[3] This chapter will examine the nature of the British debate on this subject and will try to suggest why it has been given so much attention here, as well as looking at the available evidence and the conclusions which that suggests.

On 1 January 1971, on the recommendation of the Fulton Committee, the administrative, executive and clerical classes of the British home civil service were combined into a single administration group. This study will draw upon studies of the composition of the higher civil service which were all undertaken before 1971. These studies are still relevant because the recent change will naturally take a long while to affect the social composition of the upper ranks. It is also the case that the mere abolition of the traditional 'class' divisions will not necessarily ensure that access to the upper ranks will in practice be much more open to persons initially recruited to lowly positions than it has been hitherto. The abolition of the class divisions should be seen as a move to reduce the inflexibility that existed at certain points in the civil-service structure and not as a social revolution.

In this book the dependence upon pre-1971 studies of the civil service means that reference to the higher civil service must be normally taken to be a reference to the administrative class. The administrative class was dominated by graduates, directly recruited to that class. Less than a third of its members entered the class on promotion from a lower class or on transfer from one of the specialist classes. Specialists, however senior, were not normally categorised as higher civil servants. This was perhaps indicative of the traditional dominance of the administrative class, at least in the minds of those who wrote about it.[4]

With the emergence of the British Labour party as an effective political force, and with the development of the welfare state, doubts were raised about the suitability of the higher civil service, whose essential characteristics were determined in the middle of the nineteenth century and whose recruits were largely products of the higher education system developed at the same time, for the tasks it is required to perform. As is characteristic of British political debate, few people have been prepared to go so far as to suggest either that the civil service is likely to be positively disloyal to a democratically elected government of the Left or to imply that higher civil servants are members of a cohesive 'political elite'. Labour Party leaders have been very ready to deny vehemently ideas of this kind, a fact which, it may be argued, tells us more about the ideological orientations of these politicians than it does about the predispositions of civil servants.

However, reflections on the importance of the social affiliations of civil servants, in rather more gentle and cautious terms than those suggested above, have been made fairly widely since the inter-war period. For example, Herman Finer expressed the opinion in 1937 that if members of the administrative class had personal memories[5] 'of misery, hunger, squalor, bureaucratic oppression, and economic insecurity, perhaps a quality would be added to their work in the highest situations which could not fail to impress the Minister at a loss for a policy or an argument'. Similarly, a former civil servant, H. E. Dale,[6] wrote of the difficulties posed by the possible social and educational gap between a working-class cabinet minister and a public school and Oxbridge educated higher civil servant, though the reform of the civil service was not amongst *his* suggestions for dealing with this gap.

Perhaps the most sophisticated discussion of this issue has been provided by two Americans, J. D. Kingsley[7] and S. M. Lipset.[8] Kingsley shows that the British civil service was transformed from an aristocratic into a bourgeois organisation during that period in the nineteenth century when the commercial middle class were becoming politically dominant. The British bureaucracy was thus made representative of the dominant political class, but not of course of the people as a whole. To work effectively the democratic state requires a 'representative bureaucracy', Kingsley argues, thus taking up the theme, developed also by Friedrich,[9] that the power of the civil service is such that formal constitutional controls upon its activities are insufficient. Kingsley sees the recruitment of the civil service from all sectors of the population as one means of ensuring that it is a 'responsible bureaucracy'. Kingsley's is a Jacksonian doctrine updated to fit a bureaucratic age.

Kingsley argues that prior to the Northcote-Trevelyan reforms the middle classes were 'seriously handicapped in office ... by an aristocratic civil service'[10] but is unprepared to commit himself on whether the Labour Party could be similarly handicapped in power, as he recognises that there is doubt about the extent to which the Party is an uncompromisingly proletarian party, but he goes on,[11]

What can be said, with little fear of contradiction, is that the Civil Service as now constituted would be much less representative of a State in which Labour wielded power than it has been of a State in which that prerogative belonged to the upper middle classes.... As a matter of fact [Kingsley goes on however[12]] ... the essence of responsibility is psychological rather than mechanical. It is to be sought in an identity of aim and point of view, in a common background of social prejudice, which leads the agent to act as though he were the principal. In the first instance, it is a matter of sentiment and understanding, rather than of institutional forms....

Lipset's treatment of this issue can be found in his study of the Saskatchewan socialist party, the Co-operative Commonwealth Federation. He analyses the difficulties this party found in implementing their policies once they acquired power and argues that in Britain 'dependence on a conservative bureaucracy may prove to be significant in the success or failure of the Labour Government.' Lipset supplements Kingsley's argument about the social backgrounds of civil servants by pointing out that previous experience of serving more conservative governments will also have an impact upon the behaviour of civil servants called upon to implement markedly different policies. With reference to Saskatchewan he says,[13]

Trained in the traditions of a laissez-faire government and belonging to conservative social groups, the civil service contributes significantly to the social inertia which blunts the changes a new radical government can make. Delay in initiating reform means that the new government becomes absorbed in the process of operating the old institutions. The longer a new government delays in making changes, the more responsible it becomes for the old practices and the harder it is to make the changes it originally desired to institute.

This approach to the problem squares much better with the classical theory of bureaucracy than either the legalistic approach which treats civil-service impartiality as an unalterable fact or the conspiratorial view that portrays civil servants as persons naturally committed to undermining a government of the Left. Civil servants are recruited from certain kinds of social backgrounds, given certain kinds of training, and become accustomed to working for certain kinds of people and dealing with certain kinds of problems; any new group of political masters who want to turn their attentions to new issues and problems are bound to find that they cannot easily reorient themselves. This problem might equally arise with a shift of power to the Right after a long period of rule by a party of the Left, a phenomenon that it seems possible is occurring to some extent at the time of writing (1970–1).

It is misleading to present the issue here as a conflict between individuals with differing formal political affiliations or loyalties. Those writers who attack this argument by stressing the detachment of civil servants from party politics largely miss the point. Chapman brings this out very clearly in showing the strong reservations civil servants have about party politics while at the same time possessing commitments to particular policies. He argues,[14]

However favourable to one party a civil servant is in his early years, because he works so closely with politicians, he soon becomes aware of the ineptitude of any party. After a time, it seems, he learns to think more in terms of policies and their workability, he focuses his political interests on the merits and demerits of particular policies, and since all political parties tend to have a mixture of policies, the parties are seen in a distinctly neutral light.

The implication of this is that civil servants find changes in their political masters easy to adjust to so long as they do not involve violent ideological shifts. Civil servants can operate most easily in a situation of political consensus. Where consensus does not exist, however, their role may become one of trying to create it. Graham Wallas sums this up most neatly:[15] 'The real "Second Chamber", the real "constitutional check" in England, is provided, not by the House of Lords or the Monarchy, but by the existence of a permanent Civil Service, appointed on a system independent of the opinion or desires of any politician and holding office during good behaviour'.

This argument, however, which places civil servants at a rough centre point of the ideological spectrum does not preclude the possibility that they play a role in the maintenance of a particular bias in the orientation of that spectrum.

Since the Second World War criticism of the composition of the higher civil service has centred not so much upon the possible incompatibility of civil servants and their political masters, or political tasks, as upon two issues but partially related to this central problem. First, in an age in which efforts have been made to create equality of opportunity, attention has been paid to the composition of the higher civil service, amongst other occupational groups, to provide evidence of its continuing absence. The civil service has been criticised for failing to admit sufficient persons of working-class origin, as much because it is felt that the public service should give a lead in opening its ranks to all, as because of any concern about the political consequences of a restricted entry. Thus Kelsall's[16] important contribution to the evidence on the social origin of higher civil servants is often cited in discussions of continuing inequality of opportunity.

The second point that has been recently emphasised in discussions of the composition of the British higher civil service has been the relationship between social composition and efficiency. This has been a frequent theme in recent political debates. It was given particular emphasis by Harold Wilson in the early 1960s, when he talked of the 'technological revolution' and the need for 'professionals' to replace 'amateurs' in positions of power. During this period Lord Balogh seems to have been one of the people who influenced this line of rhetoric and, in an essay first published in 1959,[17] Balogh makes a swinging attack on the amateurism of the civil service. While the main prongs of his attack are directed against the employment of[18] 'the crossword-puzzle mind, reared on mathematics at Cambridge or Greats at Oxford' and the failure to make effective use of economists, statisticians and scientists, Balogh implies that social exclusiveness goes with this intellectual exclusiveness.

This concern with efficiency has tended to shift the focus of debate about the British civil service away from the social composition issue. This is brought out very fully by the fact that the Fulton Committee on the civil service paid very little attention to social composition. Its concern was with securing the best graduates, making the most effective use of them, and with effecting a shift towards maximising expertise in general. Certainly the Fulton Committee suggested a change in recruitment policies, which might have brought into the service people from a wider range of social backgrounds, in that it recommended selective preference for students who had studied 'relevant subjects' at universities. This could have favoured students from the newer universities. However, this particular recommendation was turned down by the government in favour of the traditional emphasis upon 'quality' regardless of degree subject. Instead the civil service's response to the argument about relevance has been to step up the recruitment of specialists, particularly economists and statisticians, and to increase the scope of its training programme for administrators.[19]

Another facet of the Fulton reforms of the civil service which may have a long-run impact upon the social composition of the upper reaches of the civil service has been the adoption of a uniform grading structure to eliminate the administrative/executive distinction and the administrative/specialist distinction. As this has only been partially implemented so far, and as it is proposed to continue to make special provisions for the training and career structuring of graduate generalist entrants to the service, it is by no means certain what the impact of this reform will be. If it results in a considerable increase in the numbers of top posts going to people who entered through the 'executive' or 'specialist' gates, or their future equivalents, this may increase the proportion of such people of lower-middle-class origin and without a public school and Oxbridge educational background.

While the political debate about the origins of higher civil servants has increasingly focused upon the issue of efficiency, and the sociologists have therefore only been called upon to contribute to this debate by producing factual analyses of the educational backgrounds of civil service entrants, a minority of academics have sought to keep alive the wider questions of the relationship between social origin and political bias. Their contribution has, however, been largely disregarded in the political arena because of its tendency to take an extreme form. Thus the academic sociologists have been asking the question: What is the relationship between higher civil servants and the ruling class? Accordingly there has been a tendency, particularly noticeable in the work of Bottomore[20] and of Guttsman,[21] to treat upper-middle-class origin as synonomous with membership of the ruling class. Identity of civil servants with other elite groups is inferred in such rather crude attempts to show that the sharing of broadly similar social and educational origins is of determining importance.

Thus, in considering recent contributions from British sociologists to the continuing debate about the impact of the social affiliations of civil servants upon their behaviour in decision-making roles, one is provided with a choice between the acceptance of the wide inferences which are provided by analysts of social stratification, suggesting a close identity between higher civil servants and other ruling groups, and the rather narrower contributions which sociologists have made to the debate about efficiency. Neither of these approaches provides really useful contributions to the more subtle questions raised by Kingsley, Bendix and Lipset.

Halsey and Crewe raise,[22] but do not discuss, the important issue which lies between the two approaches. They argue that concern about social origins is relevant to the problems of the recruitment of civil servants and not just 'an obsessional professional preoccupation of sociologists', where they say:

The same process of social selection which brings individuals to diverse occupational destinations also fashions and maintains norms of outlook and shared assumptions among the members of a profession. The character of these tacit values and assumptions is surely of crucial importance in a profession such as the administrative class, which plays a vital role in the public management of the lives of all classes of society.

This raises three very interesting questions:

1 How important are values and assumptions derived from social origin, particularly in relation to the fact that there are values and assumptions related to occupational roles which may or may not conflict with them?

2 How do such values contribute to intra-organisational solidarity?

3 May not such values also contribute to interorganisational solidarity where common origins are shared with other elites, and will this solidarity add up to the more conspiratorial concepts implied by some theorists? In other words, what will be the relationship between inter- and intra-organisational solidarity?

These three points have been spelt out above in the form of separate questions but they are interrelated and will be treated as such in the following discussion. Furthermore, while these points could be pursued in the largely abstract form followed so far, it does seem appropriate here to relate the arguments to the facts available on the social and educational origins of British higher civil servants. So some information on these points will be interposed here. The following discussion is very largely based upon data provided in Halsey and Crewe's study,[23] undertaken for the Fulton Committee in 1967, of a sample of civil servants. Their

Father's occupation	All Administrative class	Direct entrants	Open competition direct entrants 1948–67	Open competition direct entrants 1961–7	Undergraduates 1961/62	University teachers 1966	Males 20–64 1951
I & II Professional and managerial	67%	79%	71%	85%	59%	60%	18%
III(i) Skilled non-manual	10%	9%	⎱ 21%	3%	12%	⎱ 32%	⎱ 52%
III(ii) Skilled manual	13%	8%	⎰	⎱ 10%	18%	⎰	⎰
IV & V Semi and unskilled	6%	3%	7%	⎰	7%	6%	28%
Other	3%	1%	—	1%	4%	2%	2%

data on members of the administrative class have been used, no attempt has been made to raise questions about the other less powerful classes in the civil service.

About a third of the members of the administrative class entered it on promotion or transfer, the remainder were direct entrants to the class. There is a tendency for the direct entrants to dominate the higher grades but this tendency is somewhat obscured by the presence in the class of people who came into the civil service by exceptional avenues during the Second World War, many of whom occupy senior positions today. This analysis will draw on two kinds of information, on members of the administrative class as a whole and on direct entrants to the class. It will be found that whereas direct entrants form a largely socially homogeneous group, the presence in the class of transferees, promotees and special wartime entrants tends to reduce this homogeneity.

The table opposite provides information on the social class origin of members of the administrative class, as defined by their fathers' occupations. Some figures on other comparable groups have been included in this table.[24]

These figures show very clearly the extent to which the administrative class recruits from social classes I and II. Of course, this is true of all occupations for which a high level of education is required, as a simple consequence of unequal educational opportunity and success, but what is striking about the higher civil service is:

1 The fact that if its recruits are compared with the undergraduate population, it will be found that they are disproportionately from classes I and II. This fact is further emphasised by the social class distribution of university teachers; though drawn from a similar population of 'good' graduates, this group contains a markedly lower proportion from social classes I and II.

2 The continuing importance of direct entrants in keeping up this high proportion from classes I and II. On this point the following figures are interesting[25]

Year of establishment	Direct entrants from social classes I and II still in the civil service
1946–50	79%
1951–55	64%
1956–60	80%
1961–65	85%

This table shows the very surprising fact that the lowest period for recruitment from classes I and II was before the recent expansion of the university population. There has been a recent downturn in the numbers recruited from classes I and II to a figure of 76 per cent for 1966–7, but this remains a very high figure.

In the tables above, social classes I and II are combined. It is unfortunately not useful to break down these figures into the two categories as the distribution of occupational groups between the two classes does not provide a very meaningful social division. For example, clergy, no matter how obscure or impoverished they are, figure in social class I while most company directors are placed in II. Significantly also while university lecturers are placed in I, members of the administrative class are in II! This weakness in the data is an unfortunate one since it makes it impossible to distinguish between entrants to the civil service who might be said to come from what might be termed 'ruling-class' backgrounds and those who are more appropriately categorised as coming from typically middle-class homes. It is necessary, therefore, to see whether data on educational backgrounds help to answer this question.

The table opposite provides information on the kinds of schools attended by administrative class civil servants, together with some comparative figures for other groups:[26]

Of course, type of schooling is here very largely a reflection of social class origins. Halsey and Crewe provide a cross-tabulation of fathers' occupation against type of schooling, but this does not really help to clarify the problem here. They summarise the position in the following way:[27]

Thus there appear to be three avenues from social class origins through school and educational qualification to the administrative class.

First, a route from middle class origins through direct grant and fee paying schools to a university first degree. This route has been of slightly increased importance for direct entrants since the war. Second, there is a path from working class origins through the L.E.A. grammar schools to sub-degree qualifications which has permitted entry to the administrative class, usually by promotion within the Civil Service. Third, there is a path to post-graduate degrees from a wide range of social origins, through the private or state schools but slightly wider through the former. These three main socio-educational routes are not, of course, mutually exclusive; all

Schools attended	All Administrative Class	Direct entrants	Open competition entrants		Arts and social science faculties of universities	
			1948–67	1961–7	Undergraduates 1961–2	Teachers 1966
Secondary modern, technical and comprehensive	2	—	} 34	—	} 58	51
LEA grammar	40	30		29		10
Direct grant	19	19	} 65	18	15	22
Public school and other fee paying	37	48		50	27	17
Schools abroad and others	2	2	1	3	—	

combinations of social origin, type of school and educational qualification are to be found and there are half as many L.E.A. grammar school boys among the direct graduate entry as public and direct grant school pupils, as well as a minority of non-graduates whose secondary schooling was in the private sector.

Kelsall tried to get a little nearer to throwing light on the 'elite' origin of higher civil servants by providing data on the number at assistant secretary level and above who attended certain 'exclusive' schools.[28] 10.8 per cent of those at or above the rank of assistant secretary in 1950 had attended one of the nine public schools figuring in the investigations of the Clarendon Commission 1861–4 (St Pauls, Merchant Taylors, Eton, Winchester, Westminster, Shrewsbury, Harrow, Charterhouse and Rugby), and 19.2 per cent had attended schools where board and tuition cost over £140 a year in 1939. The great majority of civil servants in these categories were direct entrants.

Lupton and Wilson tried to tackle a similar problem with regard to the educational backgrounds of 73 of the most senior civil servants[29] ('the twelve senior members of the Treasury Staff and the Permanent Secretaries and their immediate deputies of twenty-one other ministries'). They provide figures for the proportion who went to six specific schools—Eton, Winchester, Harrow, Rugby, Charterhouse and Marlborough. 19.2 per cent of their sample of civil servants went to these schools.

Lupton and Wilson's article is of particular interest in that it provided data on other elite groups in 1957 (see table below).

	Percentages who attended Eton	Percentage who attended any of the six 'elite' schools
Cabinet ministers and other ministers of the Crown ($N = 17$)	32.4	50
Senior civil servants ($N = 73$)	4.1	19.2
Directors of the Bank of England ($N = 18$)	33.3	66.6
Directors of the 'big five' banks ($N = 148$)	29.7	48
Directors of 'city' firms ($N = 107$)	32.7	43
Directors of large insurance companies ($N = 149$)	30.9	47

University attended	All Administrative class	Direct entrants	Open competition entrants		Arts and social science faculties of universities	
			1948-67	1961-7	Undergraduates 1963-4	Teachers 1966
Oxford and Cambridge	64%	74%	78%	73%	14%	44%
London	9%	8%	8%	5%	19%	19%
Welsh and English provincial	8%	6%	9%*	14%	50%	23%
Scottish	9%	8%	5%	4%	17%	8%
Irish and foreign	1%	1%	—	—	X	} 5%
Other (institutions of higher education other than universities)	10%	3%	—	3%	X	

*Includes Irish, foreign and others.

When looked at in this way, senior civil servants appear to be a distinctly sub-elite group, but then, of course, Lupton and Wilson's study provides a picture of British elites which will not necessarily hold so strongly today. Certainly, for example, Macmillan's 1957 cabinet was particularly remarkable for its aristocratic character.

Three-quarters of the members of the administrative class are graduates, and, as has already been seen, almost all the non-graduates will be promotees. It is of further interest, therefore, to have a look at the kinds of university education received by these graduates. The table on page 185 provides information on the universities attended by graduates in the administrative class and by some comparable groups.[30]

This information on universities provides further evidence that higher civil servants are largely drawn from a particular segment of Britain's educated population. The close correlation of parental occupation, schooling and university education suggested here does tend to indicate that higher civil servants must be regarded as in some respects a socially exclusive group.

Since it has been shown that, according to the figures provided by Kelsall and by Lupton and Wilson, only about a fifth of senior civil servants come from the major public schools, it must be asked whether the remainder were able to make up for non-possession of certain old school ties by university connections. Interestingly enough Lupton and Wilson's table on universities attended shows top civil servants in a very different position in this particular elite education league.[31]

	Percentage who attended Oxford or Cambridge
Cabinet ministers etc.	71.5
Senior civil servants	68.5
Directors of the Bank of England	50
Directors of the 'big five' banks	50
Directors of 'city' firms	34.6
Directors of insurance companies	38.3

Very few persons in any of these categories went to other universities; this must of course be related to the fact that most of these people were educated at a time when the dominance of Oxbridge was much more marked than it is today. However the higher civil service entry has changed very little in this respect. In the period 1948–56, 78 per cent of open competition direct entrants had Oxbridge degrees; and in the period 1957–63, despite the increasing criticism of Oxbridge dominance, the figure went up to 85 per cent. In the last few years this proportion has gone down a little, but this change needs to be put in perspective by reference to the dramatic increase in the number of university places outside Oxbridge and to the considerable popularity of some of the new universities. In 1968, 59 per cent of all direct entrants to the administrative class came from Oxbridge. Finally, in describing the social characteristics of the members of the British higher civil service there is a need to try to supplement the rather bare data used so far with a little more detail. Apart from the very impressionistic information provided in the many descriptions of the civil service, such as for example the books by Dale[32] and Dunnill,[33] one of the pieces of evidence provided for the Fulton Committee was a detailed study of thirty civil servants by R. A. Chapman.[34] This thirty comprised all but two of the men and women who joined the service as assistant principals in 1956 and were still in it in 1966. They were all principals, a grade which they had been in for between four and six years at the time of the study. They were thus being studied at about the time that most of them would have been beginning to become really effective members of the administrative class.

There is no point in reproducing Chapman's data on father's occupation, and on school and university education. Suffice it to say that his sample was fairly typical of the direct entrants to the administrative class during the postwar period. Where this piece of research does provide some extra information, however, is on the question already raised as to which epithet, 'ruling-class' or just 'middle-class', is most applicable to these people. And on this point Chapman's evidence is quite striking. The typical member of his sample is a family man commuting to work from an outer London suburb, owning a small family car, paying less than £100 per year in rates on the house he is buying, and describing himself as middle-class. His long hours of work cut down his recreational activities, which are likely to be varied but hardly upper-class. Only four of the sample belonged to London clubs; this is interesting in that Dale suggested that the typical higher civil servant in his time was a member of at least one club whereas Chapman found that few of his sample even aspired to become members[35] and some 'found it amusing that they should be seriously asked about membership of London Clubs'. Another interesting feature of Chapman's sample was that 17 said they voted Labour in 1966, 6 voted Conservative, 4 Liberal, 1 Scottish Nationalist (an Edinburgh-based civil servant) and 2 did not vote.[36]

1966 was, of course, a year in which a fair proportion of the middle class were prepared to give Labour a chance and, significantly, a further exploration of the political attitudes of the sample showed many of them to be floating voters with 'centrist' views:[37]

... only eight out of the thirty said they consistently voted for the same party at elections and twenty claimed (some forcefully) to be floating voters. Many answered the question about how they voted only on condition that their reasons or general views about politicians were also considered. The reasons tended to show that they did not really align themselves with the party for which they voted, but instead had voted for the man, or had some other personal reason for voting in a particular way.

The only other data we have which is in any way comparable with Chapman's study is a certain amount of information on permanent secretaries provided by Harris and Garcia[38] and some other data from the Lupton and Wilson study. Both of these studies suggest that there is a high London club membership amongst these people, but that the clubs they belong to are not those frequented by the business elite. The contrast here with Chapman's sample can be explained partly in terms of the fact that the top men largely belong to a generation who entered the civil service before the Second World War and partly in terms of their very much more senior positions. If London club membership is an indicator of social status, this contrast tends to suggest that in the case of the civil service it is an 'achieved' and not an 'ascribed' status.

Another interesting aspect of Lupton and Wilson's study is that they explored some of the kinship networks of the people from the financial and political world who were implicated by the Bank Rate Tribunal and found that, while they were able to trace a most elaborate network of interrelationships, the top civil servants tended not to have kinship links with these people.[39]

From this review of the information available on the social and educational backgrounds of higher civil servants the following conclusions can be drawn. That the core of the service, the direct entrants, are drawn from a sufficiently narrow range of backgrounds that it may be suggested that the resultant homogeneity may contribute to intra-organisational solidarity. But, on the other hand, while the partial sharing of educational backgrounds with other elite groups may contribute to the development of understanding of and ease of working with, for example, managers and financiers, we may expect that there will be an absence of close identity between civil servants and other elites since the range of social backgrounds from which civil servants are drawn appears to be rather wider than is the case with the capitalist elites.

While it must be recognised that in Britain today the extent to which the two groups are distinguishable is debatable, it may be suggested that such affinities as civil servants have with the captains of industry are with the managers rather than the capitalists. Furthermore civil servants are people who have chosen the service of the state rather than work in private industry. Only seven of Chapman's sample of civil servants[40] said they would have entered industry if they had not got into the civil service; the great majority said they would have chosen university teaching or some other form of public administration.

Studies of American civil servants have brought out very clearly the difference between the social origins of businessmen and civil servants in their country, and Lloyd Warner and his associates demonstrate how civil servants feel about business:[41] 'For them business is concerned with materialistic things. Motivation is narrowly in terms of profit and loss, of selfish interest. And while monetary rewards are much greater, it is not worth it....'

Against this emphasis upon civil servants as a group committed to the service of the state and with a tendency to left-of-centre views, it may be argued that these ideological differences from businessmen are marginal in comparison with the broad identification of civil servants with the middle class. On this, Chapman suggests, on the basis of the reluctance of his sample to place themselves in a social class, that civil servants—who, when pressed, of course place themselves in the middle class—are in many respects a classless group. This is misleading because the rejection of the concept of class is a characteristic feature of middle-class ideology, and people who argue 'we are all middle now' are merely resisting the implications of class-based theory.

Clearly it is important to recognise that the social base from which direct entrants to the higher civil service derive is a very narrow one. Yet would the widening of this base really alter the character of the higher civil service?

Jackson and Marsden[42] have suggested that working-class individuals who achieve educational success tend to be highly conformist. On this point, Robinson has argued that men who succeed in entering the administrative class of the British civil service[43]

... from much lower social strata may be just as likely to take the view that failure to rise is the result not of faulty organization of society but of the defects of those who fail. The successful industrialists who rose from the humblest origins in the nineteenth century were not generally supposed to be those with the greatest regard for their work people, as much contemporary fiction shows.... There is not really very much reason to suppose that the son of working-class parents, whether he enters the administrative class by open competition or promotion, will necessarily have greater regard to the interests of the workers than the child of middle- or upper-class parents.

Furthermore, it seems reasonable to suggest that the early training of a civil servant of working-class origin would reinforce any tendencies to conformity. Socially mobile, but class-conscious, working-class boys are only too well aware of the potential pressures upon them to conform within a bureaucratic organisation; accordingly they tend to leave such careers to their more conformist fellows, often seeking instead academic avenues of advancement which offer, initially at least, partial escape from their dilemma.[44]

Therefore it may be suggested that the pressures upon the entrant to the civil service to accept a conventional definition of his occupational role are very strong indeed. Hence, while the particular role definition involved is largely congruent with middle-class values and middle-class educational processes, it may be expected that the nonconformist of working-class origin will come under considerable pressure to modify his attitudes and values.

The emphasis upon 'apprenticeship' in the higher civil servant's training—learning the job by sitting beside more senior colleagues, rather than by formal training, the enormous importance of conformity for promotion in a hierarchical system where criteria for the judgement of performance are necessarily vague, and the presence in the British civil service of an explicit 'job ideology' (as is made clear in the writings of so many ex-civil servants)[45] all provide evidence that the new recruit is likely to come under heavy but subtle pressure to adopt a traditionally approved definition of his role.

In general terms it is suggested that there has been a tendency in discussions of the personnel of the British civil service to over-emphasise the importance of social origins and to disregard the enormous importance of the pressures upon the individual implicit in his adoption of the occupational role of administrative class civil servant.

In so far as there is here a situation in which, at present, pre-occupational and post-occupational socialisation are congruent, it may be predicted that any change in the character of recruits will be resisted. Discussions of recruitment to the higher civil service tend to raise the issue of 'cultural prejudice' in relation to the examination techniques used.

The traditional method of selection for the higher civil service involved a combination of academic examination and interview. After the Second World War this technique became known as Method I and was joined by an alternative selection system, Method II, involving an examination in general subjects followed by a series of interviews and tests modelled on the officer selection techniques devised during the War. After it was introduced, Method II steadily increased in popularity at the expense of Method I and, in 1969, Method I was abolished.

The stress upon verbal skills and the subjectivity involved in Method II led to suggestions that social biases would be likely to play a large part in this method of selection. Interestingly, however, there was evidence[46] that both methods tended to favour the products of Oxbridge and the independent schools and that Method I favoured candidates who had followed traditional syllabuses in the humanities. Pickering's study of this topic suggested[47] 'that broadly speaking the same variables are strongly associated with performance at all stages of the competitions and apply to both Method I and Method II. This points to the important conclusion that each stage—interview, written papers, CSSB tests—tends to select or reject the same type of candidate. It is certainly not the case that "redbrick" candidates fall down only on the non-academic parts of the competition.'

These findings seem to have led to a certain complacency about the Method II selection device. The fact that it is no more socially biased than a written examination does not fully dispose of the argument on this point, and certainly does not dispose of the argument that, quite apart from any social class bias, there may be a bias in favour of conformists in general. Conformity and compatibility with an established model are bound to seem important in a subjective selection scheme, particularly when some of the selectors are themselves part of the organisation for which they are selecting.

The close relationship between politics and social class in Britain has been important in bringing to the forefront the discussion of the class basis of the higher civil service. As was suggested above, this issue was originally expressed in terms of the possible difficulties involved in the relationship between civil servants and a Labour government, and accordingly debate developed at a rather crude level in which fears were expressed about potential disloyalty, and the effectiveness of particular devices to ensure political control were questioned. Inevitably the issue arose in the course of the investigations of the Fulton Committee and provoked indignant reactions from civil servants and the following comment from the Prime Minister, Harold Wilson:[48]

This idea that Ministers don't know what is going on, and that Civil Servants keep facts away from them – if I could be told the name of any Minister who is subject to that situation, I don't think he would be a Minister for very long. It rests with the Minister to control his department. I find the Civil Servants do what is required once they get a clear lead. I think you could get the situation if a Minister failed to give a clear lead, but then he shouldn't be a Minister.

It has already been made clear that this kind of huffing and puffing bears very little relation to the real issue, the 'representative bureaucracy' issue. It is interesting to note that, while nowhere else (except perhaps in France[49]) has this issue been related particularly clearly to the social class issue, in a number of federal states, the balanced representation of different regions, areas and states has been taken seriously. For example, of Germany and Switzerland, Brian Chapman says:[50]

In both countries entry to the federal civil service is to some extent dependent upon the preservation of a correct balance between the constituent states. In Switzerland further factors are taken into account. The federal authorities try to keep a balance not only between the cantons, so that each is properly represented, but also between the political parties, the religions and the languages. There are no formal rules laid down, but informal agreements are normally made. To the knowledgeable, therefore, an advertised post may be destined from the start to go to a French-speaking Roman Catholic Social Democrat from Canton Basle.

Lloyd Warner comments on a similar preoccupation with balance between states operating as an informal influence on the selection of American federal executives.[51]

In general, with the notable exceptions of Warner's study and Bendix's rather slight book on the subject,[52] it is hard to find discussions of the social origins of American higher civil servants. The primary concerns of most discussions of top civil service personnel in the United States are with effective selection, training and advancement of the best qualified people. Indeed in the United States,[53] and also in Australia,[54] concern has been rather more about how to create an 'elite corps' than with how to secure the effective penetration of such an elite by the upward-mobile sons of working-class parents.

Another peculiar aspect of the British discussion of the origins of higher civil servants has been the fact that the debate about class has coincided with a debate about efficiency. This has been due to the fact that the dominant administrative class was given its basic structure and character in the nineteenth century when the tasks of government were limited and the accepted form of education for a ruling group was the nonspecialist instruction in the humanities provided at the public schools and at Oxford and Cambridge. The irrelevance of this kind of education for the modern civil servants of the 'positive state' is gradually becoming as clear as is at the same time the restricted social spectrum from which the consumers of such education have been traditionally drawn.[55]

Yet, as the French have found,[56] to try to secure greater efficiency, by changing the nature of the education provided for the elite group and by removing formal limitations upon open access to such education, does not preclude the development of a situation in which the traditionally privileged are able to compete much more effectively for limited educational resources and thus maintain their dominance in the competitions for entry to the higher civil service. In this way we have the creation of a situation in which, according to Halsey and Crewe,[57] 'Most of this process of social selection is beyond the control of the Civil Service Commissioners: they can do nothing directly about the basis of the educational system in the primary and secondary schools from which the university students in which they are interested flow.'

So, in the last resort the case for reforming the social basis of the higher civil service may involve conflict with efficiency, in that selection of those who are most successful in the education system may mean selection from a narrow social band. Those who favour social balance will have to argue with those who insist upon selection of the 'best', or otherwise wait for reforms in the educational system.

10

Politics and Administration

In the first chapter of this book an account was given of the main lines of the debate about the impact of the growth of bureaucratic administration upon democratic government. In this and the next chapter attention is directed upon a more detailed examination of the way in which the relations between politicians and administrators are worked out in representative forms of government. They build upon some of the evidence provided in earlier chapters, provide some more detailed evidence on the ways in which complex administrative organisations prove difficult to subject to political control, and look at some approaches to solving the problems of politician/administrator relationships.

Towards the end of the nineteenth century, in the United States, Woodrow Wilson sought to develop interest in the study of administration, and explained the neglect of the subject in these terms:[1]

No one wrote systematically of administration as a branch of the science of government until the present century had passed its first youth and had begun to put forth its characteristic flower of systematic knowledge. Up to our own day all the political writers whom we now read had thought, argued, dogmatized only about the *constitution* of government; about the nature of the state, the essence and seat of sovereignty, popular power and kingly prerogative; about the greatest meanings lying at the heart of government and the high ends set before the purpose of government by man's nature and man's aims. The central field of controversy was that great field of theory in which monarchy rode tilt against democracy, in which oligarchy would have built for itself strongholds of privilege, and in which tyranny sought opportunity to make good its claim to receive submission from all competitors. Amidst this high warfare of principles, administration could command no pause for its own consideration. The question was always: Who shall make law, and what shall that law be? The other question, how law should be administered with enlightenment, with equity, with speed, and without friction, was put aside as 'practical details' which clerks could arrange after doctors had agreed upon principles.

Thus Woodrow Wilson helped to develop the study of public administration by pointing out the way in which the implementation of law was as deserving of attention as the making of law. Yet, by assuming that the implementation could be clearly distinguished from law-making, he made a distinction that has misled many students of government since his day, the distinction between 'politics' and 'administration'. In fact as far as American government was concerned he expounded the view that politicians should keep out of administration. Wilson argued that:[2]

> Most important to be observed is the truth already so much and so fortunately insisted upon by our civil-service reformers; namely, that administration lies outside the proper sphere of *politics*. Administrative questions are not political questions. Although politics sets the task for administration, it should not be suffered to manipulate its offices.

Thus at the same time as European writers, studying the representative systems that were but partially emerging in their own countries, recognised and attacked a new power in the land which was growing as government tasks increased, bureaucracy, Wilson, who clearly recognised that many European administrations could be said to have too much power, nevertheless felt that the development of good government in his own country should involve the diminution of political interference in administration. Wilson suggested that the English system represented something of an ideal in this matter, and the relative absence of concern about the balance between politics and administration in this country seems to suggest that this view has been complacently accepted by the English. There have however been some English writers who have attempted to disturb this complacency, but their arguments have been very largely attacks on the collectivist state rather than criticisms of the way in which politics and administration are distinguished in England.[3]

In many respects the debate over the distinction between politics and administration could be treated as a rather tedious and irrelevant academic discussion and the discussion confined to consideration of the actual relations between politicians and administrators, were it not for three facts. First, it must be taken into account that there is a need to have some conception of where the boundary of the subject matter lies if administration is to be discussed, given that there are no firm lines which divide administrative roles from political roles. Second, and more important, the 'is' question about what administrators or politicians do is intimately bound up with the 'ought' question about what they should do and is therefore the subject of controversy between politicians, and even sometimes between administrators and politicians. Third, it will be found that an apparently academic discussion about definitions will in practice increase understanding of both some of the important characteristics of administrative behaviour, and of some of the problems that are related to the democratic control of administration.

The traditional conception of the distinction between politics and administration, as present in the work of Wilson,[4] Goodnow[5] and Merriam,[6] seems to involve an assumption that questions which are essentially political and questions which are essentially administrative can be distinguished from each other. Simon[7] has shown that no clear criteria were specified by these traditional theorists to enable the making of this kind of distinction. It may therefore seem appropriate to ignore this kind of theory. Yet it corresponds with a widespread popular point of view, which involves arguing that particular areas of decision-making should be kept nonpolitical. It is important to recognise that this means in practice that what is being said is that certain areas of public decision-making should be removed from democratic control.

This sort of plea for the removal of aspects of decision-making from political control comes in various forms. It may involve simply a rejection of the alternatives offered by the available protagonists, the political parties, or a feeling that these alternatives are posed in terms which blur the crucial issues.[8] It may involve the view that professionals should make the decisions rather than amateur politicians. Or it may, as in the sophisticated form in which it has been presented by Woodrow Wilson and many of his successors, involve the view that certain kinds of decisions inherent in the implementation of policy are made much more efficiently out of sight of the politicians who set out the broad lines of policy.

There seem to be two alternative approaches to the distinction between politics and administration; one involves regarding all governmental behaviour apart from legislative behaviour as administration whether or not politicians are involved in it, and the other involves distinguishing in practical but not absolute terms those roles that might most appropriately be performed by politicians from those that may be reserved or left for administrators.

The first of the two alternatives raises few problems as far as the role of politicians in administration is concerned since it involves no prescriptions as to the extent to which they should engage in administrative tasks. The politicians are seen as the managing directors of their enterprises who may be expected to make their own choices as to when and how they delegate.

There is, however, one sense in which logical problems are raised by this kind of definition of the scope of administration quite apart from any organisational problem arising out of uncertainty. These logical problems concern the distinction between administration and legislative behaviour. For an American, legislation comes from Congress; not surprisingly therefore this definition of administration is used with few qualms by Simon, Smithburg and Thompson, who set it out in the following way in terms of American institutions:[9]

By public administration is meant, in common usage, the activities of the executive branches of national, state, and local government; independent boards and commissions set up by Congress and state legislatives; government corporations; and certain other agencies of a specialized character. Specifically excluded are judicial and legislative agencies within the government and non-governmental administration.

The difficulties involved in developing a comparable definition for English circumstances can be very well illustrated with reference to one current political issue, the reorganisation of secondary education. At present the development of comprehensive education is occurring within a legal framework provided by the 1944 Education Act, an act framed in sufficiently general terms to permit a range of local innovations. The pioneers in the development of comprehensive education were certain local authorities. Were they therefore legislating when they decided to change their secondary education systems? The development of comprehensive education was given impetus by a Department of Education and Science circular to local authorities in 1965 which required them to submit comprehensive plans. Was this circular a legislative act? The answer to these questions which most people would give would be, No. Yet undoubtedly the decisions described have been, at their respective levels, major political decisions. Moreover, before its electoral defeat Mr Wilson's government was proposing an Act of Parliament to compel local authorities to bring in comprehensive education schemes. What would there be about such an Act that would have marked it out, either in terms of the people who drafted it or in terms of its content, from the decisions described above as preceding it or from the wide range of no less controversial decisions about implementing the Act that would have followed it?

In general, the distinction between politics and administration made by Simon, Smithburg and Thompson is particularly difficult to apply to two important British political institutions, local government and the higher civil service. One of the salient features of British local government is enshrined in the doctrine of *ultra vires* which prevents local authorities doing anything they have not got Parliamentary permission to do. Moreover a great deal of the legislation that affects local government is mandatory rather than permissive, and central government also has a great deal of control over local authority finance, so that, all in all, most local government work involves the implementation of central government legislation. All this suggests that it is appropriate to categorise local government as 'administration'. Yet if this is done then the activities of local politicians, which are not markedly different in character from the activities of politicians in central government, are misleadingly characterised as 'administrative' behaviour; and the efforts of the Maud committee[10] to distinguish between political and administrative roles in local government, which involve essentially an attempt to enforce the Woodrow Wilson doctrine, have to be described in terms of different concepts.

The difficulty with applying the traditional politics/administration distinction to the work of the British higher civil service lies in the fact that senior civil servants are just as much involved in the political control of their departments, and often, too, in the actual legislative process, as they are in the management of administrative machinery designed to carry out political instructions. Indeed, one of the weaknesses of recent attempts to reform the British civil service has been a tendency to belittle or misunderstand the essentially political role of the 'administrative class' of the service. R. G. S. Brown's views on this point were referred to earlier in the book, and it is appropriate here to quote a little more of his argument:[11]

The effect of the Fulton proposals is to 'managerialize' the civil service. In 'pre-Fulton' terms, this means giving priority to the kind of jobs previously done by top-grade members of the executive class.

In the short term, the main sacrifice to the new managerialism may be the work formerly done by junior members of the administrative class in their capacity of 'enlightened amateurs'. The weakness is likely to be felt at the top within a generation or two. For a period, the civil service will be very strong indeed, when its junior members are deploying their technical skills in administration and their superiors, trained in the traditional school, are experts at co-ordinating and relating all these special fields to one another and to the broad stream of political consciousness. When the now numerous group of senior civil servants in their late forties and early fifties retire, they may be replaced by a group who have been brought up in quite different traditions. It is difficult to predict the results.

It may also be suggested that another, and in many respects alternative, consequence of the new commitment to managerialism could be segregation of areas of managerial or administrative decision-making in such a way as to close them to political scrutiny.

However, while in general it may be more logical to avoid making a distinction between politics and administration in the traditional way, students of public administration often feel the necessity to try to prescribe rules to enable political roles to be distinguished from administrative roles. Perhaps the main reasons why they seek to do this are that they see a need to ensure that attention is paid to professional and technical advice (in the widest senses of those concepts), to ensure that the fluctuations of political fortune are balanced by administrative continuity, and to help to protect politicians from undue involvement in detail.

In Britain during the last few years considerable attention has been given to the need to distinguish between political and administrative roles in local government. This issue particularly arose because the growing scope and complexity of local government makes increasing demands upon councillors who only have their spare time to devote to local government. This reason for concern has been naturally linked in discussions with concern about the quality of local councillors.

An interesting aspect of this debate about roles is that there has developed in English local government during the last hundred years a tradition of heading departments by professionals, whose responsibilities are seen as going beyond the mere carrying out of policies. Some Acts of Parliament lay particular responsibilities upon specific officials, rather than upon their committees; and the law relating to local government responsibilities, in general, places a duty upon officials to give advice on powers and duties. Such is the importance of officials relative to councillors that one Manchester councillor told Heclo,[12] 'policy and administration have actually been reversed. The officer formulates the policy and the committee argues about the technicalities of administering it,' and another said, 'My committee can do little more than rubber stamp things. ... Even when an officer comes to us for instructions, the committee is baffled. We have to ask him, "Well, what did you have in mind?" We're more than guided; we're directed. A councillor is dependent on the official minutes and pretty much in the hands of the officer.'

But it is more than just a matter of amateurs finding it impossible to study policy matters fully, for local authority officials jealously defend their prerogatives in ways that central government officials would never dare to express openly. In the course of a Royal Institute of Public Administrative symposium, Keith-Lucas told with approval a story about a county education officer[13] 'who was in very basic disagreement with his committee chairman; on being told to sit down at a committee meeting the officer retorted: "I am the Education Officer of this county and I have a duty to advise and I shall"—and he did.' A town clerk, G. F. Darlow,[14] supported Keith-Lucas's view and argued that one of the dangers of political party dominance in local government was 'that a political group will arrive at a decision on an extremely important matter without having had any advice at all.' Darlow went on to speak of a situation in which this occurred:

> The leader of the party who were then in control of the council walked into my office and said 'Oh, Mr Town Clerk, we have decided to do so and so ;' I said 'Oh have you? Well I am going to play golf.' He looked at me somewhat flabbergasted and asked what I meant. I said 'Well, if you are going to decide important matters of that description without a word of advice, then you do not want me or any of my colleagues: you want an army of "yes-men"!'

On the face of it this seems to involve an attack on democracy, a doctrine that might be heard from a colonial administrator in a country not yet entrusted with complete freedom. The present writer's experience of local government, however, leads him to a very ambivalent position in the face of this point of view. When his party was in power he resented the curbs on policy development imposed by officials who refused to regard certain suggestions as feasible, but in opposition was grateful for the limitations imposed on the potential 'excesses' of the dominant party. When, as in British local government at present, the electoral successes of the parties depend not upon the popularity of policies pursued locally but upon the popularity of the government at Westminster, councillors can no more lay claim to be the sole arbiters of the popular will than can officials.

The Maud Committee on the management of local government was more concerned about the undue involvement of councillors in detailed day-to-day administration, so that, as suggested in the above quotations from Manchester councillors, they are unable to devote time to issues of policy. The Maud Committee point out that in some cases committees of elected members[15] 'undertake a large miscellany of lesser functions, such as interviewing for appointments (even at assistant caretaker level in some cases), authorizing repairs to buildings, granting leave to employees to attend courses, deciding on furnishings for welfare homes and allocating individual tenancies.'

It can be seen, therefore, that there are a number of sources of pressure towards drawing distinctions between politics and administration, and that these pressures do not stem solely from the status concerns of officials, or from reservations about democracy, but also from the recognition of practical reasons for trying to define roles. Yet the difficulties involved in doing this are considerable; in the following passage the Maud Committee succinctly spells out the main dilemma:[16]

Reference has been made to the widely held view that it is necessary to distinguish between policy and administration; this is a constantly recurring theme in the written evidence. The research report gives examples of the opinion that if only policy could be separated from administration, the former to be exercised by members and the latter by officers, this would be a solution to problems and a step towards reform. In their written evidence to us Mr. D. N. Chester ... and Professor Griffith and his colleagues, make the point that 'policy' and 'administration' cannot be defined. Mr. Chester adds that what may appear to be a matter of detail when viewed from a distance may prove to be a matter of great significance when looked at locally. We do not believe that it is possible to lay down what is policy and what is administrative detail; some issues stand out as important and can be regarded as 'policy'; other matters, seemingly trivial, may involve political or social reaction of such significance that deciding them becomes a matter of policy and members feel that they must reserve to themselves consideration and decision on them. A succession of detailed decisions may contribute, eventually, to the formulation of a policy. As the research report points out, policy making can arise out of particular problems when consideration of a new case leads to the determination of general guides to action which have a general application.

Of course, in the above quotation the word 'policy' is used rather than 'politics', suggesting a certain deference to the traditional view that there is some special area of decision-making which can be distinguished from administration. It could be suggested that deciding that certain decisions are 'policy' ones implies some logical reason for investing them with importance, while calling them 'political' decisions would imply that expediency was the only criterion for distinguishing them. In practice the Maud Committee clearly regarded policy decisions as matters for politicians. There are two other ways in which it has been suggested political and administrative decisions might be distinguished, which both recognise the relevance of 'political or social reaction' like Maud, but one of which still involves some attempt to provide an absolute basis for making the distinction while the other rests upon a relative conception of political roles.

Simon, in his analysis of decision-making, suggests that all decisions are based upon factual and value premises. He points out that even the most minor decisions may involve value premises, but that decisions differ in the extent to which they involve these. His solution to the problem of distinguishing politics and administration is to see values as the province of the politican and facts as the field of the administrator.

Simon therefore suggests[17] that procedural devices should be devised to enable the effective separation of the factual and the ethical elements in decisions. Then, on the basis of such a separation, the decisions which involve important ethical issues should be the responsibility of legislatures, while those which are largely noncontroversial and involve primarily factual issues should be taken by administrators. However, 'since the legislative body must of necessity make many factual judgments, it must have ready access to information and advice', while the administration must be very sensitive to value issues and be prepared to respond to 'community values'. Finally, the complete answerability of the administrator to the legislature must be retained in all cases.

The main difficulties with these prescriptions arise from Simon's rather simplistic rationality. Factual and value premises cannot be easily disentangled. Clearly, therefore, the 'procedural devices' suggested by Simon for their disentanglement will tend to require processes in which politicians have to delve deeply into nearly all issues in search of hidden ethical implications. Where disentanglement proves possible there is likely then to be a necessity for overriding value decisions to be made to judge what weight to give to the premises on both sides of the distinction. To be able to do this the politician will have to have a considerable measure of expertise, to be able to discover the value issues which are embedded in many factual problems normally falling within the field of full-time administrators or their professional advisers. Alternatively if he is unable or unwilling to engage in so elaborate an examination of the problems which face administration, the politician will have to rely upon the administrators to select for him the issues which they consider are of an ethical kind.

So once again, surely, Simon's discussion of this problem does lead the debate in a useful direction, for 'values' may perhaps be equated with those aspects of the decisions which involve 'social and political' reactions. Even Simon refers at one point to 'controversial issues' in recognition that perhaps the acid test as to whether policy-making or administration is, or should be, involved is the presence or absence of controversy.

The final approach to the politics/administration distinction rests upon an attempt to apply organisation theory to the problem. At the most general level organisation theory involves regarding the boundaries of the organisation as meriting particular study. At its boundaries the organisation is involved in a variety of interchanges with its environment which are important for its survival.[18] It is not necessary to accept the elaborate equilibrium theory posited by some writers to acknowledge that organisations need to manage their relations with their environments to ensure their own survival. Moreover, the organisations with which we are concerned, the organs of public administration, are by definition involved in making responses to the demands and perceived needs of at least some parts of their environments; a point that may be put more strongly with regard to those public organisations that operate in a political system that aspires to be democratic. Accordingly this approach to the politics/administration distinction tends to suggest that politics is concerned with the 'boundary' relations of the administrative organisation. Such an approach corresponds with the emphases upon controversy, and upon response to social and political reactions, which have already been suggested as the crucial underlying points in other definitions. Moreover, since many governmental agencies are concerned so much of the time with the formulation, elaboration and implementation of forever changing policies, this approach tends to make it clear why making the distinction between politics and administration poses so many problems; why some areas of decision-making are so often politicised by the public—or their representatives—when they refuse to leave the administrators in peace; why in British central government such a strong tradition of civil-servant involvement in policy-making has grown up; and why semi-autonomous administrative agencies in the United States become so involved in politics.

What is really being concluded here is that public administration is not just management with politics tagged on as a minor irritant on the periphery any more than running Woolworths is just management with salesmanship as a subsidiary activity. On the contrary it is the organisation's relations with its environment that are fundamental to its existence, and in the case of public administration—unless one is to make certain of the anti-democratic assumptions discussed earlier—this means that politics is of fundamental importance. In fact, inasmuch as organisation theory draws attention to the relationships between organisations and their environments, it tends to offer two alternatives; (1) accept the very much more elaborate equilibrium or general systems analysis provided by writers like Parsons and treat the processes by which Woolworths, the Roman Catholic Church and the Department of Education and Science maintain themselves as broadly similar, or (2) acknowledge the importance of organisation theory in directing attention to the boundaries of organisations, but then to reject the attempt to include within any single general theory the kinds of relationships between different kinds of organisations and their environments. It is, of course, the second alternative which is recommended in this book.

Parker and Subramaniam make a similar point with reference to general theory, with a somewhat different emphasis:[19]

The public administrator, by the very nature of Government's integrating function, must look at *all* the organizations in society and integrate different interests into something like a general interest. Different forms of policy may shift the stress given to different interests as well as affect the process of working out a general interest, but the need to *consider* every interest always remains a corollary to the need to integrate all sub-systems in society. The Government administrator must take account of the whole where the private administrator representing a single part can restrict his field of vision.

Most students of politics would regard considering 'every interest always' as very much the hallmark of the political role. One cannot treat the study of public administration as the study of government with the politics taken out, and therefore one cannot draw any clear lines between politics and administration. Passing Acts of Parliament is very clearly 'politics' and supervising Post Office counter clerks equally clearly 'administration', but there are many governmental activities which fall between these extremes and which cannot be clearly put into one category or the other.

Furthermore it is unwise to expect politicians to be uninterested in the supervision of counter clerks or administrators to be un-involved in passing Acts of Parliament. Accordingly, it is found that in public administration career administrators and elected or appointed political functionaries play a variety of roles in decision-making processes in ways that (1) it is difficult to generalise about, and (2) do not fit with any preconceived notions of the relations between politics and administration. This is not to say, however, that it is not possible to discern a number of broad patterns in the organisation of roles in this context.

The task of examining the ways in which the roles of politicians and administrators interact, and in particular the study of the causes and consequences of the patterns of interaction discerned, must be closely related to that most fundamental question in political sociology : Who governs? Any study of the way in which an administrative system operates must be concerned with the management of the boundary between the system and the society which it 'serves' or 'rules'.

In the introductory chapter of this book three ways of studying the relations between state bureaucracy and society were suggested: by examining the social characteristics and affiliations of civil servants, by relating the characteristics of bureaucratic systems to the culture or cultures of the society within which they are contained, and by examining decision-making in order to throw light upon the distribution of power and the roles played in relation to the power structure. This chapter and the next one are particularly concerned with the last and most difficult of these three methods.

The detailed examination of decision-making in central government is made very difficult by the complexity of such processes and by the desire of many actors to conceal the roles they play. In Britain, in particular, concealment of decision-making processes is achieved by a very comprehensive veil of official secrecy. The difficulties facing a researcher in Britain are well summarised by Brown:[20]

> Individual civil servants are generally found both revealing and helpful by an outside enquirer, so long as he is not obviously wasting their time, or trying to penetrate the mysteries of an essentially political decision. Kingdom tells the story of a young American who wanted to study departmental files in order to find out what part the Chancellor of the Exchequer, the Minister of Health and their respective advisers had played in the decision to impose National Health charges in 1951, 'Wherever he went in London he received literally nothing but courtesy'.

An attempt to explore the roles of civil servants in decisions of this kind would be even more firmly squashed. Accordingly there remain, as almost the only sources of information on decision-making processes of this kind, statements, memoirs and discussions by either ex-ministers or present or past civil servants.

In recent years civil servants have been increasingly ready to write or talk about their roles. But, while it is the case that contemporary civil servants are rarely so naive as to serve up for public consumption the bland statements about their roles provided in the past by writers like Dale[21] and Bridges,[22] the characteristic modern form of public statement from such a source tends to consist of a discussion about the way civil servants 'ought' to behave.[23] Naturally the public is not told specific stories about the way people actually behaved, though such things are often anonymously leaked to journalists. It can only be supposed that civil servants hope that people will, as a result of reading or hearing statements from civil servants on the ethics of their profession, come to believe that the 'servant' aspect of the relationship between administrators and the political system is being preserved inviolate.

Ex-ministers are equally committed, when they write about their relations with civil servants, to maintaining the traditional picture of the master/servant relationship. After all, to admit to anything else would seem to be an admission of personal weakness. A typical line on this issue is to suggest that there were some initial difficulties, after which the hero, our candid autobiographer, succeeded in getting the upper hand.

There is a further difficulty about using the accounts of ex-ministers to throw light on this issue, which is that, in an institutional situation in which the politician is constitutionally supposed to be dominant, people who influence him successfully will do so by winning his support without giving him the feeling he is losing his dominance.

The conclusion to be drawn from this discussion is that the scope for the study of decision-making processes in a single, very largely closed, decision-making system is inherently very limited. The student of administration can gain considerable insight by a shrewd use of officially published information and journalists' gossip, particularly if he is prepared to regard governmental decision-making not as the sort of high-powered process many textbooks make it out to be but as a process very similar to the kinds of decision-making he sees going on around him all the while. But it would be unwise to try to develop generalisations from these very limited insights into a process in which the variations imposed by individual personalities play such a major part.

American central government is rather more open than British government to study on these lines, but one difficulty there is that the extreme complexity of the formal system tends to fog the issues and make the development of a sociological analysis difficult. However, it is in the study of American local government that most progress has been made towards clarifying some of the issues in this area. Here the task is made easier not only by the fact that in many ways local government decision-making is more easily studied, partly because the issues involved tend to be simpler and partly because the decision process is more open, but particularly because there are, operating in a broadly similar social and institutional framework, a large number of authorities whose activities can be compared. Sociological research on local power structures has been able to proceed by the standard scientific process of testing the hypotheses derived from research in one area in other areas.

American sociological studies of local government have been primarily concerned with answering questions about the locus of power. In doing so they in no way address themselves to the question this chapter has been concerned with, the relationship between politics and administration. Nevertheless, because they are concerned with throwing light upon complex political processes, surrounding decisions that in the British institutional framework would be considered administrative ones, they are relevant to this subject and they do assist in the process of achieving insights into the complex questions of the control of administration.

Newton has been engaged on an examination of the American studies of community power and, in particular, the controversy that has raged around this subject in recent years, in order to assess its applicability to the study of local politics in Britain. In a report published in a Social Science Research Council Newsletter on a Paper Newton gave to a conference on research in local politics, Cornford comments:

> Dr Newton reviewed the present state of the American debate and drew attention to the contrasts in institutional structure between city politics in Britain and the U.S.A. There seemed little inclination to dissent from his conclusion that these differences made the American debate largely irrelevant to the problems of studying the policy process in Britain.

Newton's published work suggests that Cornford has in fact distorted his view on this topic; but the comment is quoted because it represents the common tendency in British political science to assume that little can be learnt from a study of the American debate on community power. In the next chapter, however, it will be shown that there is a great deal to be gained from examining the American community power controversy and from drawing on American studies in order to bring out the contrasts between decision-making processes in Britain and America. In particular it will throw light on the fact that while in America the point at issue is the significance of the role played by powerful groups of citizens, in Britain perhaps the most significant questions concern the extent of the dominance of the full-time administrators, a group of people who are rarely mentioned in the American studies.

11

Politics and Administration in Local Government in Britain and the United States

Newton suggests that[1]

> The most basic and profound difference between American and British city politics lies in the formal structure of local government. In American local politics, as in her national politics, power is fragmented and dispersed; by comparison, power in British national and local politics is concentrated. Seldom does one come across *the* local authority in the United States. Instead each town and city is divided into myriad authorities each with its own particular and special competence, each guarding its powers, such as they are, with the utmost care, and each competing with a variety of other authorities. It is an interesting coincidence that whereas England and Wales have about 1,400 separate local authorities, New York City alone has about 1,400.

The consequence of this is that, whereas in Britain it is highly probable that power will be in the hands of the formally designated power holders, in the United States power has to be sought by informal means. The fragmentation of formal power in American towns means that effective government depends upon the skilful creation of informal coalitions. As Banfield and Wilson put it,[2] 'bits and pieces of many governments are scattered around the local scene. To make any one of the governments work, it is necessary for someone to gather up the bits and bring them into a working relation with each other.'

In this chapter three particular styles of local government will be distinguished; these will be called 'ideological politics', 'bargaining politics' and 'administrative politics'. In general terms 'bargaining politics' can be seen as the characteristic system in American local government because of the dispersion of power, while the other two styles are most commonly found in England.

The basic difference between 'ideological politics' and 'administrative politics' lies in the fact that the former style will be found only when unified political parties provide specific programmes.

English local government operates in a context of low public interest, a context in which there is little public conflict about policies. Accordingly party political conflict is absent, or muted, too; and so decision-making is largely in the hands of professional administrators.

However, the differences between the three styles are not clear cut; in Britain local politicians often act as if their system was one in which bargaining is required, while in the United States many people try to transform their systems into administrative or ideological systems.

Furthermore, the classic debate that has developed in the United States about the nature of community power, between the 'elitists' and the 'pluralists', is in many ways a debate about whether or not the bargaining aspect of local political systems is really open or whether many systems are in fact ideologically dominated with opposition effectively suppressed.

In the ensuing pages the structure of power in local government on both sides of the Atlantic will be explored in terms of the three specific styles, because an analysis of the extent to which different systems correspond with these ideal types provides insight into different kinds of political and administrative roles.

The kind of local administrative system in which the dominant style is ideological politics will be one in which the traditional distinction between politics and administration is most easily made. The ideal-type case here is one in which political parties compete to win control of a local authority by submitting distinct programmes between which the electorate can choose. Once in power the members of the different parties will be identifiable as distinct groups, with leaders, whips and other officials. They will meet as 'groups' to discuss policies and strategies from time to time, and the conduct of individual members will be regulated by rules. In particular, rules will define the duties of members, and individuals who deviate by speaking publicly or voting against the group to any marked degree, or on any major issue, may be expelled. Such a party group, once in power, may be expected to distribute patronage on party lines, and will present to the administrators certain general objectives or policies with which they expect specific measures to be compatible.

It is important to point out that the presence of a situation in which candidates for election use party labels is not in itself evidence of the presence of an organised party system within a local authority, and that equally the presence of party blocs, and even in some cases the distribution of patronage along party lines, is not evidence that issues are necessarily decided on a party basis. This is very evident from studies of American politics, not only at local levels but even in Congress. Equally Bulpitt[3] showed, in a study of politics in local government, that marked variations occurred in the extent of party organisation between different areas in a group of authorities in north-west England with very similar political compositions.

Studies of Leeds[4] and Sheffield,[5] together with an account of organisation in the former London County Council by Margaret Cole,[6] illustrate examples of strong party organisation with marked policy differences between the main parties, while all the examples studied by Bulpitt show a less firm approach to issues, and in studies of Cheshire County Council[7] and Newcastle under Lyme Rural District Council[8] ideological divisions are hardly in evidence at all.

One traditional feature of English local government is the use of a committee system in which all the major parties on a council have members on each committee. A feature of the development of ideological politics in local government has been the gradual evolution of a one-party cabinet system operating in a way that cuts across the committee system. Wiseman describes the way in which the Labour group on Leeds City Council[9] did this by operating an executive committee which devoted a considerable amount of time to policy-making prior to the cycle of official committee meetings. In the example described by Wiseman the party executive met without officials in attendance to give advice. More recently some authorities have set up policy committees served by officers on a one-party basis. For example, in the London Borough of Ealing the Conservatives set up, on gaining control of the council, a 'coordinating committee' containing only members of their own group. The Maud Committee on the Management of Local Government[10] recommended the setting up of 'management boards' but took the view that minority parties should be represented on them. It seems contradictory to recommend, as they did, changes in the management of local government in the direction of a form of cabinet government, while refusing to acknowledge the role of parties in providing the potential for a strong and unified executive.

In British local government the Labour party has played an important part in the evolution of party divisions of an ideological kind. Dilys Hill summarises this development as follows:[11]

Party politics have existed on local councils for a considerable time. From the late nineteenth century onwards there have been opposing views on local councils, though the labels have not always been those of the national parties. In the past, party divisions centred on who should hold power. With the rise of the Labour party at the beginning of this century, controversy has centred on what policies should be followed.

The aim of the Labour party was to gain power in order to change local affairs; they had programmes which they wanted to put into practice. After 1918, and particularly after 1945, the Labour party organized their council groups on formal lines. Other groups on the council coalesced into anti-Socialist opposition. After 1945 Conservative councillors were encouraged to act as organized groups, to meet Labour political activity with disciplined opposition, and to fight local elections under the Conservative label.

However, while it is generally true that the Labour party has played a major part in bringing ideological conflict into local government in Britain, this phenomenon is often interpreted in a misleading way. First, it must be pointed out that when one party is seeking to introduce changes in conformity with its own ideological position, other parties which seek to resist those changes are behaving in no less an ideological way. A 'stand pat' position is just as much an ideological position as one involving the advocacy of change. Second, when a particular political group seeks to introduce ideological conflict into a governmental authority which has hitherto operated in a nonpolitical way, it may be that the consensus that has been broken had existed because certain points of view had been un-articulated or even suppressed. The Maud Committee, true to their 'liberal' position of going half-way to meet what they saw as unpleasant necessity, concluded,[12] 'Party politics are to be deplored when they produce, as they sometimes do, irrelevant and sterile debate or stifle discussion, and when they dictate the approach towards issues which are manifestly non-political.' But subjects are often seen as manifestly non-political in situations in which ruling groups do not want particular issues raised. As was suggested in the previous chapter it cannot be predetermined whether issues are political or not. If people are concerned about an issue and succeed in getting politicians to share their concern then that issue becomes political.

It will be suggested later that ideological politics rarely appears in local government in the United States because the effective expression of the points of view of people who require innovatory policies is largely suppressed, but there is one form in which it sometimes occurs. In some, primarily upper-middle-class, areas, 'reform' movements grow up from time to time which aim at change by cutting across party lines to achieve conditions which will simplify the institutional structure and undermine the corruption and graft which are associated with the party machines.[13] Such movements are generally comparatively short-lived because they have to take as their starting points reform of the machinery of government in order to get anything done. This inevitable focus upon means rather than ends produces some unintended consequences. It either involves taking responsibilities out of the hands of politicians and putting them into the hands of professional administrators, such as city managers, or introducing devices which involve the 'people' more fully in decision-making by more elections and the introduction of referenda, or, of course, a combination of the two. The consequences of such reforms are that administrators find that they have to join in the bargaining process in order to get anything done, or even in many cases in order to survive, while new electoral devices also tend to have the effect of further complicating rather than simplifying the decision-making processes.

A situation in which a local authority is run by a dominant political group with fairly definite ideas about policy tends to make the relationship between politicians and administrators more clear cut. In an interesting comment on the relationship Darlow[14] has suggested two particular advantages of a party system for administrative officers, 'that the officer can find out what the policy is to be' instead of being faced by councillors who have vague ideas about what they want done but are unable to give a consistent direction to policy, and that 'the officer knows where the individual member stands'.

In the United States, a wide range of types of local government structures is found, in some of which as in Britain executive and legislative functions are not separated, while others provide for a strong separate executive in the form of a mayor, and yet others provide a strong permanent official as executive—the 'city manager'. It is the strong mayor form that tends to be the most conducive to a form of ideological politics. As made clear earlier there are strong pressures against the development of coherent party government so that an ideological lead is most likely to come when, as in the case of New Haven in Dahl's study,[15] power is relatively centralised in the hands of a popularly elected mayor.

Such a situation is, however, rare, as Banfield and Wilson[16] suggest, since generally the mayor is by no means the only elected official in the city. However the American system of electing key executive officials and providing them with salaries means that they are put in a very much stronger position than English councillors or aldermen to influence administrative behaviour. While in England the development of ideological politics is limited by the relative weakness of the elected representative in relation to the permanent administrator, in the United States the limitation stems from the power of other elected officials rather than from the power of administrators.

In the previous chapter it was suggested that the concept of democracy which has become accepted in British local government is very much more limited than that which prevails in central government. Administrators in local government are professionals with a strong sense of their right to expect a measure of professional autonomy. Their positions are further recognised by Acts of Parliament and the courts, so that some of their duties are prescribed by law; some of them (notably medical officers of health) cannot be appointed or dismissed without ministry approval, and some of them can be surcharged or prosecuted for negligence or misconduct. In other words their positions are something more than just 'servants' of the council. Accordingly, local government officials are more significantly threatened by ideological politics than are civil servants. They are not anonymous and may, prior to the emergence of a political party committed to its own programme, have been closely identified with specific policies. To them above all, the remarks of Morstein Marx about 'the bureaucracy between millstones' particularly applies:[17]

The dilemma of the career man lies here in the paradox of being both in and out of politics. On the one hand, he is placed, whether he likes it or not, in the cloud of dust swirled up in the conflict of party aims and economic interests. On the other hand, because he is not personally burdened with political responsibility and therefore has no device for clearing his general ledger, he cannot hope for reinforcement by the electorate. Whether he conducts himself truly as servant of the state when defending before his political superior a particular position on grounds of principle or whether in doing so he makes himself guilty of 'lack of co-operation' or even concealed sabotage, he has no recourse to the general public.

Ideological politics puts great strains upon administrators. The stability of a political system where ideological conflict is significant depends very heavily upon the ability of highly trained public servants to devote themselves wholeheartedly to the service of a particular party without at the same time compromising themselves so that they are unacceptable if an opposition party comes to power. Ideological politics requires stable administration, paradoxically it runs the risk of undermining itself if it puts the administrator under undue pressure; in Morstein Marx's words,[18]

... civil service status is a constitutional necessity under conditions of popular rule. Popular rule implies opportunity for popular choice, for peaceable change in the lawful exercise of power. The principle of alteration in political control would be put in jeopardy if the government of the day was allowed to make heavy partisan replacements in the civil service.

If politicians do not preserve a high measure of job security for full-time administrators they will find that they will receive either too much or too little loyalty. By 'too much loyalty' what is meant is that administrators will resort to corrupt practices to ensure that their masters remain in power. Less melodramatically, 'too little loyalty' means that administrators will either play very negative roles which will not really help advance policy goals or will seek to protect themselves by exploiting their offices for private gain or by leaving before their situations become dangerous.

Most of these final comments on ideological politics do not apply in Britain, but they do apply in some measure to those situations in the United States in which administrators become involved in the rare ideological conflicts, and they often apply to less secure political systems in developing countries. However, it is not unknown for local government officers to become embroiled in political conflicts in Britain in ways that are damaging for their own careers and embarrassing for their political allies.

The concept of 'bargaining politics' can be applied to situations, characteristic of the government of most large American cities, in which there is what Banfield has described as 'formal decentralisation of power'. The general nature of this type of situation is well illustrated by Banfield's description of government in Chicago:[19]

The Chicago area from *a purely formal standpoint* can hardly be said to have a government at all. There are hundreds, perhaps thousands of bodies each of which has a measure of legal authority and none of which has enough of it to carry out a course of action which other bodies oppose. Altogether, these many bodies are like a great governing committee each member of which has, in matters affecting it, an absolute veto. Moreover, the 'committee' is (from a formal standpoint) one in which the members can have no communication with each other. Each legally separate body acts (from a formal standpoint) independently and without knowledge of the others. This being the case, it is of course extremely easy (from a formal standpoint) for any opponent to forestall any action. An opponent has only to find, among the countless independent bodies whose consent is required, one which can be induced to withhold consent in order to obstruct action. From a formal standpoint, virtually nothing can be done if anyone opposes – and, of course, everything is always opposed by someone – and therefore every opponent's terms must always be met if there is to be action. Every outcome must therefore be an elaborate compromise if not a stalemate.

The consequence of this kind of situation is that the only way to achieve effective action is to overcome this formal decentralisation by a degree of informal centralisation. Such a goal can only be achieved by a very extensive bargaining process, unless there are exceptional factors operating to encourage a large number of holders of power to act in concert. It is much more probable that such collective action as is achieved will come about as a result of deals and reciprocal commitments rather than as a consequence of shared ideals.

The existence of a loosely coordinated party system in the Chicago area contributes to the achievement of informal coordination there, according to Banfield. But by English standards the Democratic Party in Chicago is a very loose coalition held together by the skill of the Party 'boss', Mayor Daley. Furthermore, Daley's

H

success stems from the fact that he uses his power to maintain the strength of the machine and not in the service of any 'ideals'. Faced by the need to make controversial decisions Banfield shows that Daley will avoid committing himself until he is fairly sure that there is a broad basis of support for the point of view he will endorse. Such a situation is clearly not conducive to the development of ideological politics, and Meyerson and Banfield's[20] study of federally supported housing programmes in Chicago suggests that innovatory plans are unlikely to get far in such a context.

In the light of this it is surprising that Banfield, and other students of American city politics, such as Dahl, who have come to similar conclusions, present the pluralist political structure they perceive as essentially open and democratic. In order to explain this paradox it is necessary to examine the debate about the nature of community power, in which Dahl and Banfield have been amongst the leading protagonists of the pluralist point of view.

The point of view which the pluralists were concerned to attack is sometimes described as the 'elitist' approach to the study of power. The leading exponent of this point of view is Floyd Hunter who studied the power structure of a Southern city in the United States[21] by a method which can be crudely described as involving asking a selected group of people, whom Hunter believed to be well informed about community affairs: Who runs this community? The conclusion Hunter drew from his study was that the community was dominated by an economic elite, whose control techniques are summarised as follows by Lane:[22]

The techniques whereby these dominant families control the political life of the community are intricate and varied. By their leverage over the economic institutions of the community, they can exercise sanctions over many of the civic leaders and professional people in town; they can intimidate workers through the control over jobs; they control the credit institutions of the community and can influence such matters as admission to a hospital or a mortgage on a house; they generally control the local press and radio; they subsidize the party (or parties) of their choice and hence influence their selection of candidates....

The political organizations are so completely dominated by the power interests (i.e. business elite) ... that there is little hope of adequate expression being fostered by them at this time. They control admission to the prestige associations and clubs; they set the patterns of approved behaviour and opinion.... Hunter speaks of the great 'silence found in the mass of citizenry of Regional City'.

The position taken by the elitists has been fairly easy to attack, particularly on account of the rather dubious methodology involved in the 'reputational' technique. In his *International Encyclopaedia of the Social Sciences* article on 'The Study of Community Power', Polsby summarises the argument on this point as follows:[23]

Perhaps the most fundamental objection has been that the identification of presumed 'influentials' is a very crude method of sampling the underlying shape of decision-making processes. Instead of focusing on how valued outcomes are distributed by those who actually distribute them in specific instances, it focuses on those who some people *say* distribute them under hypothetical circumstances.

Polsby goes on to conclude,[24]

The central methodological issue is thus one of appropriateness. Are respondents being asked questions to which they can give answers capable of unambiguous interpretation? Are respondents able to give the best available testimony on the questions they are asked? Are they able to give competent testimony? Are their responses, if correctly interpreted, capable of answering underlying questions about community decision-making processes?

It is clear, then, that the close association between the elitist theory and the reputational approach to research has made it fairly easy for the pluralists to attack this point of view. The two most telling points against the elitists are that their approach involves asking the question, Who runs this community? and not Does anyone run this community? and that they equate reputed power with actual power. The pluralists go on, therefore, to argue that the right way to study community power is to study decision-making on particular issues. In doing this they seek to find out who the protagonists are on specific issues, and whose will prevails.

There have now been a large number of studies using this 'issue-outcome' method, all of which tend to support the pluralist point of view. Perhaps the classic study in this tradition is Dahl's[25] study of New Haven, Connecticut. As a result of his study and his examination of the elitist case Dahl takes up a position which does not involve any attempt to argue that the United States, or any of its local communities, is a perfect democracy. Nevertheless he does argue that American society is pluralist, that it contains a wide variety of organised groups which compete for political power and thereby ensure that all points of view are heard. Few people play an active part in politics, but the voting powers of the mass of the people are sufficient to ensure that their interests are not disregarded. Dahl does not argue that political resources are equal but that 'the inequalities are not cumulative.'[26]

To support this point of view with specific reference to New Haven, Dahl points out that[27] 'for more than a century, indeed, New Haven's political system has been characterized by well-nigh universal suffrage, a moderately high participation in elections, a highly competitive two-party system, opportunity to criticize the conduct and policies of officials, freedom to seek support for one's views ... and surprisingly frequent alternations in office from one party to the other as electoral majorities have shifted.' Dahl also shows in the course of his study of specific issues in New Haven government a wide range of people competing to influence issue outcomes.

Dahl therefore defends the pluralist position outlined in Chapter 1 (see pages 10–11) with specific reference to community power. Newton summarises Dahl's position on this issue as follows:[28]

Although each separate group in the pluralistic system may be oligarchical, pluralistic democracy is preserved because each oligarchy has to compete with others. The end result is not a perfect democracy in operation but it is a system which eliminates the worst abuses of injustice and forces compromise solutions to political problems which give some satisfaction to all the interested groups.

Clearly the pluralists have been able to push over the rather weakly based elitist case and have, at least as far as Dahl is concerned, put a rather more sophisticated edifice in its place. However, as is so often the case when a group of people set out to undermine someone else's arguments, the pluralists' case is not so firmly founded as it appears. As Newton says of the pluralist studies[29] 'they are demolition jobs which are mainly concerned to prove the elitists wrong but much less concerned, and also less well equipped, to prove the pluralists right.'

Newton mainly rests his case on the weaknesses in Dahl's argument about the relationship between elites and non-elites. He argues[30] that some sections of society are not organized into pluralist groups, that some political inequalities are cumulative, that some political groups are considerably weaker than others, that some groups are denied access to the decision-making process and to the political stratum, that those with little or no direct influence may also have no indirect influence, and that a set of competing oligarchies does not make a pluralist system. The end result is a political system that does not distribute power at all equally and consequently a system that heavily favours some groups or sections of society against others.

An important part of Newton's argument rests upon the fact that voting is not necessarily the satisfactory source of indirect influence that Dahl presumes it to be.[31] Voters are generally forced to choose between a limited range of package deals, and elections are not a satisfactory means of protecting the interests of underprivileged minorities.

Bachrach and Baratz[32] attack these same weaknesses in 'pluralist' theory, but in a rather different way. They suggest that the 'pluralist' concern to study issues confines attention to those matters which are allowed to become the subject of public controversy. In a study of Baltimore they attempt to test pluralist theory by subjecting 'non-decisions' to attention too. They define a non-decision as[33] 'a decision that results in suppression or thwarting of a latent or manifest challenge to the values and interests of the decision-makers.' Non-decisions, they suggest, result from 'mobilisation of bias' within a community,[34] 'a set of predominant values, beliefs, rituals, and institutional procedures ("rules of the game") that operate systematically and consistently to the benefit of certain persons and groups at the expense of others. Those who benefit are placed in a preferred position to defend and promote their vested interests.'

The underlying aspect of both Bachrach and Baratz's argument and Newton's argument is that pluralist structures in which formal power is dispersed so that decision-making entails bargaining are inherently biased in favour of the status quo. Underprivileged groups need positive government in order to further their interests; the acquisition of the power to veto actions is no use to them. Privileged groups, on the other hand, are protected by a system which makes innovation very hard to attain.

To take up this kind of position against the pluralists does not entail returning to the crude conspiratorial characterisation of the elite involved in Hunter's work. To say that there is, in a particular community structure, mobilisation of bias in favour of a particular class of people does not involve any implication that this class operates in any unified manner in the protection of their own interests.

However, Banfield laid great stress upon the importance of informal centralisation as a means of overcoming the pluralistic dispersion of power. Where such centralisation is achieved there are surely grounds for suspicion that some kind of elite unification is occurring. So finally, while there is no intention here to subscribe to the reputational method of studying community power, it must not be regarded as beyond the bounds of possibility that in some cases, persons, who are not themselves formal power holders, may conspire covertly to influence local decision-making. As was suggested in Chapter 6, the powerful may often find it expedient to conceal their influence.

In the main the answer to the question: Is bargaining politics found in English local government? is, No. Formal power is very largely distributed in such a way that there are very few competing jurisdictions. Local government is subject to central government control so that there is a higher authority which keeps the structure tidy and may intervene to resolve the rare difficulties of this kind. Where local government is found to have a two- or three-tier structure, the responsibilities of upper and lower tier authorities are clearly distinguished. Obviously there are possibilities for conflict, between local authorities and Whitehall ministries, between districts and counties, and between local authorities and other public agencies (as for example, in the health service) but such conflict essentially takes the form of what will be called administrative politics rather than bargaining politics, in that such conflict is largely kept private and appeals are rarely made to the general public for support in such cases. This fact must be attributed partly to an absence of constitutional devices which would enable interorganisational differences to be fought out in public by means of elections and referenda, but perhaps more significantly to an elitist approach to government, itself of course a main cause of the absence of means of consulting the public, which makes it largely illegitimate to seek to enlist public intervention in resolving such conflicts.

However, in situations of conflict between authorities the protagonists will often act as if they are playing bargaining politics by justifying themselves by reference to their mandates, their views of what 'their' people want, and so on. The 'representative' bodies, the local authorities, are prone to attack the 'nonrepresentative' bodies, such as the Regional Hospital Boards, as organisations that act without reference to public opinion, but in practice the extent to which either kind of body can really presume to know what the public wants is very limited.

There is another sense in which people in local government in Britain tend to exaggerate the extent to which there is a bargaining element in the political system; this is in the attention that is paid to pressure groups.[35] There is a tendency for the 'rule of anticipated reactions' to operate[36] in which it is assumed that pressure groups will have electoral influence when in practice local elections are normally decided by the popularity of the political parties at the national level, and local controversies rarely have much impact.

Apart from the situation in which pressure groups are effective because of anticipated reactions there are two other ways in which they may introduce a bargaining element into decision-making in British local government. One of these is through party politics, the other is more significant where ideological politics is largely absent.

Newton has drawn attention to the way in which the open campaigns of pressure groups in the United States are replaced in Britain by the more covert phenomenon of interest aggregation by the political parties. He argues,[37] 'Local party organizations in Britain may have important interest aggregation functions in so far as established groups in the community tend to work through their connections with the party groups on their council rather than mount an independent pressure group campaign of their own.'

Inasmuch as bargaining with pressure groups occurs in this way it involves covert compromises within political parties rather than a public competition for influence. The second point made above about pressure-group activity in the absence of ideological politics will be discussed more fully when administrative politics is examined. The general point here is that in the absence of politically determined programmes, local representatives will obviously be ready prey to any interest group which can force its attention upon them. The typical situation at the moment is one in which influence of this kind is fairly haphazard, and the title 'bargaining politics' does not really apply.

If bargaining politics does not exist in anything approaching its American form in the United Kingdom it is appropriate to ask whether the 'community power debate' has any relevance for the British situation. This is a question to which Newton has addressed himself. He has shown that the only attempts to apply the reputational method to the study of a British town produced very misleading results.[38] The people picked out by this method were all people who 'hold the top positions in its [Bristol's] largest and most prestigious organizations,' and, Newton argues, 'it is difficult to believe that any of them have either the time or the inclination to devote much energy to local politics,' a conclusion born out by Clements'[39] study of the lack of interest shown by leading businessmen in local politics in Bristol.

The only other attempt to study community power in a way comparable to the American studies in a British city is Green's study of Bath.[40] Green rejected the reputational method as unworkable, and went on to show that the use of the issue-outcome method pointed directly to the formal power holders, the local-authority members.

Green distinguished between 'prescribed' or formal power and 'structural', or what may be regarded as actual power. Using this distinction Newton argues,[41]

It can never be assumed that the prescribed influentials of a city are those who wield structural power, for it is always possible that there are hidden powers behind the elected and appointed officials. Herein lies the basic problem of community power studies. . . . Although the assumption that formal office holders also wield structural power is a dangerous one to make for American city politics it was a proposition that was tested and found valid for Georgian City [Bath]. . . .

In other words, no one has yet produced a study of an English town establishing the existence of structural power holders who are not prescribed power holders, but this should not be regarded as impossible. What can be said is that the nature of the formal structure makes it very much less likely that such a situation will be found. Furthermore it is likely that researchers would find it very difficult to establish the existence of such a situation in Britain because it would be unlikely to take the open form characteristic of American bargaining politics but would be in the form of covert elite influence of the kind which, it will be suggested later, is most likely to emerge in administrative politics.

In systems of bargaining politics, administrators are forced to choose to play one of two roles: (1) to be purely passive implementers of policy, as in classical theory, or (2) to involve themselves deliberately in the political process.

It is important to recognise that bargaining politics tends to keep down the scale of effective administrative action unless, as in the rare case, someone succeeds in building an effective political coalition. Consequently the administrator is likely to be faced with a minimum of situations in which he can take action, and by grave difficulties in maintaining consistent policies. Traditionally, under bargaining politics in the United States, administrators were of little importance and many of the jobs that could be called administrative were allocated under the spoils system. Rising concern about the inability of local government to tackle the problems of the American cities has led to endeavours to professionalise local public administration. However, such reforms have tended to be abortive in the absence of other reforms to centralise authority. In practice, as suggested above, reforms to professionalise city government have often, paradoxically, been accompanied by measures to further decentralise authority. The new professionals in American city government have developed ideologies of their own which lead them to become significant advocates of planning, public housing and so on. Indeed these professions have naturally tended to attract individuals committed to such ideologies in the first place. Faced with the problem of putting such ideologies into practice in cities dominated by bargaining politics, it is not surprising that administrative professionals have learnt that they must operate within the political system or remain totally ineffective.[42]

The professional's strength particularly lies in his ability to invest his views in a certain scientific or quasi-scientific rationality, to draw upon 'facts' to support his viewpoint. The politician is vulnerable to his influence in this way because he likes to clothe his proposals, whatever their real basis, in the mantle of rationality; he is susceptible to attack if it can be suggested that his commitments make no sense to the experts. Hence the professional possesses one key weapon for use in bargaining politics. However, this weapon can be blunted by the production of experts with contrary views, as there is usually scope for more than one 'expert' viewpoint. Moreover, while the expert may be in a strong position when arguing for doing *A* rather than doing *B*, he may find it much more difficult to make a case for doing *A* rather than doing nothing—it is easier on the whole to make a case for doing nothing than for doing something that may have unknown consequences. Meyerson and Banfield's study of public housing projects in Chicago is largely an account not of 'wrong' decisions taken on account of politics but of no decisions being taken because of opposition.

Hence, in the United States, professional administrators often go much further into the bargaining process than merely trying to argue the case for action; they seek to build for themselves support groups, to find allies amongst the politicians and the pressure groups who can argue their case for them. Sometimes they are even involved in the formation of special groups to agitate and drum up support for specific projects. They will provide facts and figures to brief these political allies,[43] but will normally, of course, avoid public identification with pressure groups. It was to describe this kind of phenomenon that Selznick coined the expression 'administrative constituency'.[44]

Selznick argues that the relationship between an administrative organisation and its constituency becomes a reciprocal one; thus, while in some cases administrators may be able to find support groups within the society who back them out of purely idealistic motives, it is likely that often the process of establishing support will involve administrators in making concessions to, or developing commitments to, their allies. In this way administrators in situations of bargaining politics become totally enmeshed in the political process.

In bargaining politics, administrators are protected by the consensual nature of the process from the dangers which Morstein Marx suggested exist in ideological politics. They can be open about their commitments, but what they cannot expect if they have commitments is to be able to realise their goals. American history is littered with examples of situations in which committed administrators have been frustrated by the political process. Some of these examples were discussed in Chapter 5.

Merton's essay on the 'Role of the Intellectual in Public Bureaucracy' deals with the frustrations which the committed individual experiences in the public service. If he does not simply 'get out' he finds himself transformed:[45]

There is another way in which the orientation of intellectuals entering a bureaucracy tends to change, and this derives from the pressure for action. They tend to become, as the loose phrase has it, 'less theoretical and more practical'. To what does this refer? The closer to the actual locus of decision, the more necessary it is for broad policy to be translated into programs of action and the larger the number of considerations which must be taken into account, over and above the original formulation of policy. This 'taking into account' of additional variables generally means a partial change of the original policy; it means, 'compromise with the realities of the case'. Thus, the closer to the point of actual decision that the intellectual is located, the more he experiences a pressure to temper the wind to the shorn lamb, that is, to fit his original abstract formulations to the exigencies of the situation. This pressure, operating over a period of time, shapes the general perspectives of the bureaucratic intellectual; he comes increasingly to think in technical and instrumental terms of ways of implementing policies *within a given situation.*

The concept of administrative politics is used to describe the last of the three styles of local government because, although it will be suggested that administrators dominate the decision-making system, it will also be argued that to do this they will operate politically. In a political system which aspires to be democratic, if administrators are essentially in control, they will (1) be involved in relationships with people outside their own organisations with whom they will have to bargain, negotiate or consult, in a manner that has traditionally been regarded as 'political', and (2) be forced from time to time to legitimate their own actions by the use of what are regarded as 'democratic' devices.

In these situations of administrator dominance, politicians may have two roles. They may be treated as representatives of the public, or of particular interest groups within the general public, in which case administrators will be concerned to take their views into account and generally sell policies to them, or some of them may be, in effect, co-opted into the ranks of the administrators and be involved, as individuals and not primarily as representatives, in the general decision-making processes. J. M. Lee, in his study of Cheshire County Council, sets out the characteristics of a system of this kind: [46]

It is ... misleading to think of the County Council primarily as a body of elected representatives who make decisions of policy and then order officials to execute them. Although such a view constitutes the theory, the reality is vastly different. It is better to regard the system of county government as a body of professional people placed together in a large office at County Hall, who can call upon the services of representatives from all places throughout the area which they administer. Some of these representatives by sheer ability and drive make themselves indispensable to the successful working of the machine; others merely represent points of view which come into conflict with it. County Hall is therefore a meeting place for a community of persons in public life, formed partly of local government officers, who enjoy the privileges of various professional associations, and partly of elected representatives whose main job, either through a party organization or independently, is to keep in touch with all the interests which are affected.

It is therefore suggested that English local government tends to operate this way in the absence of strong ideological politics; and even where ideological politics does exist a very high proportion of the kind of decision-making which the outsider would consider policy-making is in the hands of the officials. Ironically, one of the consequences of the imbalance of power between the professional administrator and the spare-time councillor in Britain is that while key policy-making is too complex for the politician to handle he can easily cope with some of the routine administrative decision-making. Hence in English local government, councillors do deal with a host of trivial matters, and argue about them and really take the decisions on them. In the previous chapter evidence was quoted on this point from the Maud Committee report and from Heclo's study of Manchester councillors. Heclo's conclusions on this issue are interesting:[47]

... much of the debate on the councillors' executive (administrative) versus legislative (deliberative) duties is beside the point. The Maud Committee for example advocates increasing the local council's policy responsibilities, although most councillors report that there is not enough time for all their duties at present. It can be argued that releasing councillors from details in favour of broad policy debates will lighten the demands of council work, but as we have seen it is at least as plausible to argue that details are attended to because of the heavy demands involved in comprehending the issues at stake. The demands remain heavy in any case, and the likelihood is that increased policy duties will necessarily widen the realm of partisan conflict.

Thus Heclo acknowledges that administrative changes do not necessarily solve the problem which faced the Maud Committee, and he seems to subscribe to the point of view argued earlier in this chapter that it is primarily that phenomenon to which the Maud Committee is so ambivalent, partisan conflict, which directs councillors' attention to policies. Take away the detailed matters to which many councillors pay attention and those who are not engaged in furthering policies through ideologically motivated groups will feel really impotent.

Buxton, on the other hand, in a recent book,[48] goes very much further than this and argues that English local government fails to operate as a system involving representative democracy and that councillor intervention in policy-making involves no more than a very erratic and inconsistent form of popular democracy. He says,[49] 'Representative democracy demands that policy decisions should be taken by elected representatives, subject to control through the ballot box if the representatives decide differently from what the majority of the people want. Popular democracy demands that citizens should be able to know what the government is doing and have access to that government in particular cases.'

Buxton argues that the present system, and the reformed system proposed by the Maud Commission,[50] fails to resolve the tension between these two kinds of democracy. Representative democracy does not exist since councillors cannot cope with the critical policy issues because of a lack of time and technical expertise, and also because of the failure of the electoral process to operate as a check upon policy-making. Popular democracy does not exist because councillors are committed to being policy-makers and are not effective grass-roots representatives. Buxton therefore sees administrative politics as the rule in Britain, with professionals dominant and councillors but minor participants, as weak and inadequate representatives of *some* public interests. This view seems to suggest that the ideological politics that others have perceived in Britain is an illusion. It is certainly the case, as has already been argued (see page 212), that there is often no real political conflict within local authorities which are ostensibly dominated by political parties.[51] There is also no disputing Buxton's view that[52] 'The overwhelming majority of electors treat local elections merely as an extension of the political contest at national level, and vote for their councillors not on the record of the individual candidates, or even of the city administration, but rather according to their current view of the performance of the national government on purely national issues.' It is also conceded that Buxton successfully shows why local government fails to get to grips with the real policy issues involved in a complex matter like urban redevelopment. However, it is still the case that in some authorities, and in respect of some issues,[53] councillors do succeed in achieving some measure of control over policies when a majority are united by ideological commitment. This is not to say that this is necessarily democratic government, but that it does involve a style of government different in kind from that which obtains when administrators are almost entirely dominant.

Earlier in this book attention has been given to relationships within bureaucratic organisations and it has been suggested that forms of internal politics are likely to develop within all kinds of organisations. Local authorities are organised in such a way that internal politics are likely to be rife and it may therefore be suggested that councillors may become involved in these internal battles as allies of administrators. It has been pointed out already that local government in England is run by means of a committee system and that traditionally, and in the absence of strong party control, this system is fairly decentralised. Furthermore, many local authorities have very decentralised departmental systems linked in various ways more or less closely with their committee systems. Traditionally, too, the heads of the various departments within a local authority operate as equals.[54] Contemporary developments are leading towards greater centralisation with power concentrated in the hands of town clerks or city managers, but there are a number of factors operating to resist this centralisation. These include tradition, the special legal responsibilities of certain officers, the professional commitments of officers, and the special power that expertise provides. Obviously this decentralisation of administrative responsibilities creates tension between departments and a need for political action to override the difficulties so created. Officers find that their committees can be used as allies, and that formal conflicts between committees can provide a vehicle for interdepartmental conflicts—officers can let councillors fight their battles for them. Inter-committee conflicts are a common feature of councils where centralisation by means of strong political party discipline is absent.

A scrutiny of American studies reveals no evidence of a similar pattern of administrative politics there, indeed very little attention has been paid to the roles of professional administrators in that country. Presumably the city manager movement represents an attempt to arrive at a similar form of control in the United States.

In Britain, administrative politics may prevail despite the existence of party groups which are active at election time, either where local politics has remained largely low-key so that a tradition of independent or nonpolitical government has been maintained, or in some cases where one-party rule has been established.

In a study of local education policies in West Ham, Peschek provides a very good example of a situation in which one-party domination of an authority is associated with a lack of innovation and a situation in which policy is controlled by administrators:[55]

The political scene, too, has suffered from the effects of a rigid social structure. Labour has now ruled West Ham for forty-eight years, surely one of the longest unbroken periods of political domination in any county borough. For most of that time there has never been an effective opposition in the sense of one that stood any reasonable chance of displacing Labour at the polls.... And so one-party rule, and the lack of professional and middle-class leavening, has tended to smooth the paths of municipal government and to inhibit the growth of any great sophistication in local party politics. A characteristic feature of much political life at the local level is the absence of clearly defined local politics.

In this case, administrator domination is associated with stagnation in local politics. It is not intended to imply that administrator domination is necessarily associated with an absence of new policy initiatives. On the contrary it could be the case elsewhere that one-party government has provided the stability necessary for administrators to take bold policy initiatives under the protection of a stagnant political situation.

The situation in which party representatives generally refrain from acting in a unified way must be seen as a legacy of 'independence' in local politics. This legacy derives from an era of dominance in local government by the most powerful landowners or businessmen, an era which ended early in this century in most of the large urban areas[56] but which has not altogether ended in some country areas. In between lie those areas, in particular suburban, urban and rural districts, which lack any real sense of identity and recruit a diverse collection of people onto their councils, some with party labels and some without, some with axes to grind for the part of the district which elected them and some with a sense of noblesse oblige. Bealey and his associates describe one such district council in the following terms:[57]

... party politics is a phenomenon that scarcely troubles the Rural District Council. A rare issue, such as whether or not the sole shop on a council estate should belong to Silverdale Co-operative Society, might evoke a party response. Otherwise the Council gives the impression to the observer of discussing local issues with warmth, enjoyment and informality.

In this particular council, chairmanships are rotated annually so no centres of power develop at all. Accordingly:[58] 'In the absence of party groups and strong, long-serving committee chairmen, much of the co-ordination of present policy and even thinking about future policy has passed into the hands of the rural district officials.'

It has been suggested earlier that in this kind of situation councillors are as much the representatives of sectional groups as a cohesive ruling element on the council. It is obviously convenient to the policy-making administrator to have significant representatives of pressure groups amongst the councillors with whom he has to deal. In some cases, notably education, the committee includes representatives of local interests as well as councillors, thereby providing a further addition to the communication process. It is in the field of education administration that a particularly strong commitment to consultation of interest groups may be found, and the study by Peschek and Brand[59] suggests that such groups may often have more impact upon policy than councillors. The Liberal party in West Ham, though successful in achieving some representation on the council, was probably most significant as a pressure group since its actual political power was very limited. In the field of education, of course, perhaps the most significant pressure is provided by teachers, a group of employees who find it useful to operate as a public pressure group.

In some cases administrators may in fact find that pressure groups are a more effective threat to their policies than councillors. More often, however, pressure groups will not be much more in evidence than political parties or will confine their influence to a little discreet lobbying of officers and councillors. What this may mean in practice is that administrators will find that the sole pressure upon them comes from a small number of high-status individuals. In this sense local elites may still be influential even when they don't play an open part in local government. Clements[60] found that businessmen in Bristol were uninterested in local government in general but would contact local officials when their specific interests were at stake.

In general, then, administrators who are not faced by organised and committed party groups may have to pay very little attention to selling policies to the public. However they may have to take into account the views of a small section of the public who regard themselves, and may be regarded by the administrators and others, as an elite. There seem in many towns and counties to be customary presuppositions about the rights of certain groups to be consulted.

In many towns, particularly the smaller ones, although local government officers in general are of low status, the chief officers of the councils will have a recognised place in the local elite. They will, for example, be found amongst the members of Rotary Clubs and other social service organisations. They will thus be placed in the kinds of social positions that enable them to take note of the views and interests of local elites. There are three aspects of English society which are likely to make local elites a significant force for administrators to recognise in a general political context in which they are the key decision-makers: (1) the general aspiration of some public officials to enjoy some kind of standing with the local elites, (2) a general cultural assumption that there is such an elite (the evidence for this comes out very strongly in the procedures governments use for selecting persons to serve on the very wide range of nonelected bodies in our society, and in the common call for an improvement in the 'quality' of councillors which seems to involve an assumption that professional and managerial people should take the places vacated by the diminishing local gentry) and (3) the fact that it is very largely from the upper-middle class that protest is likely to come against the actions of particular local government bodies. (Grammar school parents are more likely to protest than secondary modern school parents, amenity societies are much more likely to exist in upper-middle-class suburbs than on council estates, and so on.) These three points reinforce each other, so that although it is impossible to define precisely who are the elite or elites in a particular community it goes without saying that top local officials are more likely to identify with some people than others, that some people are much more likely to be considered important than others and that these same people are much more likely to organise to protect their interests than others. Such a system is self-reinforcing; it exists in almost any society but it is particularly endemic in British society where democratic rights are still so often regarded as privileges to be given to those who earn them and where, therefore, administrators have quite easy consciences about taking policy-decisions in consultation only with such a minority.

Administrative politics may involve situations in which administrators have considerable freedom to innovate, particularly where they are protected from the public by a moribund political system. They may therefore secure the autonomy to put in practice their ideals and commitments, and it is for this reason that one finds occasionally in Britain striking innovations stemming from local authorities in which politicians play a minor role. For example, a great deal of progress has been made in the direction of comprehensive education by some counties where councillors have had very little to do with policy-making. But at the same time administrative politics is a paternalistic style of government in which much crucial decision-making occurs without any scrutiny by the electorate. It involves a system in which elite influence may be very significant, and yet be unnoticed.

In the United States, the scope of the decision-making process is restricted by open bargaining between governmental institutions, political parties and pressure groups; in Britain, such restriction is secured very much more covertly through low participation and behind-the-scenes influence. Ideological politics seems to provide the way to open up political debate, to enable the unification of ordinary people in class-based political conflict.

This is what Newton sees as the characteristic of British local politics, a characteristic arising from the simplicity of the lines of social cleavage in Britain:[61]

> British parties will find it rather easier than American parties to aggregate interests and act as group spearheads because of the relatively small number of lines of social and political cleavage in this country. The larger cities in America are divided into class, religion, ethnic and colour lines, which makes it somewhat difficult for parties to claim to represent all these interests. Class is the main line of division in British politics and hence different interests tend to separate out into Labour and Conservative party camps.

The rise of the Labour Party in Britain helped to open up local politics, to move it from administrative politics to ideological politics by giving voice to working-class interests. The danger now is that the cleavage within British politics will be regarded as only as complex as this. The difficulty with ideological politics is that it provides scope for the advocacy of the point of view of those interests which can be aggregated to provide an electoral majority; minority points of view may be no more effectively articulated than they are in a bargaining system, where at least they have the blunt weapon of veto-power. This is an issue Rex[62] has tackled, pointing out the existence of 'housing classes'. The middle class are able to buy good houses, and the working class have been able to use political power to acquire council housing on semi-suburban estates, but the poor and the immigrants left in the inner city areas today have neither the financial nor the political power to cope with their predicament. As the contrast between the extent of municipal housing in Britain and the United States suggests, ideological politics provides an avenue through which underprivileged majorities can seek to attain some of their needs, but it does not serve minorities so well. Administrators may be the best advocates of minority points of view in such cases, but, as was suggested earlier in the book, to rely upon the values of administrators to protect particular classes of people involves the difficulty that a diversity of influences plays upon them.

In many ways this book may have appeared to have taken an equivocal stand on issues of this kind. This is largely because the writer believes that while, on the one hand, any study of administration that is blind to the enormous significance of bureaucratisation for governmental decision-making will be inadequate and misleading, he also accepts the relevance of Gouldner's challenge on this issue:[63]

Wrapping themselves in the shrouds of nineteenth-century political economy, some social scientists seem to be bent on resurrecting a dismal science. Instead of explaining how democratic patterns may, to some extent, be fortified and extended, they warn us that democracy cannot be perfect. Instead of controlling the disease, they suggest that we are deluded, or more politely, incurably romantic, for hoping to control it. Instead of assuming responsibilities as realistic clinicians, striving to further democratic potentialities wherever they can, many social scientists have become morticians, all too eager to bury men's hopes.

References

CHAPTER 1 Bureaucracy and Democracy: The Theoretical and Philosophical Debate

1   M. Albrow, *Bureaucracy*, chapter 1.
2   Albrow, *Bureaucracy*, p. 21.
3   K. Marx and F. Engels, 'The German Ideology', in *Basic Writings on Politics and Philosophy*, ed. L. S. Feuer, p. 296.
4   F. Engels, 'The Origin of the Family, Private Property and the State', in K. Marx and F. Engels, *Selected Works*, II, p. 322.
5   M. Weber, *The Theory of Social and Economic Organization*, translated by A. M. Henderson and T. Parsons, p. 328.
6   Weber, *Theory of Social and Economic Organization*, p. 328.
7   Weber, *Theory of Social and Economic Organization*.
8   R. Bendix, *Max Weber, an Intellectual Portrait*, p. 453. The quotation is from M. Weber, *From Max Weber: Essays in Sociology*, ed. H. H. Gerth and C. W. Mills, p. 49.
9   M. Weber, *From Max Weber: Essays in Sociology*, ed. H. H. Gerth and C. Wright Mills, p. 49.
10 R. Michels, *Political Parties*, translated by Eden and Cedar Paul.
11 G. Mosca, *The Ruling Class*, translated by H. D. Kahn.
12 V. I. Lenin, *The State and Revolution*.
13 K. Kautsky, *The Labour Revolution*.
14 Lenin, *The State and Revolution*, p. 41.
15 M. Djilas, *The New Class*.
16 See P. Blumberg, *Industrial Democracy*.
17 J. Burnham, *The Managerial Revolution*.
18 Burnham, *The Managerial Revolution*, p. 182 (of Penguin edition).
19 H. H. Gerth and C. W. Mills, 'A Marx for the Managers', in C. W. Mills, *Power, Politics and People*, ed. I. L. Horowitz, p. 65. (First published in *Ethics*, 52 (1942).)
20 T. B. Bottomore, *Elites and Society*.
21 R. Miliband, *The State in Capitalist Society*, chapter 5.

22   R. Aron, 'Social Structure and the Ruling Class', *British Journal of Sociology*, 1 (1950), pp. 1–16 and 126–43.
23   S. M. Lipset, *Political Man*.
24   R. Dahl, *A Preface to Democratic Theory*.
25   R. Dahrendorf, *Class and Class Conflict in Industrial Society*.
26   J. K. Galbraith, *American Capitalism*.
27   P. Bachrach, *The Theory of Democratic Elitism*.
28   Bachrach, *The Theory of Democratic Elitism*.
29   C. W. Mills, 'Culture and Politics', in C. W. Mills, *Power, Politics and People*, ed. I. L. Horowitz, p. 237. (First published in *The Listener*, 12 March 1959.) See also C. W. Mills, *Causes of World War Three*.
30   Mills, in *Power, Politics and People*, pp. 237–8.
31   Mills, in *Power, Politics and People*, p. 244.
32   Mills, in *Power, Politics and People*, p. 246.
33   Bachrach, *The Theory of Democratic Elitism*, p. 59.
34   Mills, in *Power, Politics and People*, p. 242.
35   J. P. Nettl, 'Consensus or Elite Domination: The Case of Business', *Political Studies*, 13 (1965), p. 41.
36   R. Bendix, *Nation-Building and Citizenship*, p. 127.

CHAPTER 2   Organisation Theories

1   M. Albrow, *Bureaucracy*, p. 65.
2   See Albrow, *Bureaucracy*, chapters 1–3 for a full discussion of this.
3   M. Weber, *The Theory of Social and Economic Organization*, translated by A. M. Henderson and T. Parsons, pp. 329–41.
4   See, for example, R. G. Francis and R. C. Stone, *Service and Procedure in Bureaucracy*.
5   See R. K. Merton, 'Bureaucratic Structure and Personality', *Social Forces*, 17 (1940), pp. 560–8 reprinted in *Reader in Bureaucracy*, ed. R. K. Merton et al., and P. M. Blau, *The Dynamics of Bureaucracy*.
6   A. W. Gouldner, *Patterns of Industrial Bureaucracy*, p. 22.
7   R. V. Presthus, *The Organizational Society*.
8   V. A. Thompson, *Modern Organization*. See also V. A. Thompson, 'Hierarchy, Specialization and Organizational Conflict', *Administrative Science Quarterly*, 5 (1961), pp. 485–521, and V. A. Thompson, 'Bureaucracy and Innovation', *Administrative Science Quarterly*, 10 (1965), pp. 1–20.
9   See A. W. Gouldner, 'Cosmopolitans and Locals: Towards an Analysis of Latent Social Roles', *Administrative Science Quarterly*, 2 (1957–8), pp. 281–306 and 444–80. Also L. Reissman, 'A Study of Role Conceptions in Bureaucracy', *Social Forces*, 27 (1949), pp. 305–10.

10 See particularly Blau, *The Dynamics of Bureaucracy*.

11 For an account of these theories, see N. Mouzelis, *Organization and Bureaucracy*, chapter 4; or J. G. March and H. A. Simon, *Organizations*, chapter 2. The classic works of this school are F. W. Taylor, *The Principles of Scientific Management*; and H. Fayol, *Administration Industrielle et Générale*.

12 This is reported in F. J. Roethlisberger and W. J. Dickson, *Management and the Worker*. See also E. Mayo, *The Human Problems of an Industrial Civilization*, and *The Social Problems of an Industrial Civilization*.

13 For a good discussion of the background to the Hawthorne investigations, see J. Madge, *The Origins of Scientific Sociology*, chapter 6.

14 M. P. Follett, *Dynamic Administration*.

15 This controversy is discussed in H. A. Landsberger, *Hawthorne Revisited*.

16 A good discussion of the general implications of the Hawthorne researches, and especially the Bank Wiring Room observations, can be found in G. C. Homans, *The Human Group*.

17 See, for example, N. Walker, *Morale in the Civil Service*.

18 M. Dalton, *Men Who Manage*; and, for a discussion of the general significance of the findings for all organisational levels, see P. Selznick, 'An Approach to a Theory of Bureaucracy', *American Sociological Review*, 8 (1943), pp. 47–54.

19 C. Barnard, *The Functions of the Executive*.

20 Gouldner, *Patterns of Industrial Bureaucracy*, chapter 2.

21 Barnard, *The Functions of the Executive*, p. 123.

22 H. A. Simon, *Administrative Behavior*.

23 March and Simon, *Organizations*.

24 Simon, *Administrative Behavior*, p. 1.

25 Simon, *Administrative Behavior*, paperback ed. p. xxiv.

26 W. Wilson, 'The Study of Administration', *Political Science Quarterly*, 56, 2 (June 1887), pp. 481–506.

27 Simon, *Administrative Behavior*, pp. 169 ff.

28 Simon, *Administrative Behavior*, p. 152.

29 Parsons' main contributions on this subject are in the first two chapters of his *Structure and Process in Modern Societies*.

30 P. Selznick, *TVA and the Grass Roots*.

31 P. Selznick, *Leadership in Administration*. See also Selznick, in *American Sociological Review*, 8, pp. 47–54 and 'Foundations of the Theory of Organization', *American Sociological Review*, 13 (1948), pp. 25–35.

32 Selznick, *Leadership in Administration*, p. 5.

33 Selznick, *TVA and the Grass Roots*, p. 251.

34 A. W. Gouldner, 'Metaphysical Pathos and the Theory of Bureaucracy', *American Political Science Review*, 49 (1955), p. 504.
35 Selznick, *TVA and the Grass Roots*, paperback edition, preface.
36 Selznick, *TVA and the Grass Roots*, p. 155.
37 Selznick, in *American Sociological Review*, 13, p. 34.
38 For such an account, see D. Silverman, *The Theory of Organizations* or Mouzelis, *Organization and Bureaucracy*.

CHAPTER 3   Formal and Informal Organisation

1 H. A. Simon, D. W. Smithburg, and V. A. Thompson, *Public Administration*, p. 87.
2 See N. Mouzelis, *Organization and Bureaucracy*, pp. 146–8.
3 See A. W. Gouldner, *Patterns of Industrial Bureaucracy*, part 4.
4 R. K. Merton, 'Bureaucratic Structure and Personality', *Social Forces*, 17 (1940), pp. 560–8 (reprinted in *Reader in Bureaucracy*, ed. R. K. Merton et al).
5 T. Burns and G. M. Stalker, *The Management of Innovation*, pp. 5–6.
6 M. Albrow, *Bureaucracy*, p. 45.
7 D. C. Miller and W. H. Form, *Industrial Sociology*, p. 113.
8 C. Barnard, *The Functions of the Executive*.
9 F. M. Marx, *The Administrative State*.
10 E. Barker, *The Development of Public Services in Western Europe 1660–1930*.
11 B. Chapman, *The Profession of Government*.
12 E. Cohen, *The Growth of the British Civil Service 1780–1939*.
13 J. D. Kingsley, *Representative Bureaucracy*.
14 R. K. Kelsall, *Higher Civil Servants in Britain*.
15 H. Parris, *Constitutional Bureaucracy*.
16 T. F. Tout, *The English Civil Service in the Fourteenth Century*.
17 H. Parris, 'The Origins of the Permanent Civil Service, 1780–1830', *Public Administration*, 46 (1968), p. 143.
18 Kingsley, *Representative Bureaucracy*, p. 50.
19 *The Civil Service* (London 1968).
20 *Report of the Sub-Committee of the Inter-Departmental Committee on the Application of the Whitley Report to Government Establishments* (London 1919), p. xi.
21 *The Civil Service*, I, pp. 11–12.
22 M. J. Hill, 'The Exercise of Discretion in the National Assistance Board', *Public Administration*, 47 (1969), p. 83.
23 W. J. Mackenzie and J. W. Grove, *Central Administration in Britain*.

24 See particularly Mayo's own books, *The Human Problems of an Industrial Civilization* and *The Social Problems of an Industrial Civilization.*

25 See, for example, C. Argyris, *Integrating the Individual and the Organization*; D. McGregor, *The Human Side of Enterprise*; and A. Fox, *Industrial Sociology and Industrial Relations* (Research Paper number 3 for the Royal Commission on Trade Unions and Employers' Associations) (London 1968).

26 P. Selznick, *Leadership in Administration,* pp. 7–8.

27 See H. A. Landsberger, *Hawthorne Revisited.*

28 M. Dalton, *Men Who Manage.*

29 E. Josephson, 'Irrational Leadership in Formal Organizations', *Social Forces,* 31 (1952), pp. 116–17.

30 See Albrow, *Bureaucracy,* chapter 3.

31 H. A. Simon, *Administrative Behavior,* chapter 2.

32 Merton, in *Social Forces,* 17, pp. 560–8.

33 Gouldner, *Patterns of Industrial Bureaucracy.*

34 Dalton, *Men Who Manage,* chapter 3.

35 See R. L. Peabody, *Organizational Authority,* pp. 63–4.

36 P. M. Blau, *The Dynamics of Bureaucracy,* part 2.

37 R. G. Francis and R. C Stone, *Service and Procedure in Bureaucracy.*

38 P. M. Blau, 'Orientation towards Clients in a Public Welfare Agency', *Administrative Science Quarterly,* 5 (1960), pp. 341–61.

39 A. Fox, *A Sociology of Work in Industry* provides a more elaborate discussion of this important topic.

40 M. Crozier, *The Bureaucratic Phenomenon.*

41 J. R. Pitts, *In Search of France.*

42 See D. Lockwood, *The Blackcoated Worker.*

43 Fox, *Sociology of Work in Industry,* p. 140.

44 See, for example, H. E. Dale, *The Higher Civil Service of Great Britain.*

45 See M. Gilbert and R. Gott, *The Appeasers.*

46 See H. Thomas, *The Suez Affair* and A. Nutting, *No End of a Lesson.*

47 See R. Opie, 'The Making of Economic Policy', in *Crisis in the Civil Service,* ed. H. Thomas, pp. 53–82.

48 The Institution of Professional Civil Servants, 'Comment on H.M. Treasury's Note, "The Future Structure of the Civil Service" ', in *The Civil Service,* V, p. 287. For a fuller discussion of this issue, see chapter 8.

49 C. P. Snow, *Science and Government.*

50 See Dale, *The Higher Civil Service of Great Britain.*

51 See A. Rose, *The Power Structure,* chapter 7 for a discussion of the evidence on this point.

52 Dale, *The Higher Civil Service of Great Britain*, pp. 176–7.
53 R. A. Chapman, *The Higher Civil Service in Britain*, pp. 110–11. Some of this evidence is discussed further in chapter 9.
54 Blau, *The Dynamics of Bureaucracy,* chapter 2.
55 Blau, *The Dynamics of Bureaucracy*, pp. 187–93.
56 Hill, in *Public Administration,* 47, p. 82.
57 Blau, *The Dynamics of Bureaucracy*, p. 26.
58 Blau, *The Dynamics of Bureaucracy*, p. 215.
59 Blau, *The Dynamics of Bureaucracy*, p. 142.

CHAPTER 4   Administrative Discretion

1 This phenomenon is by no means unique to Britain; see, for example, the discussion of American 'regulatory agencies' in H. A. Simon, D. W. Smithburg and V. A. Thompson, *Public Administration,* p. 52.
2 See J. R. Lambert, *Crime, Police and Race Relations* for a further discussion of this issue.
3 Justice, *The Citizen and the Administration,* pp. 17–18.
4 Tony Lynes, 'The Secret Rules', *Poverty,* 4 (Autumn 1967), pp. 7–9.
5 D. Marsden, *Mothers Alone,* p. 242.
6 See M. J. Hill, 'The Exercise of Discretion in the National Assistance Board', *Public Administration,* 47 (1969), pp. 79–80.
7 Hill in *Public Administration,* 47, pp. 75–90.
8 Hill in *Public Administration,* 47, pp. 78–9.
9 *Committee on Local Authority and Allied Personal Social Services* (London 1968), para. 685.
10 Olive Stevenson, 'Problems of Individual Need and Fair Shares for All', *Social Work Today,* 1, 1 (1970), p. 21.
11 J. Lambert, 'The Police Can Choose', *New Society,* 18 September 1969, p. 430.
12 See B. Allen, 'Administration of Discretion', *Case Conference,* June 1968, pp. 43–8.
13 Olive Stevenson in *Social Work Today,* 1, 1, ⲣ. 15.
14 Second reading by the House of Lords of the Ministry of Social Security Act 1966.
15 H. A. Simon, *Administrative Behavior,* pp. 57–8.
16 See, for example, D. Bell, *The End of Ideology* and S. M. Lipset, *Political Man.*
17 See Bob Hepple, *Race, Jobs and the Law in Britain,* 2nd ed.
18 *Council Housing Purposes, Procedures and Priorities* (ninth report of the Housing Management Subcommittee of the Central Housing Advisory Committee) (London 1969).

19 For a discussion of the evidence, see P. Blumberg, *Industrial Democracy*.

20 P. M. Blau, *The Dynamics of Bureaucracy*.

21 R. G. Francis and R. C. Stone, *Service and Procedure in Bureaucracy*.

22 J. Jacobs, 'Symbolic Bureaucracy: A Case Study of a Social Welfare Agency', *Social Forces*, 47 (1969), p. 414.

23 A good discussion of some of the problems entailed in adopting legal controls is in R. M. Titmuss, 'Welfare Rights, Law and Discretion', *Political Quarterly*, 42, 2 (April 1971), pp. 113–32.

24 See Justice, *The Citizen and the Administration*.

25 See K. Bell, *Tribunals in the Social Services*.

26 See Hill in *Public Administration*, 47, pp. 83–5.

27 Ministry of Housing and Local Government, *Management of Local Government* (London 1967).

28 *Council Housing Purposes, Procedures and Priorities*, p. 43.

29 Simon, *Administrative Behavior*, p. 58.

30 C. J. Friedrich, 'The Nature of Administrative Responsibility', *Public Policy*, 1 (1940), pp. 3–24.

31 The Calouste Gulbenkian Foundation, *Community Work and Social Change*, chapter 7.

32 Gulbenkian Foundation, *Community Work and Social Change*, p. 86.

33 H. Kaufman, *The Forest Ranger*.

34 Simon, Smithburg and Thompson, *Public Administration*, p. 371.

35 A. Keith-Lucas, *Decisions about People in Need*.

36 'The Truth about the Welfare Rackets', *Spectator*, 6 September 1969, pp. 300–2.

37 J. Q. Wilson, *Varieties of Police Behavior*, p. 283.

38 P. M. Blau, 'Orientation towards Clients in a Public Welfare Agency', *Administrative Science Quarterly*, 5 (1960), p. 351.

39 P. Selznick, *Leadership in Administration*, p. 5.

CHAPTER 5 Organisational Goals

1 C. Perrow, 'The Analysis of Goals in Complex Organizations', *American Sociological Review*, 26 (1961), p. 854.

2 P. M. Blau and W. R. Scott, *Formal Organizations*, p. 5.

3 Blau and Scott, *Formal Organizations*, pp. 229–30.

4 N. Mouzelis, *Organization and Bureaucracy*, p. 4.

5 Mouzelis, *Organization and Bureaucracy*, p. 57.

6 M. Albrow, 'The Study of Organizations – Objectivity or Bias?', in *Penguin Social Sciences Survey 1968*, ed. J. Gould, p. 153.

7   For a good discussion of these misleading approaches see D. Silverman, *The Theory of Organizations*, pp. 9–11.

8   Albrow in *Penguin Social Sciences Survey 1968*, p. 160.

9   H. A. Simon, 'On the Concept of Organizational Goal', *Administrative Science Quarterly*, 9 (1964), p. 2.

10   T. Parsons, *Structure and Process in Modern Societies*, p. 63.

11   Albrow in *Penguin Social Sciences Survey 1968*, p. 162.

12   A. Etzioni, 'Industrial Sociology: the Study of Economic Organizations', *Social Research*, 25 (1958), p. 303.

13   Perrow, in *American Sociological Review*, 26, p. 855.

14   Blau and Scott, *Formal Organizations*, p. 229.

15   Simon, in *Administrative Science Quarterly*, 9. pp. 1–22.

16   R. K. Merton, 'Bureaucratic Structure and Personality', *Social Forces*, 18 (1940), pp. 560–8, reprinted in R. K. Merton, *Social Theory and Social Structure*, revised ed., pp. 195–206.

17   E. Gross, 'The Definition of Organizational Goals', *British Journal of Sociology*, 20, 3 (1969), p. 282.

18   R. Michels, *Political Parties*, translated by Eden and Cedar Paul.

19   J. P. Roche and S. Sachs, 'The Bureaucrat and the Enthusiast', *Western Political Quarterly*, 8 (1955), p. 261.

20   Gross, in *British Journal of Sociology*, 20, pp. 277–94.

21   C. Barnard, *The Functions of the Executive*.

22   P. Selznick, *Leadership in Administration*.

23   A. Fox, *A Sociology of Work in Industry*, p. 58.

24   Fox, *A Sociology of Work in Industry*, p. 59.

25   Simon, in *Administrative Science Quarterly*, 9, pp. 1–22.

26   Simon, in *Administrative Science Quarterly*, 9, p. 21.

27   Simon, in *Administrative Science Quarterly*, 9, p. 21.

28   Gross, in *British Journal of Sociology*, 20, p. 284.

29   Merton, *Social Theory and Social Structure*, p. 199.

30   B. R. Clark, 'Organizational Adaption and Precarious Values', *American Sociological Review*, 21 (1956), pp. 327–36.

31   Clark, in *American Sociological Review*, 21, p. 328.

32   B. M. Gross, *Organizations and their Managing*, p. 290.

33   D. V. Donnison et al., *Social Policy and Administration*, pp. 240–1.

34   P. Selznick, *TVA and the Grass Roots*.

35   E. C. Banfield, *Government Project*.

36   See, for example, S. Baldwin, *Poverty and Politics*.

37   See D. P. Moynihan, *Maximum Feasible Misunderstanding* and R. M. Kramer, *Participation of the Poor*.

38   See, for example, H. A. Simon, D. W. Smithburg and V. A. Thompson, *Public Administration*.

39   M. J. Hill, 'Selectivity for the Poor', in P. Townsend and N. Bosanquet, *Labour and Inequality*.

40   See R. Holman (ed.), *Socially Deprived Families in Britain*, p. 176.
41   For a discussion of this, see R. J. Buxton, *Local Government*.
42   See K. Coates and R. Silburn, *Poverty: the Forgotten Englishmen*.
43   N. Dennis, *People and Planning*, p. 354.
44   M. J. Hill and R. M. Issacharoff, *Community Action and Race Relations*.
45   B. R. Clark, *Adult Education in Transition*.
46   *Immigration from the Commonwealth* (Cmnd. 2739), p. 16.
47   Clark, *Adult Education in Transition*.
48   P. Marris and M. Rein, *Dilemmas of Social Reform*, p. 34.
49   J. D. Thompson and W. J. McEwan, 'Organizational Goals and Environment', *American Sociological Review*, 23 (1958), pp. 23–31.
50   Thompson and McEwan, in *American Sociological Review*, 23, p. 25.
51   Thompson and McEwan, in *American Sociological Review*, 23, p. 25.
52   Thompson and McEwan, in *American Sociological Review*, 23, p. 26.
53   Thompson and McEwan, in *American Sociological Review*, 23, p. 27.
54   Thompson and McEwan, in *American Sociological Review*, 23, p. 28.
55   Thompson and McEwan, in *American Sociological Review*, 23, p. 28.
56   See, for example, J. P. Dean and A. Rosen, *A Manual of Intergroup Relations*, M. Ross, *Community Organization: Theory and Principles* and R. Lippitt et al., *The Dynamics of Planned Change*.
57   R. Morris and M. Rein, *Social Work Practice*, pp. 127–45.
58   See M. Meyerson and E. C. Banfield, *Politics, Planning and the Public Interest*.
59   See, for example, Dennis, *People and Planning* and D. M. Hill, *Participating in Local Affairs*.

CHAPTER 6   Authority

1   R. Bierstedt, 'The Problem of Authority' in *Freedom and Control in Modern Society*, ed. M. Berger, T. Abel and C. H. Page.
2   H. A. Simon, D. W. Smithburg and V. A. Thompson, *Public Administration*, pp. 180–210.
3   Simon, Smithburg and Thompson, *Public Administration*, p. 181.
4   H. A. Simon, *Administrative Behavior*, pp. 133–4.
5   Simon, Smithburg and Thompson, *Public Administration*, p. 198.

6 A. Fox, *A Sociology of Work in Industry*, pp. 30–1.
7 R. V. Presthus, 'Authority in Organizations' in *Concepts and Issues in Administrative Behavior*, ed. S. Mailick and E. H. van Ness, p. 123.
8 Presthus in *Concepts and Issues in Administrative Behavior*, p. 135.
9 Presthus in *Concepts and Issues in Administrative Behavior*, p. 135.
10 R. L. Peabody, *Organizational Authority*, chapter 7.
11 V. A. Thompson, *Modern Organization*.
12 Thompson, *Modern Organization*, p. 120.
13 See Bierstedt in *Freedom and Control in Modern Society*, R. Bierstedt, 'The Sociology of Majorities', *American Sociological Review*, 13 (1948), pp. 700–10 and R. Bierstedt, 'An Analysis of Social Power', *American Sociological Review*, 15 (1950), pp. 730–8.
14 Bierstedt in *Freedom and Control in Modern Society*, p. 73.
15 Bierstedt in *Freedom and Control in Modern Society*, p. 77.
16 R. V. Presthus, *The Organizational Society*.
17 W. Buckley, *Sociology and Modern Systems Theory*, pp. 176–85.
18 Fox, *A Sociology of Work in Industry*, p. 37.
19 Buckley, *Sociology and Modern Systems Theory*, p. 196.
20 Buckley, *Sociology and Modern Systems Theory*, p. 196.
21 Fox, *A Sociology of Work in Industry*, p. 50.
22 R. K. Merton, *Social Theory and Social Structure*, revised ed., chapter 4.
23 A. Etzioni, *A Comparative Analysis of Complex Organizations*.
24 Etzioni, *A Comparative Analysis of Complex Organizations*, pp. 21–2.
25 Etzioni, *A Comparative Analysis of Complex Organizations*, p. 14.
26 Etzioni, *A Comparative Analysis of Complex Organizations*, p. 31.
27 Etzioni, *A Comparative Analysis of Complex Organizations*, p. 40.
28 Fox, *A Sociology of Work in Industry*, p. 71.
29 Fox, *A Sociology of Work in Industry*, p. 71.
30 Etzioni, *A Comparative Analysis of Complex Organizations*, p. 90.
31 Etzioni, *A Comparative Analysis of Complex Organizations*, p. 93.
32 Etzioni, *A Comparative Analysis of Complex Organizations*, p. 91.

33 A. Bavelas, 'Leadership: Man and Function', *Administrative Science Quarterly,* 5 (1960), pp. 491–8.

34 M. Weber, *The Theory of Social and Economic Organization,* translated by A. M. Henderson and T. Parsons, p. 328.

35 Bavelas in *Administrative Science Quarterly,* 5, p. 492.

36 P. Pigors, *Leadership Domination.*

37 C. A. Gibb, 'Leadership' in *Handbook of Social Psychology,* ed. G. Lindzey, p. 889.

38 D. Cartwright and A. Zander (eds), *Group Dynamics,* 3rd ed., p. 305.

39 S. A. Richardson, 'Organizational Contrasts on British and American Ships', *Administrative Science Quarterly,* 1 (1956), pp. 189–207.

40 W. B. Miller, 'Two Concepts of Authority', *American Anthropologist,* 57 (1955), pp. 271–89.

41 K. Lewin, 'The Consequences of Authoritarian and Democratic Leadership', in *Studies in Leadership,* ed. A. W. Gouldner. See also R. White and R. Lippitt, *Autocracy and Democracy.*

42 D. C. Korten, 'Situational Determinants of Leadership Structure', *Journal of Conflict Resolution,* 6 (1962), pp. 222–35.

43 C. A. Gibb, 'The Principles and Traits of Leadership', *Journal of Abnormal and Social Psychology,* 42 (1947), pp. 267–84. Reprinted in *Leadership,* ed. C. A. Gibb, p. 211.

44 F. E. Fiedler, 'Personality and Situational Determinants of Leadership Effectiveness' in *Group Dynamics,* ed. D. Cartwright and A. Zander, 3rd ed., p. 379.

45 Bavelas in *Administrative Science Quarterly,* 5, p. 498.

46 M. Crozier, *The Bureaucratic Phenomenon.*

47 P. M. Blau, *The Dynamics of Bureaucracy.*

48 See *The Civil Service* (London 1968), I.

49 Crozier, *The Bureaucratic Phenomenon.*

50 D. Katz and R. L. Kahn, *The Social Psychology of Organizations,* chapter 2.

51 P. Selznick, *Leadership in Administration.*

52 Cartwright and Zander, *Group Dynamics,* p. 306.

53 Cartwright and Zander, *Group Dynamics,* p. 308.

54 A. Etzioni, 'Dual Leadership in Complex Organizations', *American Sociological Review,* 30 (1965), p. 696.

55 Gibb in *Handbook of Social Psychology,* p. 897.

56 R. G. S. Brown, *The Administrative Process in Britain,* p. 232.

57 Selznick, *Leadership in Administration,* p. 75.

58 Selznick, *Leadership in Administration,* p. 154.

59 R. K. Merton, 'Role of the Intellectual in Public Bureaucracy', *Social Forces,* 23, (1945), pp. 405–15.

CHAPTER 7 Bureaucracy and Personality

1 See, for example, W. H. Whyte, *The Organization Man.*
2 For example, P. Galdos, *Miau,* translated by J. M. Cohen and H. de Balzac, *Les Employées.*
3 R. K. Merton, *Social Theory and Social Structure,* revised ed. pp. 195–206.
4 Merton, *Social Theory and Social Structure,* p. 197.
5 Merton, *Social Theory and Social Structure,* p. 200.
6 F. M. Marx, *The Administrative State,* p. 97.
7 Marx, *The Administrative State,* pp. 102–3.
8 Merton, *Social Theory and Social Structure,* p. 205.
9 The Psychological Research Centre, 'The Recruitment of Graduates to the Civil Service: Survey of Student Attitudes', in *The Civil Service,* III (2) (London 1969), pp. 309–421.
10 R. A. Chapman, *The Higher Civil Service in Britain,* p. 54.
11 R. V. Presthus, *The Organizational Society,* p. 12.
12 Presthus, *The Organizational Society,* p. 15.
13 C. Argyris, *Integrating the Individual and the Organization.*
14 C. Argyris, 'The Individual and the Organization: Some Problems of Mutual Adjustment', *Administrative Science Quarterly,* 2 (1957), p. 22.
15 In addition to Argyris, see D. McGregor, *The Human Side of Enterprise.*
16 D. J. Levinson, 'Role, Personality and Social Structure in an Organizational Setting', *Journal of Abnormal and Social Psychology,* 58 (1959), pp. 178–81.
17 See M. Banton, *Roles.*
18 P. M. Blau, 'Orientation toward Clients in a Public Welfare Agency', *Administrative Science Quarterly,* 5 (1960), pp. 341–61.
19 A. K. Davis, 'Bureaucratic Patterns in the Navy Officer Corps', *Social Forces,* 27 (1948–9), pp. 143–53.
20 A. W. Gouldner, *Patterns of Industrial Bureaucracy.*
21 M. Crozier, *The Bureaucratic Phenomenon,* p. 208.
22 Merton, *Social Theory and Social Structure,* chapter 7.
23 M. Abrahamson, *The Professional in the Organization,* p. 6.

CHAPTER 8 Expertise and Professionalism

1 F. F. Ridley, *Specialists and Generalists,* p. 11.
2 See, G. K. Fry, *Statesmen in Disguise,* p. 69, n. 4.
3 *Report on the Indian Civil Service* (London 1845), reprinted in *The Civil Service* (London 1968), I, p. 123.
4 *Hansard,* Commons 10 July 1833, col. 525, quoted in R. A. Chapman, *The Higher Civil Service in Britain,* p. 12.

5 See, for example, C. H. Sisson, *The Spirit of British Administration.*

6 *The Civil Service,* (London 1968), I, p. 18.

7 B. M. Gross, *Organizations and their Managing,* p. 37.

8 Ridley, *Specialists and Generalists,* p. 191.

9 R. G. S. Brown, *The Administrative Process in Britain.*

10 See, for example, A. A. Shonfield, *Modern Capitalism* and B. Chapman, *British Government Observed.*

11 See A. Meynaud, *Technocracy,* translated by P. Barnes.

12 For a good discussion of this, see R. A. Dahl, 'The Science of Public Administration: Three Problems', *Public Administration Review,* 7 (Winter 1947), pp. 1–11.

13 P. M. Blau and W. R. Scott, *Formal Organizations,* p. 172.

14 H. A. Simon, D. W. Smithburg and V. A. Thompson, *Public Administration,* p. 281.

15 A. Etzioni, 'Authority Structure and Organizational Effectiveness', *Administrative Science Quarterly,* 4 (1959), pp. 43–67.

16 Simon, Smithburg and Thompson, *Public Administration,* chapter 13.

17 Simon, Smithburg and Thompson, *Public Administration,* chapter 13.

18 V. A. Thompson, *Modern Organization.*

19 Thompson, *Modern Organization,* p. 129.

20 *The Civil Service,* II, p. 82, para 303.

21 Simon, Smithburg and Thompson, *Public Administration,* p. 282.

22 Etzioni, in *Administrative Science Quarterly,* 4, pp. 43–67.

23 See the discussion of this in D. E. Regan, 'The Expert and the Administrator: Recent Changes at the Ministry of Transport', *Public Administration,* 44 (1966), pp. 149–67.

24 See C. Headrick, *The Town Clerk.*

25 See Ministry of Housing and Local Government, *Management of Local Government,* (London 1967), I, pp. 55–6.

26 Thompson, *Modern Organization,* p. 6.

27 Gross, *Organizations and their Managing,* pp. 216–18.

28 Gross, *Organizations and their Managing,* p. 217.

29 Gross, *Organizations and their Managing,* p. 218.

30 An interesting, but perhaps rather complacent, account is given in F. Dunnill, *The Civil Service: Some Human Aspects,* chapters 6–8.

31 *The Civil Service* (London 1968), p. 57.

32 R. Opie, 'The Making of Economic Policy', in *Crisis in the Civil Service,* ed. H. Thomas, p. 73.

33 M. Nicholson, *The System,* pp. 299–300.

34 A Fabian Group, *The Administrators,* p. 17.

35 See Fry, *Statesmen in Disguise,* p. 233.

36 See S. Brittan, *The Treasury under the Tories 1951–64.*

I

37 See M. Dalton, 'Conflicts between Staff and Line Managerial Officers', *American Sociological Review*, 15 (June 1950), pp. 342–51.
38 Brown, *The Administrative Process in Britain*, pp. 77–8.
39 S. Brittan, 'The Irregulars', *Crossbow*, 37 (1966), pp. 30–3.
40 Opie, in *Crisis in the Civil Service*, pp. 53–82.
41 S. Brittan, *Steering the Economy*, p. 313.
42 Brittan, *Steering the Economy*. See also W. Davis, *Three Years' Hard Labour*.
43 Opie, in *Crisis in the Civil Service*, p. 61.
44 *The Civil Service*, I, p. 58.
45 *The Civil Service*, I, p. 60.
46 A. Etzioni, *The Semi-Professions and their Organization*, p. x.
47 See, for example, F. A. R. Bennion, *Professional Ethics*.
48 H. L. Wilensky, 'The Professionalization of Everyone', *American Journal of Sociology*, 70 (1964), p. 138.
49 E. Greenwood, 'Attributes of a Profession', *Social Work*, 2, 3 (July 1957), p. 48 (emphasis added).
50 Bennion, *Professional Ethics*.
51 Wilensky, in *American Journal of Sociology*, 70, p. 146.
52 Wilensky, in *American Journal of Sociology*, 70, p. 148.
53 See H. Eckstein, *Pressure Group Politics: The Case of the BMA*.
54 See H. and S. Rose, *Science and Society*.
55 See D. S. Greenberg, *The Politics of American Science*.
56 Wilensky, in *American Journal of Sociology*, 70, p. 147.
57 W. J. Goode, 'Community within a Community: the Professions', *American Sociological Review*, 22 (1957), p. 197.
58 Simon, Smithburg and Thompson, *Public Administration*, p. 77.
59 A. W. Gouldner, 'Cosmopolitans and Locals: towards an Analysis of Latent Social Roles', *Administrative Science Quarterly*, 2 (1957–8), pp. 281–306 and 444–80.
60 R. K. Merton, *Social Theory and Social Structure*, revised ed., chapter 10.
61 Gouldner, in *Administrative Science Quarterly*, 2, p. 290.
62 Merton, *Social Theory and Social Structure*, p. 222.
63 C. P. Snow, *Science and Government*.
64 L. Reissman, 'A Study of Role Conceptions in Bureaucracy', *Social Forces*, 27 (1949), pp. 305–10.
65 B. G. Glaser, 'The Local-Cosmopolitan Scientist', *American Journal of Sociology*, 69 (1963), p. 258.
66 B. Chapman, *The Profession of Government*, p. 43.
67 Chapman, *The Profession of Government*, p. 134.
68 H. Finer, 'Administrative Responsibility in Democratic Government', *Public Administration Review*, 1, 4 (1941), pp. 335–50.

69 C. J. Friedrich, 'The Nature of Administrative Responsibility', *Public Policy*, 1, (1940), pp. 3–24.

70 R. A. Chapman, 'Official Liberality', *Public Administration*, 48 (1970), pp. 123–36.

71 M. Albrow, 'Public Administration and Sociological Theory', The Lister Lecture to the British Association for the Advancement of Science, Durham 1970, p. 15.

CHAPTER 9 The Social Backgrounds of Higher Civil Servants

1 S. M. Lipset, *Agrarian Socialism*, p. 271.

2 R. Bendix, 'Bureaucracy: The Problem and its Setting', *American Sociological Review*, 12 (1947), p. 494.

3 A. H. Halsey and I. M. Crewe, 'Social Survey of the Civil Service', in *The Civil Service* (London 1969)), III (1).

4 For a further discussion of the definition of the higher civil service, see R. A. Chapman, *The Higher Civil Service in Britain*.

5 H. Finer, *The British Civil Service*, p. 49.

6 H. E. Dale, *The Higher Civil Service of Great Britain*.

7 J. D. Kingsley, *Representative Bureaucracy*.

8 Lipset, *Agrarian Socialism*.

9 C. J. Friedrich, 'The Nature of Administrative Responsibility', *Public Policy*, 1. (1940), pp. 3–24.

10 Kingsley, *Representative Bureaucracy*, p. 279

11 Kingsley, *Representative Bureaucracy*, p. 279.

12 Kingsley, *Representative Bureaucracy*, p. 282.

13 Lipset, *Agrarian Socialism*, p. 272.

14 Chapman, *The Higher Civil Service in Britain*, p. 120.

15 G. Wallas, *Human Nature in Politics*, p. 262.

16 R. K. Kelsall, *Higher Civil Servants in Britain*.

17 T. Balogh, 'The Apotheosis of the Dilettante', in *The Establishment*, ed. H. Thomas reprinted in *Crisis in the Civil Service*, ed. H. Thomas, pp. 11–52.

18 Balogh, in *Crisis in the Civil Service*, p. 37.

19 See D. Keeling, 'The Development of Central Training in the Civil Service 1963–70' *Public Administration*, 49 (1971), pp. 51–71.

20 T. B. Bottomore, *Elites and Society*, chapter 4.

21 W. L. Guttsman, *The British Political Elite*, chapters 11 and 12.

22 Halsey and Crewe, in *The Civil Service*, III (1), p. 398.

23 Halsey and Crewe, in *The Civil Service*, III (1).

24 Adapted from Halsey and Crewe, in *The Civil Service*, III (1), Tables 3.19, 3.20 and 3.21, pages 54–6.

25 Adapted from Halsey and Crewe, in *The Civil Service*, III (1), Table 3.19, p. 54.

26 Adapted from Halsey and Crewe, in *The Civil Service*, III (1), Tables 3.33, 3.34, and 3.35, pp. 70–3.
27 Halsey and Crewe, in *The Civil Service*, III (1), pp. 80–1.
28 Kelsall, *Higher Civil Servants in Britain*, chapter 6.
29 T. Lupton and C. S. Wilson, 'The Social Background and Connections of "Top Decision Makers"', *Manchester School of Economic and Social Studies*, 27, 1 (1959), pp. 30–52.
30 Adapted from Halsey and Crewe, in *The Civil Service*, III (1), Tables 3.45, 3.46 and 3.47, pp. 84–6.
31 Adapted from Lupton and Wilson, in *Manchester School of Economic and Social Studies*, 27, 1, p. 37.
32 Dale, *The Higher Civil Service of Great Britain*.
33 F. Dunnill, *The Civil Service: Some Human Aspects*.
34 R. A. Chapman, 'Profile of a Profession: the Administrative Class of the Civil Service', in *The Civil Service*, III (2) (London 1968), pp. 1–29.
35 Chapman, in *The Civil Service*, III (2), p. 6.
36 Chapman, in *The Civil Service*, III (2), p. 9.
37 Chapman, *The Higher Civil Service in Britain*, p. 116.
38 J. S. Harris and T. V. Garcia, 'The Permanent Secretaries: Britain's Top Administrators', *Public Administration Review*, 26, 1 (1966), pp. 31–44.
39 Lupton and Wilson, in *Manchester School of Economic and Social Studies*, 27, 1, pp. 38–43.
40 Chapman, *The Higher Civil Service in Britain*, p. 56.
41 W. L. Warner et al,' *The American Federal Executive*, p. 224.
42 B. Jackson and D. Marsden, *Education and the Working Class*.
43 K. Robinson, 'Selection and Social Background of the Administrative Class', *Public Administration*, 33 (1955), pp. 387–8.
44 See *Sixth Report of the Select Committee on Estimates 1964–5*, Recruitment to the Civil Service, Evidence provided by T. Smith and D. Lawrence.
45 See, for example, C. H. Sisson, *The Spirit of British Administration*.
46 See C. H. Dodd and J. F. Pickering, 'Recruitment to the Administrative Class, 1960–64', *Public Administration*, 45 (Spring and Summer 1967), pp. 55–80 and 169–99.
47 Dodd and Pickering, in *Public Administration*, 45, p. 186.
48 Interview with Harold Wilson reprinted in *The Listener*, 9 February 1967, p. 184.
49 See H. Parris, 'Twenty Years of L'Ecole Nationale d'Administration', *Public Administration*, 43 (1965), p. 406.
50 B. Chapman, *The Profession of Government*, pp. 84–5.
51 Warner et al., *The American Federal Executive*, chapter 3.
52 R. Bendix, *Higher Civil Servants in American Society*.

53 See, for example, D. T. Stanley, *The Higher Civil Service* and J. J. Corson, and R. S. Paul, *Men Near the Top*.

54 See V. Subramaniam, 'Graduates in the Public Services: a Comparative Study of Attitudes', *Public Administration*, 35, 4 (1957), pp. 373–94 and S. Encel, 'The Recruitment of University Graduates in the Commonwealth Public Service', *Public Administration*, 32, 2 (1954), pp. 217–28.

55 See G. K. Fry, *Statesmen in Disguise*.

56 Parris, in *Public Administration*, 43, pp. 395–412.

57 Halsey and Crewe, in *The Civil Service*, III (1), p. 398.

CHAPTER 10   Politics and Administration

1 W. Wilson, 'The Study of Administration', *Political Science Quarterly*, 56, 2 (June 1887), pp. 481–506.

2 Wilson, in *Political Science Quarterly*, 56, 2, pp. 481–506.

3 For example, Lord Hewart, *The New Despotism*.

4 Wilson, in *Political Science Quarterly*, 56, 2, pp. 481–506.

5 F. J. Goodnow, *Politics and Administration*.

6 C. E. Merriam, *The New Democracy and the New Despotism*.

7 H. A. Simon, *Administrative Behavior*.

8 See, for example, S. Brittan, *Left or Right: the Bogus Dilemma*.

9 H. A. Simon, D. W. Smithburg and V. A. Thompson, *Public Administration*, p. 7.

10 Ministry of Housing and Local Government, *Management of Local Government* (London 1967), I.

11 R. G. S. Brown, *The Administrative Process in Britain*, pp. 62–3.

12 H. H. Heclo, 'The Councillor's Job', *Public Administration*, 47 (Summer 1969), p. 188.

13 'Who are the Policy-Makers?' *Public Administration*, 43 (Autumn 1965), p. 272.

14 *Public Administration*, 43, p. 276.

15 Ministry of Housing and Local Government, *Management of Local Government*, I, p. 14.

16 Ministry of Housing and Local Government, *Management of Local Government*, I, p. 30.

17 Simon, *Administrative Behavior*, pp. 57–8.

18 See, for example, T. Parsons, *Structure and Process in Modern Societies* or P. Selznick, *Leadership in Administration*.

19 R. S. Parker and V. Subramaniam, 'Public and Private Administration', *International Review of Administrative Sciences*, 30 (1964), p. 365.

20 Brown, *The Administrative Process in Britain*.

21 H. E. Dale, *The Higher Civil Service of Great Britain*.

22 Sir Edward Bridges, *Portrait of a Profession*.

23 For example, C. H. Sisson, *The Spirit of British Administration* and T. D. Kingdom, 'The Confidential Advisers of Ministers', *Public Administration,* 44 (Autumn 1966), pp. 267–74.

CHAPTER 11 Politics and Administration in Local Government in Britain and the United States

1 K. Newton, 'City Politics in Britain and the United States', *Political Studies,* 17, 2 (1969), p. 209.
2 E. C. Banfield and J. Q. Wilson, *City Politics,* p. 76.
3 J. G. Bulpitt, *Party Politics in English Local Government.*
4 H. V. Wiseman, *Local Government at Work.*
5 W. Hampson, *Democracy and Community.*
6 M. Cole, *Servant of the County.*
7 J. M. Lee, *Social Leaders and Public Persons.*
8 F. Bealey, J. Blondel and W. P. McCann, *Constituency Politics.*
9 H. V. Wiseman, 'The Working of Local Government in Leeds', *Public Administration,* 41 (Spring and Summer 1963), pp. 51–70 and 137–56.
10 Ministry of Housing and Local Government, *Management of Local Government* (London 1967), I.
11 D. M. Hill, *Participating in Local Affairs,* p. 101. For an example of this process, see G. W. Jones, *Borough Politics.*
12 Ministry of Housing and Local Government, *Management of Local Government,* I, p. 114, para. 388.
13 See, for example, O. P. Williams and C. R. Adrian, *Four Cities.*
14 G. F. Darlow's contribution to the symposium, 'Who are the Policy-Makers?' *Public Administration,* 43 (Autumn 1965), p. 276.
15 R. A. Dahl, *Who Governs?*
16 Banfield and Wilson, *City Politics.*
17 F. M. Marx, *The Administrative State,* p. 160.
18 Marx, *The Administrative State,* p. 74.
19 E. C. Banfield, *Political Influence,* p. 235.
20 M. Meyerson and E. C. Banfield, *Politics, Planning and the Public Interest.*
21 F. Hunter, *Community Power Structure.*
22 R. E. Lane, *Political Life,* pp. 257–8.
23 N. Polsby, 'The Study of Community Power', in *Encyclopedia of the Social Sciences,* III, p. 158. See also A. M. Rose, *The Power Structure,* chapter 8.
24 Polsby, in *Encyclopedia of the Social Sciences,* III, p. 159.
25 Dahl, *Who Governs?*
26 K. Newton, 'A Critique of the Pluralist Model', *Acta Sociologica,* 12, 4 (1969), p. 213.

27 Dahl, *Who Governs,* p. 311.
28 Newton, in *Acta Sociologica,* 12, 4, p. 213.
29 Newton, in *Acta Sociologica,* 12, 4, p. 209.
30 Newton, in *Acta Sociologica,* 12, 4, p. 213.
31 Newton, in *Acta Sociologica,* 12, 4, p. 215.
32 P. Bachrach and M. S. Baratz, *Power and Poverty.*
33 Bachrach and Baratz, *Power and Poverty,* p. 44.
34 Bachrach and Baratz, *Power and Poverty,* p. 43. The concept of mobilisation of bias is taken from E. E. Schattschneider, *The Semi-Sovereign People,* p. 71.
35 See, for example, Hampson, *Democracy and Community,* chapter 9, for a discussion of the activities and impact of local pressure groups.
36 See R. G. Gregory, 'Local Elections and the Rule of Anticipated Reactions', *Political Studies,* 17, 1 (1969), pp. 31–47.
37 Newton, in *Political Studies,* 17, 2, p. 213.
38 K. Newton, *City Politics in Britain and America* (University of Birmingham Discussion Papers, Series E number 10) (1968), p. 14. The study discussed is D. C. Miller, 'Decision-Making Cliques in Community Power Structures: a Comparative Study of an American and an English City', *American Journal of Sociology,* 64, (1958), pp. 299–310.
39 R. V. Clements, *Local Notables and the City Council.*
40 B. S. R. Green, 'Community Decision-Making in Georgian City', University of Bath Ph.D. thesis, 1968.
41 Newton, in *Political Studies,* 17, 2, p. 211.
42 See Meyerson and Banfield, *Politics, Planning and the Public Interest.*
43 See Banfield, *Political Influence.*
44 P. Selznick, *TVA and the Grass Roots.*
45 R. K. Merton, *Social Theory and Social Structure,* revised ed. p. 218. (The essay was first published in *Social Forces,* 23 (1945)).
46 Lee, *Social Leaders and Public Persons,* p. 214.
47 H. H. Heclo, 'The Councillor's Job', *Public Administration,* 47 (Summer 1969), p. 201.
48 R. J. Buxton, *Local Government.*
49 Buxton, *Local Government,* p. 12.
50 *Report of the Royal Commission on Local Government.* Buxton's argument is also applicable to the very much less radical reform proposed in the White Paper, *Local Government in England* (London 1971).
51 See Bulpitt, *Party Politics in English Local Government.*
52 Buxton, *Local Government,* p. 79. See also Gregory, in *Political Studies,* 17, 1, pp. 31–4 and L. J. Sharpe et al., *Voting in Cities.*
53 See, for example, Hampson, *Democracy and Community.*

54 See C. Headrick, *The Town Clerk in English Local Government*.
55 D. Peschek and J. Brand, *Policies and Politics in Secondary Education* (Greater London Papers, number 11), p. 63.
56 See Jones, *Borough Politics* and Lee, *Social Leaders and Public Persons*.
57 Bealey et al., *Constituency Politics*, p. 338.
58 Bealey et al., *Constituency Politics*, p. 339.
59 Peschek and Brand, *Policies and Politics in Secondary Education*.
60 Clements, *Local Notables and the City Council*.
61 Newton, in *Political Studies*, 17, 2, p. 213.
62 J. A. Rex, 'The Sociology of a Zone of Transition', in *Readings in Urban Sociology*, ed. R. E. Pahl.
63 A. W. Gouldner, 'Metaphysical Pathos and the Study of Bureaucracy', *American Political Science Review*, 49 (1955), p. 507.

Works Cited in the Text

Abrahamson, M., *The Professional in the Organization* (Chicago, Rand McNally 1967).

Albrow, M., 'The Study of Organizations – Objectivity or Bias?' in *Penguin Social Sciences Survey 1968*, ed. J. Gould (Harmondsworth, Penguin Books 1968), pp. 146–67.

Albrow, M., *Bureaucracy* (London, Pall Mall 1970).

Albrow, M., 'Public Administraion and Sociological Theory' *Lister Lecture to the British Association for the Advancement of Science*, Durham 1970.

Allen, B., 'Administration of Discretion', *Case Conference*, June 1968 pp. 43–8.

Argyris, C., *Integrating the Individual and the Organization* (New York, Wiley 1964).

Argyris, C., 'The Individual and the Organization: Some Problems of Mutual Adjustment', *Administrative Science Quarterly*, 2 (1957), pp. 1–24.

Aron, R., 'Social Structure and the Ruling Class', *British Journal of Sociology*, 1 (1950) pp. 1–16 and 126–43.

Bachrach, P., *The Theory of Democratic Elitism* (London, University of London Press 1969).

Bachrach, P., and Baratz, M. S., *Power and Poverty* (New York, Oxford University Press 1970).

Baldwin S., *Poverty and Politics* (Chapel Hill, University of North Carolina Press 1968).

Balzac, H. de, *Les Employées* (Paris 1836).

Banfield, E. C., *Government Project* (Glencoe, Illinois, Free Press 1951).

Banfield, E. C., *Political Influence* (New York, Free Press 1961).

Banfield E. C. and Wilson, J. Q., *City Politics* (Cambridge, Mass., Harvard University Press 1963).

Banton, M., *Roles* (London, Tavistock 1965).

Barker, E., *The Development of Public Services in Western Europe 1660–1930* (London, Oxford University Press 1944).

Barnard, C., *The Functions of the Executive* (Cambridge Mass., Harvard University Press 1938).

Bavelas, A., 'Leadership: Man and Function' *Administrative Science Quarterly*, 5 (1960), pp. 491–8.

Bealey, F. Blondel, J. and McCann, W. P., *Constituency Politics* (London, Faber 1965).

Bell, D., *The End of Ideology* (New York, Free Press 1960).

Bell, K., *Tribunals in the Social Services* (London, Routledge and Kegan Paul 1969).

Bendix, R., 'Bureaucracy: The Problem and Its Setting', *American Sociological Review*, 12 (1947), pp. 493–507.

Bendix, R., *Higher Civil Servants in American Society* (Boulder, University of Colorado Press 1949).

Bendix, R., *Max Weber: An Intellectual Portrait* (London, Heinemann 1960).

Bendix, R., *Nation-Building and Citizenship* (New York, Wiley 1964).

Bennion, F. A. R., *Professional Ethics* (London, Charles Knight 1969).

Berger, M. Abel, T. and Page, C. H., (eds), *Freedom and Control in Modern Society* (New York, Van Nostrand 1954).

Bierstedt, R., 'The Sociology of Majorities' *American Sociological Review*, 13, (1948), pp. 700–10.

Bierstedt, R., 'An Analysis of Social Power', *American Sociological Review*, 15 (1950), pp. 730–8.

Bierstedt, R., 'The Problem of Authority', in *Freedom and Control in Modern Society*, ed. M. Berger, T. Abel and C. H. Page (New York, Van Nostrand 1954).

Blau, P. M., *The Dynamics of Bureaucracy* (Chicago, University of Chicago Press 1955).

Blau, P. M., 'Orientation towards Clients in a Public Welfare Agency', *Administrative Science Quarterly*, 5 (1960), pp. 341–61.

Blau, P. M. and Scott, W. R., *Formal Organizations* (London, Routledge and Kegan Paul 1963).

Blumberg, P., *Industrial Democracy* (London, Constable 1968).

Bottomore, T. B., *Elites and Society* (London, Watts 1964).

Bridges, Sir Edward, *Portrait of a Profession* (London, Cambridge University Press 1950).

Brittan, S., *The Treasury under the Tories 1951–64* (Harmondsworth, Penguin Books 1964).

Brittan, S., 'The Irregulars', *Crossbow*, (1966), pp. 30–3.

Brittan, S., *Left or Right: The Bogus Dilemma* (London, Secker and Warburg 1968).

Brittan, S., *Steering the Economy* (Harmondsworth, Penguin Books 1971).

Brown, R. G. S., *The Administrative Process in Britain* (London, Methuen 1970).

Buckley, W., *Sociology and Modern Systems Theory* (Englewood Cliffs N J, Prentice Hall 1967).

Bulpitt, J. G., *Party Politics in English Local Government* (London, Longmans 1967).

Burnham, J., *The Managerial Revolution* (London, Putnam 1942).

Burns, T. and Stalker, G. M., *The Management of Innovation* (London Tavistock 1961).

Buxton, R. J., *Local Government* (Harmondsworth, Penguin Books 1970).

Calouste Gulbenkian Foundation, *Community Work and Social Change* (London, Longmans 1968).

Cartwright, D. and Zander, A., (eds), *Group Dynamics,* 3rd ed. (New York, Harper and Row 1968).

Chapman, B., *The Profession of Government* (London, Allen and Unwin 1959).

Chapman, B., *British Government Observed* (London, Allen and Unwin 1963).

Chapman, R. A., 'Official Liberality', *Public Administration,* 48 (1970), pp. 123–36 .

Chapman, R. A., *The Higher Civil Service in Britain* (London, Constable 1970).

Clark, B. R., *Adult Education in Transition* (Berkeley, University of Califonia Press 1956).

Clark, B. R., 'Organizational Adaption and Precarious Values', *American Sociological Review,* 21 (1956), pp. 327–36.

Clements, R. V., *Local Notables and the City Council* (London, Macmillan 1969).

Coates, K. and Silburn, R., *Poverty: the Forgotten Englishmen* (Harmondsworth, Penguin Books 1970).

Cohen, E., *The Growth of the British Civil Service 1780–1939* (London, Allen and Unwin 1941).

Cole, M., *Servant of the County* (London, Dobson 1956).

Corson, J. J. and Paul, R. S., *Men Near the Top* (Baltimore, Johns Hopkins 1966).

Crozier, M., *The Bureaucratic Phenomenon* (Chicago, University of Chicago Press 1964).

Dahl, R. A., 'The Science of Public Administration: Three Problems', *Public Administration Review,* 7 (1947), pp. 1–11.

Dahl, R. A., *A Preface to Democratic Theory* (Chicago 1956).

Dahl, R. A., *Who Governs?* (New Haven, Yale University Press 1961).

Dahrendorf, R., *Class and Class Conflict in Industrial Society* (London, Routledge and Kegan Paul 1959).

Dale, H. E., *The Higher Civil Service of Great Britain* (London, Oxford University Press 1941).

Dalton, M., 'Conflicts Between Staff and Line Managerial Officers', *American Sociological Review,* 15, (1950), pp. 342–51.

Dalton, M., *Men Who Manage* (New York, Wiley 1959).

Davis, A. K., 'Bureaucratic Patterns in the Navy Officer Corps', *Social Forces,* 27 (1948-9) pp. 143-53.

Davis, W., *Three Years Hard Labour* (London, Andre Deutsch 1968).

Dean, J. P. and Rosen, A., *A Manual of Intergroup Relations* (Chicago, Chicago University Press 1955).

Dennis, N., *People and Planning* (London, Faber and Faber 1970).

Djilas, M., *The New Class* (London, Thames and Hudson 1957).

Dodd, C. H. and Pickering, J. F., 'Recruitment to the Administrative Class 1960-64', *Public Administration,* 45 (1967), pp. 55-80 and 169-99.

Donnison, D. V., et al., *Social Policy and Administration* (London 1965).

Dunnill, F., *The Civil Service: Some Human Aspects* (London, Allen and Unwin 1956).

Eckstein, H., *Pressure Group Politics: The Case of the BMA* (Stanford, Stanford University Press 1960).

Encel, S., 'The Recruitment of University Graduates in the Commonwealth Public Service', *Public Administration,* 32 (1954) pp. 217-28.

Etzioni, A., 'Industrial Sociology: the Study of Economic Organizations', *Social Research,* 25 (1958), pp. 303-324.

Etzioni, A., 'Authority Structure and Organizational Effectiveness', *Administrative Science Quarterly,* 4 (1959), pp. 43-67.

Etzioni, A., *A Comparative Analysis of Complex Organizations* (New York, Free Press 1961).

Etzioni, A., 'Dual Leadership in Complex Organizations' *American Sociological Reveiw,* 30 (1965), pp. 688-98.

Etzioni, A., *The Semi-professions and their Organization* (New York, Free Press 1969).

Etzioni, A., (ed.), *A Sociological Reader on Complex Organizations,* 2nd ed. (New York, Holt, Rinehart and Winston 1969).

A Fabian Group, *The Administrators* (London, Fabian Tract 355 1964).

Fayol, H., *Administration Industrielle et Générale* (Paris 1916).

Finer, H., *The British Civil Service* (London, Allen and Unwin 1937).

Finer, H., 'Administrative Responsibility in Democratic Government', *Public Administration Review,* 1 (1941), pp. 335-50.

Follett, M. P., *Dynamic Administration* (London, Management Publications Trust 1941).

Fox, A., *Industrial Sociology and Industrial Relations* (Research Paper no. 3 for the Royal Commission on Trade Unions and Employers Associations) (London, HMSO 1968).

Fox, A., *A Sociology of Work in Industry* (London, Collier Macmillan 1971).

Francis, R. G. and Stone, R. C., *Service and Procedure in Bureaucracy* (Minneapolis, University of Minnesota Press 1956).

Friedrich, C. J., 'The Nature of Administrative Responsibility', *Public Policy*, 1 (1940), pp. 3–24.

Fry, G. K., *Statesmen in Disguise* (London, Macmillan 1969).

Galbraith, J. K., *American Capitalism* (New York, Houghton Mifflin 1952).

Galdos, P., *Miau*, translated by J. M. Cohen (London, Methuen 1963).

Gerth, H. H. and Mills, C. W., 'A Marx for the Managers', *Ethics*, 52 (1942).

Gibb, C. A., 'The Principles and Traits of Leadership', *Journal of Abnormal and Social Psychology*, 42 (1947), pp. 267–84.

Gibb, C. A., 'Leadership', in *Handbook of Social Psychology*, ed. G. Lindzey (Reading Mass., Addison-Wesley 1954).

Gibb, C. A., (ed.), *Leadership* (Harmondsworth, Penguin Books 1969).

Gilbert, M. and Gott, R., *The Appeasers* (London, Weidenfeld and Nicolson 1963).

Glaser, B. G., 'The Local-Cosmopolitan Scientist', *American Journal of Sociology* 69 (1963) pp. 249–259.

Goode, W. J., 'Community within a Community: The Professions' *American Sociological Review*, 22 (1957), pp. 194–200.

Goodnow, F. J., *Politics and Administration* (New York, Macmillan 1900).

Gouldner, A. W., *Patterns of Industrial Bureaucracy* (Glencoe, Ill., Free Press 1954).

Gouldner, A. W., 'Metaphysical Pathos and the Theory of Bureaucracy' *American Political Science Review*, 49 (1955), pp. 496–507.

Gouldner, A. W., 'Cosmopolitans and Locals: Towards an Analysis of Latent Social Roles', *Administrative Science Quarterly*, 2 (1957–8) pp. 281–306 and 444–80.

Green, B. S. R., 'Community Decision-Making in Georgian City' University of Bath Ph.D. thesis, 1968.

Greenberg, D. S. *The Politics of American Science* (Harmondsworth, Penguin Books 1969).

Greenwood, E., 'Attributes of a Profession', *Social Work*, 2 (1957), pp. 45–55.

Gregory, R. G., 'Local Elections and the Rule of Anticipated Reactions', *Political Studies*, 17 (1969), pp. 31–47.

Gross, B. M., *Organizations and their Managing* (New York, Free Press 1968).

Gross, E., 'The Definition of Organizational Goals', *British Journal of Sociology*, 20 (1969), pp. 277–94.

Guttsman, W. L., *The British Political Elite* (London, McGibbon and Kee 1963).

Hall, A. S., 'Client Reception in a Social Service Agency', *Public Administration*, 49 (1971), pp. 25–42.

Hampson, W., *Democracy and Community* (London, Oxford University Press 1970).

Harris, J. S. and Garcia, T. V., 'The Permanent Secretaries: Britain's Top Administrators', *Public Administration Review*, 26 (1966), pp. 31–44.

Headrick, C., *The Town Clerk* (London, Allen and Unwin 1962).

Heclo, H. H., 'The Councillor's Job', *Public Administration*, 47 (1969), pp. 185–202.

Hepple, Bob, *Race, Jobs and the Law in Britain*, 2nd ed. (Harmondsworth, Penguin Books 1970).

Lord Hewart, *The New Despotism* (London 1929).

Hill, D. M., *Participating in Local Affairs* (Harmondsworth, Penguin Books 1970).

Hill, M. J., 'The Exercise of Discretion in the National Assistance Board', *Public Administration*, 47 (1969), pp. 75–90.

Hill, M. J., 'Selectivity for the Poor' in P. Townsend and N. Bosanquet, *Labour and Inequality* (London, Fabian Society 1972).

Hill, M. J. and Issacharoff, R. M., *Community Action and Race Relations* (London, Oxford University Press 1971).

Holman, R., (ed.), *Socially Deprived Families in Britain* (London, Bedford Square Press 1970).

Homans, G. C., *The Human Group* (London, Routledge and Kegan Paul 1951).

Hunter, F., *Community Power Structure* (Chapel Hill, University of North Carolina Press 1963).

Jackson, B. and Marsden, D., *Education and the Working Class* (London, Routledge and Kegan Paul 1962).

Jacobs, J., 'Symbolic Bureaucracy: A Case Study of a Social Welfare Agency', *Social Forces*, (1969), pp. 413–22.

Jones, G. W., *Borough Politics* (London, Macmillan 1969).

Josephson, E., 'Irrational Leadership in Formal Organizations', *Social Forces*, 31 (1952) pp. 109–17.

Justice, *The Citizen and the Administration* (London, Stevens 1961).

Katz, D. and Kahn, R. L., *The Social Psychology of Organizations* (New York, Wiley 1966).

Kaufman, H., *The Forest Ranger* (Baltimore, Johns Hopkins Press 1960).

Kautsky, K., *The Labour Revolution* (London, Allen and Unwin 1925).

Keeling, D., 'The Development of Central Training in the Civil Service 1963–70', *Public Administration*, 49 (1971), pp. 51–71.

Keith-Lucas, A., *Decisions about People in Need* (Chapel Hill, University of North Carolina Press 1957).

Kelsall, R. K., *Higher Civil Servants in Britain* (London, Routledge and Kegan Paul 1955).

Kingdom, T. D., 'The Confidential Advisers of Ministers', *Public Admiration*, 44 (1966), pp. 267–74.

Kingsley, J. D., *Representative Bureaucracy* (Yellow Springs, Ohio, Antioch Press 1944).

Korten, D. C., 'Situational Determinants of Leadership Structure', *Journal of Conflict Resolution*, 6 (1962), pp. 222–35.

Kramer, R. M., *Participation of the Poor* (Engelwood Cliffs NJ, Prentice Hall 1969).

Lambert, J. R., 'The Police Can Choose', *New Society*, 18 September 1969, p. 430.

Lambert, J. R., *Crime, Police and Race Relations* (London, Oxford University Press 1970).

Landsberger, H. A., *Hawthorne Revisited* (Ithaca N.Y., Cornell University Press 1958).

Lane, R. E., *Political Life* (Glencoe Ill., Free Press 1959).

Lee, J. M., *Social Leaders and Public Persons* (London, Oxford University Press 1963).

Lenin, V. I., *The State and Revolution* (Moscow, Foreign Language Publishing House, n.d.).

Levinson, D. J., 'Role, Personality and Social Structure in an Organizational Setting', *Journal of Abnormal and Social Psychology*, 58 (1959), pp. 178–81.

Lewin, K., 'The Consequences of Authoritarian and Democratic Leadership', in *Studies in Leadership* ed. A. W. Gouldner (New York, Harper and Row 1950).

Lippitt, R., et al., *The Dynamics of Planned Change* (New York, Harcourt Brace 1958).

Lipset, S. M., *Agrarian Socialism* (Berkeley, University of California Press 1950).

Lipset, S. M., *Political Man* (London, Heinemann 1960).

Litterer, J. A., (ed.), *Organizations*, 2nd ed. (New York, Wiley 1969).

Lockwood, D., *The Blackcoated Worker* (London, Allen and Unwin 1958).

Lupton, T., and Wilson, C. S., 'The Social Background and Connection of "Top Decision Makers" ', *Manchester School of Economic and Social Studies*, 27 (1959), pp. 30–52.

Lynes, T., 'The Secret Rules', *Poverty*, 4 (1967), pp. 7–9.

Mackenzie, W. J. and Grove, J. W., *Central Administration in Britain* (London, Longmans 1957).

Madge, J., *The Origins of Scientific Sociology* (London, Tavistock 1963).

Mailick, S. and van Ness, E. H., *Concepts and Issues in Administrative Behavior* (Engelwood Cliffs NJ., Prentice Hall 1962).

March, J. G. and Simon, H. A., *Organizations* (New York, Wiley 1958).

Marris, P. and Rein, M., *Dilemmas of Social Reform* (London, Routledge and Kegan Paul 1967).

Marsden, D., *Mothers Alone* (London, Allen Lane 1969).

Marx, F. M., *The Administrative State* (Chicago, University of Chicago Press 1957).

Marx, K., and Engels, F., *Selected Works* (Moscow, Foreign Languages Publishing House 1958).

Marx, K. and Engels, F., *Basic Writings on Politics and Philosophy*, ed. L. S. Feuer (New York 1959).

Mayo, E., *The Human Problems of an Industrial Civilization* (Cambridge Mass., Harvard University Press 1933).

Mayo, E., *The Social Problems of an Industrial Civilization* (Cambridge Mass., Harvard University Press 1945).

McGregor, D., *The Human Side of Enterprise* (New York, McGraw Hill 1960).

Merriam, C. E., *The New Democracy and the New Despotism* (New York, McGraw Hill 1939).

Merton, R. K., et al. (eds.), *Reader in Bureaucracy* (Glencoe Ill., Free Press 1952).

Merton, R. K., *Social Theory and Social Structure* (Glencoe Ill., Free Press 1957).

Meyerson, M. and Banfield, E. C., *Politics, Planning and the Public Interest* (Glencoe Ill., Free Press 1955).

Meynaud, A., *Technocracy* translated by P. Barnes (London, Faber 1968).

Michels, R., *Political Parties*, translated by E. and C. Paul (London, Constable 1915).

Miliband, R., *The State in Capitalist Society* (London, Weidenfeld and Nicolson 1969).

Miller, D. C., 'Decision-making Cliques in Community Power Structures', *American Journal of Sociology*, 64 (1958), pp. 299–310.

Miller, D. C., and Form, W. H., *Industrial Sociology* (New York, Harper 1964).

Miller, W. B., 'Two Concepts of Authority', *American Anthropologist*, 57 (1955), pp. 271–89.

Mills, C. W., *The Causes of World War Three* (New York, Simon and Schuster 1958).

Mills, C. W., *Power, Politics and People*, ed. I. L. Horowitz (New York, Oxford University Press 1963).

Morris, R., and Rein, M., *Social Work Practice* (New York, Columbia University Press 1962).

Mosca, G., *Elementi di Scienza Politica* ed. A. Livingston and translated by H. D. Kahn as *The Ruling Class* (New York, McGraw Hill 1939).

Mouzelis, N., *Organization and Bureaucracy* (London, Routledge and Kegan Paul 1967).

Moynihan, D. P., *Maximum Feasible Misunderstanding* (New York, Free Press 1969).

Nettl, J. P., 'Consensus or Elite Domination: The Case of Business', *Political Studies,* 13 (1965) pp. 22–44.

Newton, K., *City Politics in Britain and America* (University of Birmingham Discussion Papers, Series E, number 10) (Birmingham 1968).

Newton, K., 'City Politics in Britain and the United States' *Political Studies,* 17 (1969), pp. 208–18.

Newton, K., 'A Critique of the Pluralist Model,' *Acta Sociologica,* 12, 4 (1969).

Nicholson, M., *The System* (London, Hodder and Stoughton 1967).

Nutting, A., *No End of a Lesson* (London, Constable 1967).

Opie, R., 'The Making of Economic Policy', in *Crisis in the Civil Service,* ed. H. Thomas (London, Blond 1968), pp. 53–82.

Parker, R. S. and Subramaniam, V., 'Public and Private Administration', *International Review of Administrative Sciences,* 30 (1964), pp. 354–66.

Parris, H., 'Twenty Years of L'Ecole Nationale d'Administration', *Public Administration,* 43 (1965), pp. 395–412.

Parris, H., 'The Origins of the Permanent Civil Service 1780–1830', *Public Administration,* 46 (1968), pp. 143–66.

Parris, H., *Constitutional Bureaucracy* (London, Allen and Unwin 1969).

Parsons, T., 'Suggestions for a Sociological Approach to the Theory of Organizations', *Administrative Science Quarterly,* 1 (1956), pp. 63–85 and 225–239.

Parsons, T., *Structure and Process in Modern Societies* (Glencoe Ill., Free Press 1960).

Peabody, R. L., *Organizational Authority* (New York, Prentice Hall 1964).

Perrow, C., 'The Analysis of Goals in Complex Organizations', *American Sociological Review,* 26 (1961), pp. 854–66.

Peschek, D. and Brand, J., *Policies and Politics in Secondary Education* (Greater London Papers No. 11) (London, L.S.E. 1966).

Pigors, P., *Leadership Domination* (New York, Houghton Mifflin 1935).

Pitts, J. R., *In Search of France* (Cambridge Mass., Harvard University Press 1963).

Polsby, N., 'The Study of Community Power', in *Encyclopaedia of the Social Sciences* (New York, MacMillan 1968).

Presthus, R. V., 'Authority in Organizations' *Public Administration Review* 20 (1960) pp. 86–91.

Presthus, R. V., *The Organizational Society* (New York, Knopf 1962).

Regan, D. E., 'The Expert and the Administrator: Recent Changes at the Ministry of Transport', *Public Administration,* 44 (1966), pp. 149–67.

Reissman, L., 'A Study of Role Conceptions in Bureaucracy', *Social Forces,* 27 (1949), pp. 305–10.

Rex, J. A., 'The Sociology of a Zone of Transition', in *Readings in Urban Sociology* ed. R. E. Pahl (Oxford, Pergamon 1968).

Richardson, S. A., 'Organizational Contrasts on British and American Ships', *Administrative Science Quarterly,* 1 (1956) pp. 189–207.

Ridley, F. F., *Specialists and Generalists* (London, Allen and Unwin 1968).

Robinson, K., 'Selection and Social Background of the Administrative Class' *Public Administration,* 33 (1955), pp. 387–8.

Roche, J. P. and Sachs S., 'The Bureaucrat and the Enthusiast', *Western Political Quarterly,* 8 (1955) pp. 248–61.

Roethlisberger, F. J. and Dickson, W. J., *Management and the Worker* (Cambridge Mass., Harvard University Press 1939).

Rose, A., *The Power Structure* (New York, Oxford University Press 1967).

Rose, H. and S., *Science and Society* (Harmondsworth, Penguin Books 1969).

Ross, M., *Community Organization: Theory and Principles* (New York, Harper and Row 1955).

Royal Institute of Public Administration symposium: 'Who are the Policy-Makers?', *Public Administration,* 43 (1965).

Schatteschneider, E. E., *The Semi-Sovereign People* (New York, Holt, Rinehart and Winston 1961).

Selznick, P., 'An Approach to a Theory of Bureaucracy', *American Sociological Review,* 8 (1943), pp. 47–54.

Selznick, P., 'Foundations of the Theory of Organization', *American Sociological Review,* 13 (1948) pp. 25–35.

Selznick, P., *TVA and the Grass Roots* (Berkeley, University of California Press 1949).

Selznick, P., *Leadership in Administration* (New York, Harper and Row 1957).

Sharpe, L. J., et al, *Voting in Cities* (London, Macmillan 1967).

Schonfield, A. A., *Modern Capitalism* (London, Oxford University Press 1965).

Silverman, D., *The Theory of Organizations* (London, Heineman 1970).

Simon, H. A., *Administrative Behavior* (New York, Macmillan 1945).

Simon, H. A., Smithburg, D. W. and Thompson, V. A., *Public Administration* (New York, Knopf 1950).

Simon, H. A., 'On the Concept of Organizational Goal', *Administrative Science Quarterly,* 9 (1964), pp. 1–22.

Sisson, C. H., *The Spirit of British Administration* (London, Faber 1959).

Snow, C. P., *Science and Government* (Cambridge Mass., Harvard University Press 1960).

Stanley, D. T., *The Higher Civil Service* (Washington, Brookings Institution 1964).

Stevenson, O., 'Problems of Individual Need and Fair Shares for All', *Social Work Today,* 1 (1970), pp. 15–21.

Subramaniam, V., 'Graduates in the Public Services: a Comparative Study of Attitudes', *Public Administration,* 35 (1957), pp. 373–94.

Taylor, F. W., *The Principles of Scientific Management* (New York, Hooper 1911).

Thomas, H., (ed.), *The Establishment* (London, Blond 1959).

Thomas, H., *The Suez Affair* (London, Weidenfeld and Nicolson 1967).

Thomas, H., (ed.), *Crisis in the Civil Service* (London, Blond 1968).

Thompson, J. D. and McEwan, W. J., 'Organizational Goals and Environment', *American Sociological Review,* 23 (1958), pp. 23–31.

Thompson, V. A., *Modern Organization* (New York, Knopf 1961).

Thompson, V. A., 'Hierarchy, Specialization and Organizational Conflict', *Administrative Science Quarterly,* 5 (1961) pp. 485–521.

Thompson, V. A., 'Bureaucracy and Innovation', *Administrative Science Quarterly,* 10 (1965), pp. 1–20.

Titmuss, R. M., 'Welfare Rights, Law and Discretion', *Political Quarterly,* 42 (1971), pp. 113–32.

Tout, T. F., *The English Civil Service in the Fourteenth Century* (Manchester, Manchester University Press 1916).

Walker, N., *Morale in the Civil Service* (Edinburgh, Edinburgh University Press 1961).

Wallas, G., *Human Nature in Politics* (London, Constable 1948).

Warner, W. L., et al., *The American Federal Executive* (New Haven, Yale University Press 1963).

Weber, M., *The Theory of Social and Economic Organization,* translated by A. M. Henderson and T. Parsons (Glencoe Ill., Free Press 1947).

Weber, M., *From Max Weber: Essays in Sociology,* ed. H. H. Gerth and C. W. Mills (London, Routledge and Kegan Paul 1948).

White, R. and Lippitt, R., *Autocracy and Democracy* (New York, Harper and Row 1960).

Whyte, W. H., *The Organizational Man* (New York, Simon and Schuster 1956).

Wilensky, H. L., 'The Professionalization of Everyone', *American Journal of Sociology,* 70 (1964), pp. 137–58.

Williams, O. P. and Adrian, C. R., *Four Cities* (Philadelphia, University of Pennsylvania Press 1963).

Wilson, J. Q., *Varieties of Police Behavior* (Cambridge Mass., Harvard University Press 1968).

Wilson, W., 'The Study of Administration', *Political Science Quarterly,* 56, 2 (June 1887) pp. 481–506.

Wiseman, H. V., 'The Working of Local Government in Leeds', *Public Administration,* 41 (1963), pp. 51–70 and 137–56.

Wiseman, H. V., *Local Government at Work* (London, Routledge and Kegan Paul 1967).

Woll, P., (ed.), *Public Administration and Policy* (New York, Harper 1966).

Government Publications

Report on the Indian Civil Service 1845

Report of the Sub-Committee of the Inter-Departmental Committee on the Application of the Whitley Report to Government Establishments 1919

Immigration from the Commonwealth Cmnd. 2739 1965

Sixth Report of the Select Committee on Estimates 1964–65 1965

Ministry of Housing and Local Government *Management of Local Government* 1967

Committee on Local Authority and Allied Personal Social Services Cmnd. 3703 1968.

The Civil Service (Report of, and evidence to, the Fulton Committee) 1968 Vols. 1–5

Royal Commission on Local Government in England 1966–69 1969 3 vols.

Council Housing Purposes, Procedures and Priorities Ninth Report of the Housing Management Sub-Committee of the Central Housing Advisory Committee 1969

Supplementary Benefits Commission *Supplementary Benefits Handbook* 1970

Local Government in England Cmnd. 4584 1971

Guide to Selected Reading

CHAPTER 1

Martin Albrow's book *Bureaucracy* provides, in the course of a discussion of the varieties of meaning attached to that concept, the best general account of the various approaches to the relations between bureaucracy and democracy. Bachrach's *The Theory of Democratic Elitism* is useful too, though rather more concerned with the philosophical issues. Dahrendorf's *Class and Class Conflict in Industrial Society* is also useful in dealing with some of the arguments between the Marxists and those who emphasise the power dimension in social stratification, though naturally much of this ranges over a much wider field than our concern. A similar useful but wide-ranging work is Bottomore's *Elites and Society*.

As far as more original sources are concerned, Weber's *The Theory of Social and Economic Organization* Part 3, Mosca's *The Ruling Class* and Lenin's *State and Revolution* are the most relevant. Merton's *Reader in Bureaucracy* contains some useful excerpts from the 'classics', and is, despite the fact that it was compiled nearly twenty years ago, still the best selection of short pieces on our subject. Aron's essay 'Social Structure and the Ruling Class' puts the pluralist case well, and Miliband's very sophisticated statement of a contemporary Marxist position, *The State in Capitalist Society,* is recommended.

CHAPTER 2

The problem for the reader looking for discussions of organisation sociology is that, although there are a vast number of books available, so many of them are over long, unreadable and only marginally relevant for students of public administration. Two recent books, Silverman's *The Theory of Organizations* and Mouzelis' *Organization and Bureaucracy* provide useful, if sometimes contentious, overviews of this field. Two useful readers on the subject are Etzioni's *A Sociological Reader on Complex Organizations* and Litterer's two-volume *Organizations*.

Barnard's *The Functions of the Executive,* Simon's *Admin-*

istrative Behavior, and two books by Selznick, *TVA and the Grass Roots,* and *Leadership in Administration* have all had a big impact upon this book as a whole.

Simon, Smithburg and Thompson's textbook *Public Administration* is relevant to this chapter, and also to chapters 3, 6, 7 and 8. It contains many examples drawn from public administration in the United States.

CHAPTER 3

The references given for Chapter 2 are applicable to this chapter too. In addition, Blau's *The Dynamics of Bureaucracy* and Francis and Stone's *Service and Procedure in Bureaucracy* are valuable as both sources of theory and sources of evidence on the working of public agencies in the United States. It will be evident from the text that Dalton's *Men Who Manage* is important too, for although it deals with an industrial firm it provides some fascinating insights into the dynamics of 'informal' behaviour.

CHAPTER 4

The neglect of the topic of discretion in the literature makes it very difficult to provide satisfactory recommendations for further reading for this chapter. Kaufman's *The Forest Ranger,* an account of the way in which responsibilities are delegated in the US Forest Service, is one of the few books that deal with this subject. Two valuable articles, which have been published since this chapter was written, are Anthony Hall's 'Client Reception in a Social Service Agency' and Professor Titmuss' 'Welfare Rights, Law and Discretion'. Two sources dealing with social welfare agencies in the United States, Jacobs' article 'Symbolic Bureaucracy' and Keith-Lucas' *Decisions about People in Need,* are also partly relevant, together with the book by Blau mentioned in connection with Chapter 3.

CHAPTER 5

There are a number of interesting articles providing theoretical discussions of goals, notably Perrow's 'The Analysis of Goals in Complex Organizations', Simon's 'On the Concept of Organizational Goal', Thompson and McEwan's 'Organizational Goals and Environment', and Albrow's 'The Study of Organizations – Objectivity or Bias?' The writings of B. R. Clark on this subject are of value, particularly his *Adult Education in Transition.* Selznick's *TVA and the Grass Roots* is sufficiently important to be mentioned again here. Goal displacement in social reform programmes has been a central concern of Martin Rein's ; see Marris and Rein's *Dilemmas of Social Reform* and pages 127–45 of Marris and Rein's *Social Work Practice.* This is also an issue which is considered very fully in

Community Action and Race Relations by the present author and Ruth Issacharoff, particularly in Chapter 7.

CHAPTER 6

The theoretical discussions of authority in organisations which are particularly worthy of note are those by Bierstedt in 'The Problem of Authority', Fox in *A Sociology of Work in Industry*, Etzioni in *A Comparative Analysis of Complex Organization*, and Presthus in 'Authority in Organizations'.

Gibb has written a good account of the work of social psychologists on the subject of leadership in *Handbook of Social Psychology* edited by G. Lindzey. He has also edited a useful Penguin reader, *Leadership*.

CHAPTER 7

Merton's essay 'Bureaucratic Structure and Personality', which is reprinted both in his *Reader in Bureaucracy* and in his *Social Theory and Social Structure*, has been enormously influential amongst organisational sociologists. Presthus' book, *The Organizational Society*, Argyris' 'The Individual and the Organization', and Levinson's 'Role, Personality and Social Structure in an Organizational Setting' are also recommended for their theorising on bureaucratic personalities. F. M. Marx's *The Administrative State* has a great deal to say on the personalities and behaviour of public servants. Crozier's *The Bureaucratic Phenomenon* is in general interesting in providing a very different approach to this topic from that of most of the American writers in the field.

CHAPTER 8

Victor Thompson's *Modern Organization* represents the most interesting theoretical treatment of line/staff conflict from the American organization theorists. Dalton's book, recommended for Chapter 3, is also very relevant to this chapter.

The British arguments about the role of specialists in the civil service are found in the Fulton Report, R. G. S. Brown's *The Administrative Process in Britain*, and Ridley's *Specialists and Generalists*. The first part of Brittan's *Steering the Economy* deals interestingly with the role of economists in British government.

Professional roles are examined in Abrahamson's reader, *The Professional in the Organization*, Greenwood's 'Attributes of a Profession', and Wilensky's 'The Professionalization of Everyone'. Reissman's 'A Study of Role Conceptions in Bureaucracy' and Merton's 'Role of the Intellectual in Public Bureaucracy' (reprinted in his *Social Theory and Social Structure*) are two valuable articles whose titles speak for themselves.

CHAPTER 9

Some of the general arguments on the relevance of the social backgrounds of civil servants are found in Bendix's *Higher Civil Servants in American Society* and in Kingsley's *Representative Bureaucracy.* Kingsley's book was published in 1944 and seems rather dated in some respects but nevertheless deals with some of the most significant issues; the same is true of another rather old book, Dale's *The Higher Civil Service of Great Britain,* which presents a rather out-of-date picture of the social lives of civil servants, but has some very pertinent things to say about working relationships which are relevant to this and the next chapter.

Volume 3 of the Fulton Report contains the important study of the social characteristics of civil servants by Halsey and Crewe. This should be supplemented by R. A. Chapman's *The Higher Civil Service in Britain,* while two older works, Lupton and Wilson's 'The Social Background and Connections of "Top Decision Makers" ' and Kelsall's *Higher Civil Servants in Britain,* will be of interest to the reader who wants to go more deeply into this subject.

CHAPTER 10

Woodrow Wilson's essay on the relationship between politics and administration, together with some interesting views on the same subject by Long, Finer and Friedrich, is reprinted in *Public Administration and Policy* edited by P. Woll. Simon's contribution on this subject is found in Chapter 3 of his *Administrative Behavior.* Brown's book, recommended for Chapter 8, is also relevant for this topic.

CHAPTER 11

The most useful discussions of the relations between politicans and administrators in English local government are found in the Maud Report on the *Management of Local Government,* Buxton's *Local Government,* Heclo's article 'The Councillor's Job', and the *Public Administration* symposium 'Who are the Policy-Makers?'

The best-known protagonists in the 'community power debate' are Hunter (*Community Power Structure*) and Dahl (*Who Governs?*), but the most effective contributions to this on-going controversy have been Bachrach and Baratz's *Power and Poverty* and Ken Newton's 'A Critique of the Pluralist Model'. Newton's discussion of the relevance of the controversy to Britain, 'City Politics in Britain and the United States', is also valuable. The best general work on American city politics is Banfield and Wilson's *City Politics.*

Index

Abortion Act, 1967, 164
administration, and discretionary decisions, 61–85; goals, 89–90, 93, 95, 98, 101, 103–4; and local government, 214, 216; and politics, 195–209; specialist and non-specialist, 140–7, 154; theory, 15–33
Albrow, M., bureaucracy, 2, 15, 37; goals, 87–9; professionalism, 171
Argyris, C., bureaucratic behaviour, 133, 136
Aron, R., authority, 10
'assistant-to', 54
authority, 105–26; area of acceptance, 27; and bureaucracy, 3–14, 119, 123, 125; and compliance, 23–5, 105–6, 113, 115; delegated authority, 111; importance of status symbols, 110; and influence, 110–12; and leadership, 115–26; legitimation, 109; organisational attitudes towards, 112; types of authority, 107; 'zone of indifference', 23–4, 27

Bachrach, P., authority, 11, 12; 'pluralist' theory, 221
Balogh, Thomas, 177
Banfield, E. C., Chicago, 217, 226; elected officials, 215; farm resettlement programme, 97; local government, 210; 'pluralist' theory, 218, 222
Bank Rate Tribunal, 188
Baratz, M. S., 'pluralist' theory, 221
'bargaining', as cooperative strategy, 101–3
'bargaining politics', local government, 217–26
Barker, E., European civil services, 36
Barnard, C., administrative behaviour,

22–5, 27, 30, 34, 38; authority, 23–5; goals, 88, 92; 'zone of indifference', 24
Bath, community power, 224
Bavelas, A., decision-making, 119; leadership, 115–16
Bealey, F., local government, 232
Bendix, R., American civil service, 193; bureaucracy, 4, 172, 179; German civil service, 13
Bennion, F. A. R., professionalism, 163
Bierstedt, R., authority, 110–12
Blau, P. M., administrative theory, 86; discretionary decisions, 79; goals, 87–90; law-enforcement agency, 57–60, 119–20; peer-group influence, 84; public welfare agency, 48–9, 57–60, 136; staff-line distinction, 146
Bottomore, T. B., civil service, 9, 178; élites, 178
Brand, J., pressure groups and local government, 232
Bridges, Sir Edward, civil servants, 207
Bristol, local government, 224, 233
Brittan, S., professionalism, 166; staff-line distinction, 158–9
Brown, George, 160
Brown, R. G. S., decision-making, 207; Department of Economic Affairs, 158; Fulton Committee, 124, 144, 199–200
Buckley, W., authority, 112
budgets, comparison between central and local government budgets, 74–5
Bulpitt, J. C., local government, 212
bureaucracy, and authority, 3–14, 119, 123, 125; and behaviour, 137–8; career structure, 129; conformity, 128–39; definition, 16, 35; delega-